AFTERNESS

Columbia Themes in Philosophy, Social Criticism, and the Arts

Afterness

FIGURES OF FOLLOWING IN MODERN THOUGHT
AND AESTHETICS

GERHARD RICHTER

COLUMBIA UNIVERSITY PRESS   NEW YORK

COLUMBIA UNIVERSITY PRESS
Publishers Since 1893
NEW YORK   CHICHESTER, WEST SUSSEX

Copyright © 2011 Columbia University Press

All rights reserved

Library of Congress Cataloging-in-Publication Data
Richter, Gerhard, 1967–
  Afterness : figures of following in modern thought and aesthetics / Gerhard Richter.
    p. cm.—(Columbia themes in philosophy, social criticism, and the arts)
  Includes bibliographical references and index.
  ISBN 978-0-231-15770-4 (cloth : alk. paper)
  ISBN 978-0-231-53034-7 (e-book)
  1. Philosophy, Modern—21st century. 2. Time—Philosophy. 3. Aesthetics. I. Title.
  B805.R53 2011
  190.9'051—dc22

                                                        2011012670

Columbia University Press books are printed on permanent and durable acid-free paper.
This book is printed on paper with recycled content.

Printed in the United States of America

c 10 9 8 7 6 5 4 3 2 1

References to Internet Web sites (URLs) were accurate at the time of writing. Neither the author nor Columbia University Press is responsible for URLs that may have expired or changed since the manuscript was prepared.

After philosophy comes philosophy. But it is altered by the after.
—Jean-François Lyotard

Even the death of Christ was only his beginning.
—Ernst Bloch

Only the How is repeatable. The past—experienced as actual historicity—is anything but the Over [*das Vorbei*].
—Martin Heidegger

Modernity exists in the form of a desire to wipe out whatever came earlier, in the hope of reaching at last a point that could be called a true present, a point of origin that marks a new departure.
—Paul de Man

Contents

Introduction: The Logic of Afterness   1
1. Afterness and Modernity: A Genealogical Note   27
2. Afterness and Critique: A Paradigmatic Case   39
3. Afterness and Aesthetics: End Without End   54
4. Afterness and *Rettung*: Can Anything Be Rescued by Defending It?   72
5. Afterness and Translation: The Politics of Carrying Across   88
6. Afterness and the Image (I): Unsettling Photography   118
7. Afterness and the Image (II): Image Withdrawal   139
8. Afterness and Experience (I): Can Hope Be Disappointed?   154
9. Afterness and Experience (II): Crude Thinking Rethought   169
10. Afterness and Experience (III): Mourning, Memory, and the Fictions of Anteriority   186
11. Afterness and Empty Space: No Longer and Not Yet   199
    Afterwards: After-Words   206

Acknowledgments   211
Notes   213
Index   247

AFTERNESS

Introduction

The Logic of Afterness

As a recent doctoral student discussed with me how best to structure his dissertation, the contours of which were only beginning to take shape, he suggested writing an introduction followed by the individual chapters. Almost without hesitation, I replied by articulating a largely unspoken writerly strategy. To the great bafflement of my student—who up to that point had never written a book-length text—I advised against his plan, explaining that introductions almost always are written *after* the fact, in other words, *last*. What experienced writers know—that introductions come first but almost always are composed as an afterthought to what already has been written— bespeaks an irreducible belatedness in language and thought. That which introduces, points forward to, explains, and situates something that is not yet present always already will have been preceded by what it itself claims to precede. Hovering between proceeding and preceding, introductions are retroactively invented by what they tacitly claim to call into presence, an *after* in the guise of another temporality, another allegiance, another direction.

It is no different with the present introduction, whose pages will have been written after the chapters that follow it had long since been completed.

Why start the book with this basic reflection on the relationship between the before and the after, between preceding and following? By commenting on the situatedness of the introduction in the wake of an *after* that actually is a *before*, and a *before* that is actually an *after*, we have already entered the terrain that this study wishes to delimit, interrogate, engage in, and contextualize in ever-shifting modulations, media, frames of reference, and conceptual registers.

After all, this book is concerned with a particular figure of modernity, that of following, coming after, having survived, outlived, or succeeded something or someone: what in broad terms I wish to call *afterness*. But what does it really mean for something to "follow" something else, either in language or as a concept? Can the "after" ever fully emancipate itself from its predecessor, or does it in fact remain in the latter's ghostly and largely unacknowledged debt? The after is not merely a temporal dimension. A sustained reading of afterness has far-reaching implications for how we view the thought, aesthetic production, and ethico-political concerns of modernity—from the afterness of Kant's Copernican revolution in speculative thought (yielding, in his view, a genuinely *critical* philosophy after the phases of its *dogmatic* allegiances) to a postlapsarian Western culture famously said to come "after Auschwitz." But our understanding of the after itself first must be understood. Interrogating this understanding without explaining away its irreducible difficulties and its resistances to understanding by pretending to know what the after is in advance of this or that particular manifestation is the task of this study.

Not a history of afterness in which one after is assumed simply to follow a previous after in a teleo-chronological succession of afters, this study instead is concerned with certain *structural* and *conceptual* features of afterness that traverse the spectral reverberations of any act of following. A useful way of conceptualizing the problem to which my investigation of afterness attempts to respond is to recall Walter Benjamin's preoccupation with the concept of *Nachleben* (living on, living after, surviving, afterlife, or following) in modernity. Drawing on art historian Aby Warburg's coinage of the term *Nachleben* in the field of iconography and in the context of a revolutionary theory of the history of art and aesthetics, Benjamin was attracted to the idea that works, lives, languages, and media possess a historicity that cannot be reduced to the continuum of temporal unfolding preferred by the nineteenth-century German historicism associated with such proper names as Leopold von Ranke. As the French art historian Georges Didi-Huberman reminds us, in "Warburg's work, the term *Nachleben* refers to the survival (the continuity or afterlife and metamorphosis) of images and motifs—as opposed to their renascence after extinction or, conversely, their replacement by innovations in image and motif." He continues: "Almost every section of Warburg's *Kulturwissenschaftliche Bibliothek* opens with a collection of documents related to artistic survivals," yielding a conception of *Nachleben* that "must profoundly alter, if taken seriously, our understanding of what a historical phenomenon or fact is."[1]

Although Warburg's introduction of concepts such as *das Nachleben der Antike*, or "the afterlife of antiquity," as an art historical category would serve as a touchstone for art historians and theorists as heterogeneous as Ernst Gombrich, Erwin Panofsky, and Fritz Saxl, Benjamin's later mobilization of *Nachleben* would effect an even more radical, enigmatic, and encompassing transformation of the philosophy of history and modernity. From Benjamin's perspective, the concept of *Nachleben* inflects the fates of art, media, history, philosophy, and the ethico-political dimensions of modernity. He articulates these concerns in their most advanced formulations in the notes that comprise *The Arcades Project*. There, in the section on the theory of knowledge, Benjamin explains his conception:

> Geschichtliches "Verstehen" ist grundsätzlich als ein Nachleben des Verstandnen zu fassen und daher ist dasjenige was in der Analyse des "Nachlebens der Werke," des "Ruhmes" erkannt wurde, als die Grundlage der Geschichte überhaupt zu betrachen.
>
> [Historical "understanding" is to be grasped, fundamentally, as an afterlife of that which is understood; and what has been recognized in the analysis of the "afterlife of works," in the analysis of "fame," is therefore to be considered the foundation of history in general.][2]

If the task of historical understanding first of all is to understand what understanding means—that is, to presuppose a theory of interpretation or even a radical hermeneutics—then, for Benjamin, the *Verstehen* that is to be grasped (*zu fassen*) must be sought in the *Nachleben* in which a work or an idea first becomes recognizable as the challenge and provocation that it is. This understanding of understanding unfolds in the spectral mode of its afterlife, when its putative moment of cognition has long passed. The foundational moment of historical understanding, what Benjamin terms the *Grundlage der Geschichte überhaupt*, would therefore not be a moment of presence, lucidity, and transparent awareness of an object that is available and identical to itself, but rather would call for a rigorous engagement with that which, within a work or text, bespeaks a radical nonsynchronicity of understanding.

What *Nachleben* evokes is not merely a reconsideration of the historical but a repetition of understanding that gives what was presumed to have been understood over to historical understanding in ever-new and unpredictable ways. *Nachleben* therefore is the figure of a repetition that does not repeat, a living on and after that both remains attached to what came before and, precisely through an analysis of that abiding yet often invisible attachment, departs from it in ever-new directions.

To the extent that *Nachleben* requires us to think in a nonsychronist, nonpresentist manner, every encounter with an object or a thought also must be read in terms of what it is no longer and what it is not yet—that is to say, in terms of the object's or thought's fore- and after-history. This fore- and after-history calls upon us, in the elusive critical act, both to read what is no longer and to read what was never written. As Benjamin argues, it "is the present that polarizes the event into fore- and after-history [*die Gegenwart, die das Geschehen in Vor- und Nachgeschichte polarisiert*]."[3] He expands on this conception when he writes that the "present determines where, in the object from the past, that object's fore-history and after-history diverge in order to circumscribe its nucleus."[4] If *Nachleben* teaches us to think in terms of *Vorgeschichte* and *Nachgeschichte*, it thereby also teaches us that the experience of historical time is never that of presence alone. The after upon which *Nachleben* and *Nachgeschichte* pivot is the site where temporal experience (and there can be no other) is beckoned, even fundamentally determined, by an elsewhere, an intuition that the object or thought under scrutiny cannot yet (or no longer) be fully understood, because the moment of its actuality is never lodged in the *Gegenwart* of its presence or present tense. In this way, there can be no *Nachleben*, and no engagement with a fore-history and an after-history, that does not require us to learn to engage with absolute absence—either in the guise of the "no longer" or in the form of a nonanticipatable "not yet." Thought here becomes a form of living on, a mode of survival in a world in which nothing ever is what it seems.

One of the lessons to be drawn from this analysis is that the most fruitful historical inquiry is one whose primary interests are invested *elsewhere*. As Benjamin suggests:

Für den materialistischen Historiker ist jede Epoche, mit der er sich beschäftigt, nur Vorgeschichte derer, um die es ihm selber geht. Und eben darum gibt es für ihn in der Geschichte den Schein der Wiederholung nicht, weil eben die ihm am meisten angelegenen Momente des Geschichtsverlaufs durch ihren Index als "Vorgeschichte" Momente dieser Gegenwart selber werden und je nach dieser katastrophaler oder siegreicher Bestimmung ihren eignen Character ändern.

[For the materialist historian, every epoch with which he occupies himself is only fore-history with respect to the one that really matters to him. And this is why, for him, there can be no semblance of repetition in history, because precisely those moments in the course of history that matter most to him, by virtue of their index as "fore-history," become moments of this present itself and change their specific character according to whether this determination is catastrophic or triumphant.][5]

If the time with which the historian is concerned is always only the *Vorgeschichte* to something else—perhaps not unlike Benjamin's own nonsynchronous engagement with the German baroque mourning play as an index of modernity as such, or his later obsession with Baudelaire's Paris of the nineteenth century as a fore-history to the issues that preoccupied him throughout the late 1920s and the 1930s—then that which is at hand, even in the moment of its "present" analysis, deserves to be conceptualized also as an after, an after-history or afterthought to something that in the moment of reflection still remains to be written.

Benjamin himself furnishes us throughout his work with reverberations and direct as well as indirect echoes of the figure of *Nachleben* that, taken together, conspire to yield something akin to the task of the critic. Among these variously modulated mobilizations are his conception of a *Nachleben* of works through quotation, whereby a work lives on precisely when parts of it have been isolated and more or less violently extracted from their so-called original context in such a way as to signify in completely foreign, always unanticipatable contexts (a fate to which all language—as a system of iteration and iterability—is subject). Forms of *Nachleben* also are at work in, among other areas, Benjamin's analyses of technical reproducibility in visual media such as film and photography, in his engagements with Bertolt Brecht's epic theater and its tendency to make gestures "citable" and thus repeatable in works to come, and in the tenacious survival of theological motifs and figures of thought even after the undoing of theology as a category of insight. In "The Task of the Translator," *Nachleben* is enriched by such semantic neighbors as *Nachreifen*, or "after-ripening," a gradual ripening of language after the fact; *Überleben*, or "surviving"; and *Fortleben*, or "living on," to designate the structural fate of language when seen from the perspective of its translation and translatability with respect to the demands of *reine Sprache*, "pure language."[6] The particular *Nachleben* that is the *Überleben* of a text translates and cites language as language, indeed, makes us see what language is when it carries language across into another language, or into another con-text, where a cited or translated text may survive, but no longer simply as itself.

Taking my point of departure from, while at the same time reaching beyond, Benjamin's own preoccupations, I wish to suggest that the manifold implications of a wrestling with the ghostly *Nach* may be put to work under the auspices of a general and expanded concept of afterness in which what has superseded or outlived remains intricately indebted to the very thing it has outlived or overcome. There can be no after without a debt, an unsettled relation, a haunting. It is to this constellation of the after that the present book returns again and again—from ever-shifting perspectives and in ever-changing specific contexts and exemplarities, in different media, in response to different historical exigencies, and in relation to specific texts by a variety of heterogeneous writers, thinkers, and artists of modernity, from eighteenth-century authors such as Kant and Schiller all the way to twentieth-century proper names such as Franz Kafka, Ernst Bloch, Martin Heidegger, Theodor W. Adorno, and Jacques Derrida. While every instance of afterness retains a singularity that resists assimilation by any conceptual "system," each instance *also* enacts a specific figure of thought—of following or coming after—that will allow us to illuminate a more general concept of afterness.

In "Too Late," one of the autobiographically inflected miniatures that Benjamin's *Berlin Childhood around 1900* situates in a lyrical constellation, the subjective narrative voice finds itself suddenly seized by a memory that enacts the fundamental experience of belatedness and afterness: "The clock in the schoolyard looked damaged because of me. It read 'too late.' And, in the hall, through the classroom doors I brushed by, murmurs of secret deliberations reached my ears. . . . Or else all was silent, as though someone were expected. Inaudibly, I touched the door handle. Sunshine flooded the spot where I stood." Benjamin continues: "No one seemed to know me, or even to see me. Just as the devil takes the shadow of Peter Schlemihl, the teacher had taken my name at the beginning of the hour. I could no longer get my turn. I worked noiselessly with the others until the bell sounded. But there was no blessedness in it."[7] Questions of temporal experience and its relation to the measuring of time, discourses of guilt and the other, the thematics of the name, the subject, and the continual deferral of redemption are all condensed here into a scene of having-missed, of a certain dis-appointment. Writing from the perspective of a child playing on the threshold to the twentieth century, Benjamin allegorizes a fundamental mood of the discourse of modernity, one in which the unsettling feeling of always already having arrived too late gives rise to the experience of a certain after that consciousness is now forced to inhabit. Whether existing among the ruins and traces of what has long since outlived its usefulness, experiencing modernity as a process of increasing secularization, or feeling no longer entirely at home in this or that systematic world order: the after conditions whatever it is still possible to think and experience in modernity. That no blessedness lies in the awareness of this after, as Benjamin's poetic image apodictically claims, raises a number of questions that are inscribed in the heart of modernity.

"We must get accustomed to the fact that the concept is not something that simply goes without saying," we read in one of the philosopher Hans Blumenberg's posthumously published papers. As he reminds us, "to say, 'This is an elephant' presupposes the question, 'What is this?' The question is rooted in the fact that to have seen what it is and what it means, this thing that is encountered, presumed, or expected at a given time, is by no means self-evident. What can be perceived, and how it might affect our behavior, is not regulated in advance. The situation of the question, and hence that of the answer in which the concept is implied, is one of indeterminacy."[8] In this study, the after of afterness will prove to be just such a situation. At first sight, however, the question of the after seems to bear no relation to the purported self-evidence and everydayness of this temporal preposition. One thing follows another in a temporal sequence that appears always to have been conceptually regulated and epistemologically determined in advance. Yet: the inferiority felt by the Romans toward their own culture in comparison with Greek culture that went before it; Schelling's epoch-defining philosophy of nature, which understood itself, in a fundamental sense, as coming after Fichte's philosophy of consciousness; the long shadow of Goethe, from which later nineteenth-century German-language writers such as Keller, Stifter, Raabe, and Platen struggled to liberate themselves, since this shadow seemed to condemn them to a kind of epigonal literary existence; the "anxiety of influence," to evoke literary critic Harold Bloom's once-famous phrase, felt by British Romantic poets when, in the wake of such previous canonical poetry as Milton's, they strove desperately to devise a nonderivative, supposedly "original" poetic voice; the lyric poetry of Hölderlin, written after, and in view of, the flight of the Greek gods in modernity; the political philosophy that crystallized in the aftermath of the French Revolution; or so-called media aesthetics, which advertises itself today as an existential form coming after humanism and after the ascension of the computer to worldwide supremacy—what all these and many other variegated forms of experienced afterness have in common is that they entail far more than a simple sequential progression in time. They call upon us to view the after in a new light, one that brings its often unperceived ways of subtly channeling our habits of thought and behavior into sharper relief and demonstrates that its spectral indeterminacy can never entirely be dispelled by its apparent self-evidence.

A rigorous thinking of the after, even of an expansive, encompassing state of afterness, should not return us to the language of various "post-isms," the "end" of this or that paradigm, or the alleged "no-longer-possibles" that have proved so irresistible to intellectuals and scholars in the course of the past few decades. Rather, something else, something more fundamental, is at stake. In reflecting upon the logic and figure of afterness in modern discourse, we are prompted to reconceive a thinking of the after as a kind of after-thought or thinking-after, a *Nach-denken*. Our interrogation of the hyphen that both separates and connects *nach* and *denken* provokes a series of questions: What is meant when one thing is said to "follow" another? Does what follows mark a clear break with what comes before, or does it paradoxically perpetuate its predecessor by remaining bound to the concepts and conditions of that from which it was thought to have taken its leave? Is not the very act of breaking with, and then following upon, a way of retroactively constructing and consolidating that which, in the instance of being farewelled, has set into motion the very movement of following? For example, by declaring their independence from the English motherland, the American colonists laid claim to an afterness that was predicated on a break with colonial authority. However, in the very act of declaring their independence, the colonists also unwittingly reaffirmed colonial authority.[9] One breaks with something or someone—declaring and explaining one's decision to that something or someone—only insofar as one also recognizes that something or someone as possessing the authority that would dictate the necessity of such a declaration in the first place. A truly independent subject would have no need to justify its independence to another if that subject did not also, in the very act of asserting independence, aspire to usurp the right to make such declarations. Seen from this perspective, a break with something that gives way to a following upon it is not only itself but also its opposite—that is, both a negation of what is broken away from and at the same time an affirmation, even if through negation, of the very same thing. It is at once a negation of what is being rejected and a confirmation of the same. The question of supersession and of the after is itself contaminated by a kind of afterness, a central, if previously only peripherally articulated thought-figure in the discourse of speculative thought and modern aesthetics. Matters of following are properly matters of an afterness that holds us in its grip.

My neologism *afterness* (*Nachheit* in German) denotes a rhetorical, intellectual, and experiential phenomenon that emerges from our understanding of lateness, supersession, and posteriority. The term seems necessary insofar as related notions, such as the psychoanalytic concept of retroactivity or deferred action (*Nachträglichkeit*), for all their undisputed relevance to a thinking of afterness, cannot do justice to the full scope of the afterness phenomenon. Furthermore, the concept of afterness represents an attempt to acknowledge—in an unconventional way, to be sure—the theoretical consequences of a semantic element that is central to the German language. The extent to which the centrality of the word *nach*, or "after," in German may or may not be replicated in other languages is a matter of secondary importance, for it may well be the case that a subterranean connection of thought-figures and possibilities is brought to light in German that in other languages—"post-" or *après*—has not been retained in this form or even may be obscured by them.

The German *nach* can be found in such variegated semiotic fields and compound nouns as *nachahmen* (to imitate), *Nachfolger* (successor), and *Nachfahre* (descendent) and in words like *nachher* (afterward), *nachgerade* (positively), *nachhaltig* (lasting), *nachträglich* (retroactive, belated), *nacheinander* (sequentially), *Nachname* (last name), *Nachfrage* (demand, follow-up), *Nachkomme* (offspring), *nachäffen* (aping), *Nachricht* (news), *Nachruf* (obituary), *Nachtisch* (dessert), *Nachdruck* (emphasis, reprint), *Nachtrag* (supplement), *Nachwort* (afterword), *Nachrede* (hearsay, defamation), *nachprüfen* (to check), *nachlässig* (careless), *Nachschlag* (second helping), *nachschlagen* (to look something up), *Nachschub* (additional supply), *nachschicken* (to forward), *Nachhall* (echo), *nacheifern* (to emulate), *nachdenken* (to contemplate, to reflect on something), *nachbessern* (to correct), *nachgeben* (to give in, to give way), *nachfüllen* (to refill), *nachprüfen* (to verify), *Nachschlagewerk* (reference work), *nachtragend* (unforgiving), *Nachsichtigkeit* (leniency), *nachrücken* (to move up), *nachgiebig* (indulgent), and many more. The history of the German word's adverbial and prepositional usages permits us to recognize a certain structure of signification that is pertinent to our discussion. Uses of the word *nach* that indicate a direction or a spatial or temporal succession derive from the Old High German *nah*. Understood as an adverb, it means "near, almost, after"; understood as a preposition, it means "near, around, behind, according to."¹⁰ It is further related to the Old English *neah*, the source of the modern "near." What is remarkable about this etymology is that *nach* originally meant "close to, in the vicinity of," then "toward something," and finally "behind something" or "according to." *Nach* thus initially designated a spatial relation, having its roots in the common origin of *nach* and *nahe*, "after" and "near," discernable today in the German term for those who live nearby: *Nachbarn* (neighbors). Only later was this spatial relation translated into a temporal one. *Nach* as a temporal preposition accordingly takes the place of the after that it appears merely to indicate, and hence embodies a double afterness. The co-belonging of *nach* and *nah*, "after" and "near," within the same lexical history points to a conceptual affinity between the two as well, since the temporal after, which connects what is surpassed and that which has surpassed it, always also constitutes an often *unthought* form of ongoing proximity. To live *nach* does not mean to emancipate oneself fully from what went before but, on the contrary, to be subterraneously determined by it to a greater or lesser degree.

The concept of afterness and its double figure of *nah* and *nach* also invites us to reconsider, among many other things, the logic and movements of mourning and melancholia; the experience of loss, trauma, and survival; and the inexplicable emotions connected with living on. Is the logic of afterness not also connected to the "experience of trauma" that Cathy Caruth, following Freud, characterizes as "the fact of latency" that would seem "to consist, not in the forgetting of a reality that can hence never be fully known, but in an inherent latency within the experience itself"?¹¹ Afterness, in fact, could be said to figure as a certain traumatic crisis of experience itself. As Caruth reminds us in her reading of Freud, psychoanalysis's "difficult thought provides a deeply disturbing insight into the enigmatic relation between trauma and survival: the fact that, for those who undergo trauma, it is not only the moment of the event, but of the passing out of it that is traumatic; that *survival itself*, in other words, *can be a crisis*."[12] The trauma of afterness and the afterness of trauma are such a crisis.

Other syntactically related figures include the echo, the dream, and repetition. A forceful staging of the specific afterness of the echo can be found in the ancient myth of Narcissus and Echo, in which the mountain nymph Echo responds to her beloved Narcissus only by repeating the final phrase of what the latter has uttered in his previous statement—but, precisely in this way, bestowing new meanings on language that is "merely" cited. As a form of afterness, the language of echo is always the language of the other. What is suggested by the myth of Narcissus and Echo—especially as it is developed in Ovid's version—is that language itself is but an echo, a reverberating network of responses, citations, and reworkings that are not simply tethered to a specific voice, all without an "original" speaker or a "first" instance or principle of utterance.[13] The figure of the echo, like the historical transmissions of myth itself, stages the afterness of language, whose origin and originality always are *derived*, even in its seemingly most original instantiations. Like the echo, the dream belatedly returns us to the scene of a previous utterance or experience, albeit typically in a reconfigured and dissimulated form. Whether as a retroactive working-through, as wish fulfillment, or as the manifestation of ambivalence and anxiety, the dream unfolds its own forms and rhythms of psychological afterness, as Freud's *Interpretation of Dreams* was among the most prominent Western theories to articulate. Along similar lines, the figure of repetition, especially as it emerges in thinkers such as Kierkegaard (*Repetition*) and Gilles Deleuze (*Difference and Repetition*), can be viewed in terms of an afterness that re-presents one more time that which was held to be originary—all in an act in which difference, rather than the reproduction of an alleged prior identity, determines repetition. Finally, it could be argued that a thinking of afterness also opens onto spaces and sites such as the museum. What is a museum other than the concretized space in which the after is staged in particular and ever-shifting relations to social, historical, and aesthetico-political force fields of associations, expectations, and imbrications? More than a culture's *lieu de mémoire*, to use French historian Pierre Nora's phrase, the museum, in its particular and self-consciously overdetermined relationship to temporality, can be read as the site in which a certain idea of afterness ex-poses itself, opening itself to interrogation.

By the same token, the figure of afterness sheds new light on discourses of religion and secularization in modernity. Tied to the allegedly fully rational, scientific, and transparently reason-based commitments of enlightened thought, secularization is said to have superseded the superstitions and mythical structures of religious modes of consciousness and theological rhythms of argumentation. An interrogation of the assumptions of secularization from the perspective of afterness can work to show that religious structures of thought continue to be at play even in the most secularized thought-formations, codetermining consciousness and its practical commitments in often unacknowledged ways. Here, it would be necessary to return to the complex accounts of religion and faith in such heterogeneous thinkers on religion as Nietzsche (on the transvaluation of all values after Christianity), Bloch (especially *The Principle of Hope*), Freud (especially *The Future of an Illusion*), Emmanuel Levinas (especially *Of God Who Comes to Mind* and *Otherwise than Being or Beyond Essence*), Gianno Vattimo (especially such works as *Belief*; his book with Richard Rorty, *After Christianity*; *The Future of Religion*; and his book with John D. Caputo, *After the Death of God*); Derrida (especially such essays as "Faith and Knowledge: The Two Sources of 'Religion' at the Limits of Reason Alone"); and Jürgen Habermas's conversation with Joseph Ratzinger (now Pope Benedict XVI) on the dialectic of secularization in the context of faith and reason (*Dialektik der Säkularisierung: Über Vernunft und Religion*), among many others.[14] Far from propagating religion or denigrating secularization, the logic of afterness can be employed to demonstrate that an apparently rational position that claims to have overcome the faith-based structures of religion once and for all is one of the most religious positions conceivable.

From a slightly different perspective, the subterranean determining character of the *nach* hardly can be understood without considering the figure of the *end*. After all, from the viewpoint of the after, the end is not identical with itself. Not simply a delimitable *telos*, the end poses questions of its own that resist the articulation of any definitive answer. The famous German research group Poetics and Hermeneutics, for example, ponders what it might mean to divest the end of its putative self-evidence as a figure of thought. "The end is by no means a presuppositionless category," literary critics Karlheinz Stierle and Rainer Warning remind us, "that is useful solely for ascertaining what is the case."[15] They proceed to ask: "Does not the factual end as such always require an implicit narrative structure that causes the end to arise from a beginning? And does not the difference between beginning and end always first require hermeneutic interpretation? Yet, is not the end a problematic category for the reason that nothing which comes to an end can be exhausted by its being an end?"[16] As such, the multiple forms that the end can take may be understood as highly artificial categories for articulating the different endings experienced by consciousness and framed within aesthetic and philosophical discourse. To read such imaginings of the end as historically and intellectually contingent, and hence highly mutable, is to be confronted with the question of afterness, which clings to the figure of the end as an ever-postponed finality. Thus Hegel, in the *Differenzschrift*, draws attention to the endlessness of the end, which results from the fact that the end can always equally be regarded as a possible beginning: "The question should rather be whether this end, incapable as it is of being an end, could possibly be the beginning of something."[17] The question of the end posed by Hegel in spatial terms could equally be understood as a question of afterness, such that whatever happens in the aftermath of an assumed end represents the beginning of an after that no thinking of the end can ever fully exhaust. Afterness, in this sense, is an experiential and conceptual figure which requires that the conventional understanding of beginning and end be considered from a new perspective. Situated in rather different philosophical and cultural-theoretical discourses, Heidegger (in *Über den Anfang* [*On the Beginning*], 1941) and Edward Said (in *Beginnings*) have helped us begin to think through the complex question of the beginning as an intellectual task, and to confront the question of an unforeseeably assumed or anticipated end.[18] In the discourse of literary modernity, writers such as Robert Musil, in his collection of thought-images *Nachlaß zu Lebzeiten* (1936), or Maurice Blanchot, in "Après Coup," his belatedly composed meditation on his 1957 novel *Le ressassement éternel*, have reflected on a form of afterness in which the end always also represents the deferred, palely shimmering condition of possibility of some future beginning.[19]

This future beginning can be thought not only as the other yet to come but also as something that, for all its otherness and futurity, already or still inhabits us. In the context of his work on theatricality, Samuel Weber suggests that in "order to share and partake, there must . . . be a concomitant dividing or investing, a *parting* or, perhaps more precisely, a departing, a taking leave, a *partitioning* in order to *im-part*."[20] As he reminds us, "all of this is uncannily condensed in the English phrase 'parting with.' The 'with' suggests that parting entails a departure, not simply as the dissolving of a relationship, but rather as a singular way of (re)constituting one"; in this sense, one might say, "to remain in relation *with* precisely by departing" becomes one of the central features of any thinking of arrival and departure.[21] If *to part with* implies that what is left behind is also taken along, if what is abandoned is at the time *brought with* on one's journey elsewhere, it suggests that any parting with something also stages the implicit structure of an afterness whose logic still remains to be thought and appreciated more fully.²²

Although afterness relentlessly demands to be interpreted as the by-product of a differently understood end, one that *lives on* and thus is not merely and not always the end, it nonetheless brings a singular conception of the after into circulation. In his brief meditation on the work of the American conceptual artist Joseph Kosuth, Jean-François Lyotard remarks: "After philosophy comes philosophy. But it is altered by the after."²³ Lyotard's apodictic, seemingly straightforward observation reveals itself, upon closer inspection, to have far-reaching consequences for our own inquiry. For what gives itself to be thought here is a figure of the after that allows precisely that with which it breaks, and which it succeeds in the break itself, to continue existing, hence a figure that not only is aware of the posthumous survival of what has been left behind, but appropriates its own obsolescence as a constitutive lack, so to speak, as a more or less subterranean aftershock of the undead. Were it permissible to draw on this thought-figure to illuminate particular discourses of modernity, proper names from the intellectual history of modernity would have to include Hegel, Freud, Benjamin, Heidegger, Lyotard, Levinas, de Man, and Derrida. What the writings of these rather different thinkers have in common is that they all seek to come to terms, in the idiom of their own concerns and in a manner as consequential as it is heterogeneous, with a certain trope of afterness. In Hegel's aesthetics, the alleged end of art cannot be thought of apart from a reevaluation of the relationship between concepts and their concrete aesthetic manifestations. According to Freud's psychoanalytic model, it is only through a certain delayed action or retroactivity, his famous *Nachträglichkeit*, that the subject encounters the particular iterations of the fact that it is fundamentally not at home with itself, unable to assign to this or that experience, even the experience of trauma, a binding meaning that could not be relativized by what is to come. Whereas, for Benjamin, true historical insight demands that history be read against the grain of its supposedly natural and noncontingent narrative exposition, Heidegger, in his "ecstatic" interpretations of the temporality of *Dasein*, takes his leave of a model of three-dimensional time, insisting instead, in response to the supposedly ahistorical phenomenological method of his teacher Husserl, on the temporalization of the unfolding of historicity itself. In Levinas's ethically inflected meditations on afterness and the movement of succession, we repeatedly come across the concept of the *passé absolu*, a past that, in contrast to that of the Cartesian model, was never present to itself in the first place. This trope of the *passé absolu* is then implicitly taken up by Lyotard and Derrida. For Lyotard, all thought that arises in connection with the *episteme* that is sometimes, rather too hastily, called "postmodernity" belongs to a movement that breaks with the master narratives of the West and self-consciously emerges in their afterness. Derrida, for his part, interrogates the so-called fiction of anteriority, the assumption that the present was fully present to itself in the past. This fiction can only apparently circumvent the transience and tenuousness of self-presence, which continually threaten to put in question the experience of the now as one of unmitigated immediacy. The linguistic inflections of these considerations of afterness, their rhetorical predicament, reemerge in de Man's insistence on the allegorically structured rhetoric of temporality, in which what he terms the constitutive temporal element of presentation allows us to confront, through the rhetorical *figure*, the ways in which language both posits and threatens to unravel itself in its own deferral. In all these thinkers of the after, afterness in its various forms gives itself to be recognized as an almost spectrally undecidable provocation, a provocation that at the same time, however, points to key questions of experienceability and thinkability.

The experience and thinking of afterness would have to unfold always in terms of their hauntedness, the ways in which the after stages a hauntedness of what has been overcome or superseded by what has been, or is believed to have been, overcome or superseded. Afterness always would be a form of spectrality, a matter of the ghostly other that continues to haunt and that will not stay buried. In *Specters of Marx*, Derrida not only provides an account of the logics and aporias of spectrality, he also recalls us to the responsibility that imposes itself on us, if we let it, to learn to inherit a legacy that is at odds with itself and that shows itself to us only in the form of elusive ghosts. "If the readability," he writes, "of a legacy were given, natural, transparent, univocal, if it did not call for and at the same time defy interpretation, we would never have anything to inherit from it."[24] This is so, Derrida argues, because we "would be affected by it as by a cause—natural or genetic. One always inherits from a secret—which says 'read me, will you ever be able to do so?'"[25] The readability of the legacy of spectrality and of the inheritance of the many ghosts that continue to haunt us even when we believe ourselves to be "done" with something only can be confronted in a proper fashion when this very readability also threatens to break down. There can only be a true inheritance of something, even of the ghost, when we do not know what it would mean to inherit *this particular* ghost, assume *this singular* legacy.[26] If the mode of reading the legacy of a ghost were already given in advance, there would be nothing to consider, nothing to learn, nothing to interpret, nothing to agonize over: in short, nothing to inherit. Derrida's perspective on spectrality illuminates the task of coming to terms with afterness as well. Afterness possesses its own ghosts, causes something to live on in a spectral fashion, and as such belongs to the order of the secret. The secret of afterness will always call upon us to "inherit" it one more time, place it in a tradition of other afters and other secrets, even as we attempt to learn to respect its idiomatic and singular secret. Afterness must be read and it resists being read; but it can only be read and analyzed in the emphatic sense *because* of, rather than in spite of, this perpetual resistance. This simultaneous invitation and resistance will have been its secret and its spectral inheritance.

In *Aus der Erfahrung des Denkens* (*From the Experience of Thinking*), Heidegger's 1947 collection of prose poems, the experience of thinking an afterness conceived along such lines is made uncannily vivid, albeit not necessarily easier to grasp. There, we read the following stanzas:

Das Älteste des Alten kommt in unserem Denken
hinter uns her und doch auf uns zu.

Darum hält sich das Denken an die Ankunft des
Gewesenen und ist Andenken.

Alt sein heißt: rechtzeitig dort innehalten, wo der
einzige Gedanke eines Denkweges in sein Gefüge
eingeschwungen ist.

Den Schritt zurück aus der Philosophie in das Denken des Seyns dürfen wir wagen, sobald wir in der
Herkunft des Denkens heimisch geworden sind.[27]

[The oldest of the old comes, in our thinking,
after us and yet toward us.

Therefore thinking orients itself on the arrival of
what-has-been and is remembrance.

> To be old means: to pause in time there where the
> only thought of a path of thinking is
> swung into its joint.
>
> We may dare to take the step back out of philosophy
> into the thinking of Being as soon as we have
> come to feel at home in the provenance of thinking.]

If, for the lyrical voice of this haunted versification of thought, the oldest of the old comes after us and follows us in, as, and through thinking, this following implies a spectral bifurcation and even reversal of temporality. What is behind us, chases us (*hinter uns her*), also is that which is still to come, moving our way from an elsewhere that we have not yet visited. Staging the idea of a certain afterness, the kind of thinking that is enabled by this out-of-jointness of the after and the before, illuminates the ways in which afterness is never a clean break but acts as the figure of an unfinished business that still is in need of being understood.

The thinking of afterness would have to confront the moment of arrival (*Ankunft*) of something that has already passed, a having-been-ness (*Gewesenes*). As such, this thinking is also always a matter of remembrance, commemoration, and memorialization, concepts condensed in *Andenken*. It is hardly an accident that Heidegger here employs the term *Andenken*, for this is also the title of a canonical poem by Hölderlin, the poet to whom Heidegger devoted so many of his thoughts and words. Like in Hölderlin, the commemoration and memorialization that *Andenken* here encodes is always intertwined with the logic of an *An-denken*, a *denken an*, a "thinking-of" or "thinking-toward," in which memory and thought emerge as the siblings that they are. If Heidegger's intuition is right that great thinkers all think but a single thought, his general idea, alluded to in this specific poem with the phrase *der einzige Gedanke eines Denkweges* (the thought of a disjunction of time) is the moment when the thought of an afterness both comes into its own and is installed in and as its frame or its destiny (*in sein Gefüge eingeschwungen*). To depart from the precepts of mere philosophy by stepping back into a more orginary *thinking* of Being (it is noteworthy that Heidegger here uses Hölderlin's old spelling *Seyn*, rather than the modern *Sein*, to make his point) presupposes that we have learned to feel at home in the provenance of thought (*Herkunft des Denkens*). Only as such, in a step forward into thinking that is simultaneously a step back (*Schritt zurück*) may a true and as yet unknown thinking occur. Being on the way to language, this thinking confronts with each trope or turn anew the question of its temporal disjunction, of the before and the after, without ever being merely a now. A poetic and speculative reading of afterness, seen from this perspective, would treat afterness as one of the ghostly names for the future task of thinking itself.

The orientation of Heidegger's poem here parallels that of aspects of his essay on the poetry of Georg Trakl, "Die Sprache im Gedicht" (Language in the Poem). There, his aesthetically mediated concerns with a temporality that is out of joint and that remains unthought focus on Trakl's poem "Jahr." Heidegger writes apropos of Trakl's poetic evocation of the end:

> Das Ende ist hier nicht die Folge und das Verklingen des Anbeginns. Das Ende geht, nämlich als das Ende des verwesenden Geschlechtes, dem Anbeginn des ungeborenen Geschlechtes vorauf. Der Anbeginn hat jedoch als die frühere Frühe das Ende schon überholt. . . . Aber die wahre Zeit ist Ankunft des Gewesenen. Dieses ist nicht das Vergangene, sondern die Versammlung des Wesenden, die aller Ankunft voraufgeht, indem sie als solche Versammlung sich in ihr je Früheres zurückbirgt. Dem Ende und seiner Vollendung entspricht [Trakls] "dunkle Geduld."[28]

> [Here, the end is not the sequel and fading echo of the beginning. The end—being the end of the decaying race—precedes the beginning of the unborn race. But the beginning, the earlier earliness, has already overtaken the end. . . . True time, however, is the arrival of that which has been. This is not what is past, but rather the gathering of essential being, which precedes all arrival in gathering itself into the shelter of what, each time, it was earlier. The end and its perfection correspond to [Trakl's] "dark patience."][29]

Implicitly taking up the trope of the so-called ecstasies of time from *Being and Time*, Heidegger here imagines an uncanny involution of beginning and end in which nothing is what it seems. Because the inception of a beginning has already left behind and outpaced the end, what is to be thought as time is not the perpetual and gradual unfolding of a sequentiality but rather the arrival of the what-has-been, *des Gewesenen*.[30] The what-has-been is not simply identical to the past, if by "past" is meant the anteriority of a former point in the unfolding of linear time. Rather, in keeping with the precepts of his general thinking, Heidegger implies that the *Gewesene* is *wesentlich* (essential) also because it *west* (presences), as it were, and in the form of such a presencing allows for the gathering (*Versammlung*) of all the former "formers." Only in the form of such a gathering of the former formers in a temporality that looks back yet is always already ahead of itself, ready to receive *from* the future what is not simply *of* the future, does the arrival of the what-has-been become thinkable at the crossroads of the before and the after, without being reducible to either. Parting with an Aristotelian understanding of time as the dimension of a quantitative or qualitative calculation of duration, one that remains structured by the thinking of sequentiality, Heidegger's insistence on the nonsequential, ecstatic, disjointed experience of time points to its essence as something that refuses the binary opposition of beginning and end. We might say that this unorthodox interpretation of time provides insight into the workings of afterness, in which before and after, now and then, beginning and end, arrival and departure, destruction and perpetuation are also at issue. Any thinking of afterness may ultimately very well require the "dark patience," the *dunkle Geduld*, of which Trakl's poem strangely sings.

It is as though Heidegger here, by taking recourse to Trakl's verse, elaborated on elements of his engagement with the uncanniness of temporality that he had first outlined, three decades earlier, in his 1924 lecture before the Marburg theologians, "The Concept of Time." There, he suggests:

> Die Betrachtung der Geschichte, die in der Gegenwart aufwächst, sieht in ihr nur unwiederbringliche Betriebsamkeit: das, was los war. Die Betrachtung dessen, was los war, ist unerschöpflich. Sie verliert sich im Stoff. Weil diese Geschichte und Zeitlichkeit der Gegenwart gar nicht an die Vergangenheit herankommt, hat sie nur eine andere Gegenwart. Vergangenheit bleibt so lange einer Gegenwart verschlossen, als diese, das Dasein, nicht selbst geschichtlich ist. Das Dasein ist aber geschichtlich an ihm selbst, sofern es seine Möglichkeit ist. Im Zukünftigsein ist das Dasein seine Vergangenheit; es kommt darauf zurück im Wie. Die Weise des Zurückkommens ist unter anderem das Gewissen. Nur das Wie ist wiederholbar. Vergangenheit—als eigentliche Geschichtlichkeit erfahren—ist alles andere denn das Vorbei. Sie ist etwas, worauf ich immer wieder zurückkehren kann.[31]

[The view of history that is growing up in the present sees in it only an irretrievable busyness: that which went on. The reflection on what went on is inexhaustible. It loses itself in the material. Because this history and temporality of the present does not even reach the past, it only has another presence. The past remains closed off from a present as long as the latter, as *Dasein*, is itself not historical. But *Dasein* is historical upon itself, in as far as it is its possibility. In futureness *Dasein* is its past; it returns to it in the How. The mode of returning is, among other things, conscience. Only the How is repeatable. The past—experienced as actual historicity—is anything but the Over. It is something to which I can always return.]

For the interpretation of *Dasein* to grasp the latter's radically temporal core, it must not simply think of the past as a series of former instances or manifestations of the present that have moved on into the past. Rather, the futurity of *Dasein*, which is a matter of the future precisely because it names that which remains still to be thought and experienced, is the temporal space in which the past comes into its own. Here, the past is not simply a *Vorbei*; it resides, rather, in a certain citability or repeatability of the How. But this repeatability, the space of a possible returning, can never be simply a matter of a clear division between *das Vergangene* and *Zukünftigkeit* as they relate in specifiable ways to the utterances that are spoken from the vantage point of a stable, identifiable Now. Time and *Dasein* are one because, among other things, they relate the experience of being-in-the-world to a haunting *Vorbei* that is both unavoidable and indeterminate. From Heidegger's perspective, *Dasein* is the possibility of its own *Vorbei* and its simultaneous inability to grasp this *Vorbei* as a determinable content. There can hardly be a *Dasein* that does not struggle with the experience of a *Vorbei* that is both past and yet to be confronted. This *Vorbei*, even in its most finite form of absence and death, names an afterness that holds us in its grip.

At this point, the objection could be raised that no phenomenon can ever withdraw from a purely temporal afterness—in other words, that there is nothing that does *not* temporalize a before and an after. In this sense, little could be gained from a thinking of the concept of afterness; its explanatory powers would be far too general for it to lead to any genuine insights. One could respond to this objection by pointing out that the attempt to reflect on afterness in a sustained way by no means amounts to the resurrection of a purely formal understanding of time as succession, nor does it entail a perspective fixed on the mere generality of thinking in temporal sequences. Rather, a thinking of afterness will have to be concerned with investigating under what conditions, and with which rhetorical and intellectual presuppositions, the experience of afterness gives expression to a largely unconscious ideology of supersession that warrants critical examination. This critical interrogation of afterness would have to be more than mere ideology critique. It would have to make visible a gesture that mistakenly holds itself to be self-evident, denigrating what has come before in the name of an alleged progress, whether this be conceived in ideological, political, aesthetic, economic, or techno-scientific terms. What needs to be taken into account is the idea that the essence of afterness is not of a purely temporal nature, even if any given instance of afterness must always also appear in a temporal sequence. In reflecting on each instance of afterness, a comportment of vigilance is elicited that sets itself the task of clarifying each time anew the reciprocal and ever-shifting *relations* among thought, experience, and afterness.

While it returns time and again to the manifold and variegated iterations of the after in modern thought and aesthetics, this study does not wish to constitute a history of afterness in modernity, nor does it strive in any way for comprehensiveness. Rather, its aim is to make vivid—in a few crucial tropes, situations, and media—certain key principles of afterness that haunt us always one more time. Rather than strive for the illusion of completeness or closure, this study takes its cue from Hegel's remark, in the *Phenomenology of Spirit*, that "the known is, precisely because it is *known*, not *cognized* [*Das Bekannte überhaupt ist darum, weil es* bekannt *ist, nicht* erkannt]. It is the most common deception of oneself and of others to presuppose, in the act of cognition, something as known."[32] He reminds us that "this knowledge, for all its back and forth and without knowing what is happening to it, cannot make any headway."[33] In keeping with Hegel's insight, this study will not presuppose the after as a known category about which one could simply write a history—for histories, to the extent that they are always histories *of* something, must methodologically presuppose a certain unity, familiarity, and presumed knowledge of their objects of study. Here, by contrast, the after will be kept open—that is, will be shown always *to have kept itself open*—as the site of competing significations and claims that have the capacity to surprise us in their idiomatic singularity and in their refusal to be absorbed without remainder into the master narratives, valuable and reassuring as they are, of causal and linear unfolding. The book focuses, rather, on a limited number of issues and strictly contoured contexts relating to the after that, in their exemplarity, illuminate the problem of afterness from ever-new perspectives and with ever-shifting emphases. The chapters simultaneously engage and displace each other in a polyphony that resonates around a common core.

Following chapter 1, which situates the problem of afterness in the genealogical context of post-Kantian modernity, chapter 2, "Afterness and Critique: A Paradigmatic Case," interrogates the problem of afterness in one of its most representative formulations—as it emerges in the moment of critique. Critique, which derives from the Greek *krinein* (to sever, to separate, to distinguish, to decide), names that which remains attached and indebted, in a subterranean way, to what it criticizes and to that from which it believes itself to have departed. This logic becomes understandable through a consideration of the moment of critique in three canonical thinkers—Kant, Heidegger, and Adorno—especially when enriched by a reflection on pertinent moments in Benjamin and Michel Foucault.

Chapter 3, "Afterness and Aesthetics: End Without End," analyzes a poetic and philosophical thought-image from Adorno's *Minima Moralia* in the context of his larger theoretical models furnished by *Negative Dialectics* and *Aesthetic Theory*. This chapter shows how Adorno envisions an aesthetic and epistemological thinking of the concept of afterness that defers the end-bound, teleological closure favored by conventional propositional theories of the artwork.

Chapter 4, "Afterness and *Rettung*: Can Anything Be Rescued by Defending It?," argues that there can be no gesture of rescuing that is not deeply inscribed in the logic of an afterness. Pursuing the vexed concept of *Rettung* in the actual and conceptual dialogue between Adorno and Benjamin allows us to view the postlapsarian status of the gesture of rescuing as a way of approaching the categories of historical experience and rescuing critique in a new way. Rather than embodying stable concepts to be employed by a self-identical critical consciousness (as exemplified by the Habermasian model), these categories emerge as correlates of the relentless demand in thinking to show oneself responsible to the ways in which rescuing something or someone is inseparable from a confrontation with this action's most successful dialectical failures.

Chapter 5, "Afterness and Translation: The Politics of Carrying Across," focuses on the form of afterness that goes by the name of "translation." It analyzes Heidegger's often neglected concept of translation as *Über-setzen*, or "carrying across," elucidating the ways in which this concept is lodged at the core of Heidegger's philosophy of language. Through its emphasis on the afterness of translation, this chapter reads Heidegger's ideas on translation in light of his 1936/1937 Freiburg seminar on Schiller's *Letters on the Aesthetic Education of Mankind*. Through an analysis of Heidegger's idiosyncratic appropriation of Schiller, it becomes possible to understand how translation provides Heidegger with a privileged paradigm for conceptualizing the problematic relation between a so-called original and the translation commonly thought of as following it in a straightforward sense. Here, the vexed relationship between his troublesome political involvements in 1933 and 1934 are reexamined in light of the "afterness" that emerges in his remarks on translation in such works as his lecture courses on *Hölderlin's Hymn "The Ister"* and on *Parmenides*, but also in such essays as "Building Thinking Dwelling" and "The Question Concerning Technology."

Chapter 6, "Afterness and the Image (I): Unsettling Photography," engages the medium of photography as a telling instantiation of the relation between the figure of following and its representations. The chapter places the theories of photography found in Kafka's writings and those that emerge in Derrida's work into a constellation. By situating Kafka's and Derrida's reflections on photography in the context of the work of German photographer Stefan Moses, the chapter problematizes the afterness of a photograph and its relation to an allegedly referential original subject, particularly with regard to Moses's series "Selbst im Spiegel" (Self in the Mirror), a subtly self-conscious and richly textured collection of photographic self-portraits of well-known German writers, philosophers, scientists, and artists.

Proceeding from the notion of an afterimage, chapter 7, "Afterness and the Image (II): Image Withdrawal," pursues the question of whether, given the uncanny "thereness" of the image today, one might nevertheless theorize a certain *withdrawal* of the image. Through an engagement with four singular and enigmatic articulations of the relation among image, essence, and truth-content, furnished by Benjamin, Heidegger, Blanchot, and Deleuze, the image in withdrawal claims our attention as the sign of a modernity that stages itself in terms of a perpetual leave-taking.

Chapters 8 through 10 each take up a specific form of the *experience* of afterness. "Afterness and Experience (I): Can Hope Be Disappointed?" examines the experiential category of hope that animates Bloch's oeuvre. Asking to what extent post-Enlightenment artists and scholars are still permitted to harbor, in their works and texts, hope for a future that is yet to come and therefore not foreclosed by dominant discourses of power, this chapter locates hope precisely in its disappointability, what Bloch calls an inescapable but deeply productive *Enttäuschbarkeit*. "Afterness and Experience (II): Crude Thinking Rethought" focuses on a different experience of afterness: the mode of thinking that differentiates between subtle and crude analysis. Taking its cue from playwright Bertolt Brecht's concept of "crude thinking" (*plumpes Denken*) and Benjamin's theoretical commentary on it, this chapter considers the afterness of a specific modality of thinking as a test case for modernity's political investments. Finally, "Afterness and Experience (III): Mourning, Memory, and the Fictions of Anteriority" investigates questions of memory, recollection, and remembrance as instantiations of afterness. Analyzing Derrida's innovative reworking of the two Hegelian concepts of memory for which there is only one English term, *Gedächtnis* (a conceptual, thought-based form of memory) and *Erinnerung* (a form of interiorizing memory that is irreducible to conceptual recall), this chapter shows how instances of historical and personal memory illustrate an afterness that vexingly complicates the historical relationship of past to present, of recollection to futurity. Engaging Derrida's language of mourning as it emerges in several of his texts, the chapter suggests that what he calls the "fiction of anteriority"—that is, the belief that something in the past was once simply present-to-itself as a transparent and accessible category of insight—sheds important light on an entire modern preoccupation with containing the specters of following and its inevitable afterness. For Derrida, the task is to call into question the notion of an anteriority unencumbered by the elusiveness of self-presence that our experience of presence as present contemporaneity so intractably stages.

Finally, chapter 11, "Afterness and Empty Space: No Longer and Not Yet," pursues the question of whether afterness can be thought to have a space, a *Zeitraum*, in which its movements can be thought. By turning to Hannah Arendt's notion of "empty space," a historical and experiential no-man's-land in which what lies between the after and the before cannot be reduced to the presence of a "now," we may approach afterness as both an openness and a form of traumatic survival.

Taken together, then, the chapters of this book engage the concept of afterness as a privileged trope and experiential category of modernity in a variety of iterations and modulations. The various analyses—across a heterogeneous collection of modern writers and thinkers, diverse historical moments of articulation, and a range of media—conspire to illuminate the notion that in the realms of aesthetics, politics, experience, media, and speculative thinking considered in this book, modernity can be understood as a question of the after. Through a series of close readings and broader conceptual contemplation, this book puts forward the wager that much hinges on our interpretation of the after. After all, our most fundamental assumptions concerning modern aesthetic representation, conceptual discourse, community, and politics are at stake.

To revise Lyotard's apodictic statement about the after in light of what will have "come to language" in this study, we could say: "After the after comes the after. But it is altered by the after." This singular, nonidentical moment of the afterness of critique, insofar as it can be accessed at all, harbors within itself a thinking and praxis to come that, in withholding their consent to what exists, would once again, as gestures of *krinein*, separate and decide. The after is thus the scene of an interminable transference, of perpetual marginality, and still-pending supersession. As Adorno's *Negative Dialectics* puts it in its final sentence, a kind of after-word that conditions all the sentences of criticism and commentary still to come: "Only if what is can be changed is that which is not all [*Nur wenn, was ist, sich ändern läßt, ist das, was ist, nicht alles*]."[34] This possibility would be an always already assumed, and thus anticipated, afterness of critique. *Too late* would then always also mean *not yet*.

1 *Afterness and Modernity*
A Genealogical Note

In our interrogation of the variegated conceptual aspects of afterness thus far, the words "modern" and "modernity" have made more than one appearance. In fact, one might say that by retroactively glossing terms that already have been in circulation, my sentences in this chapter perform a kind of afterness of their own. That is, what the following sentences introduce and attempt to justify already has preceded them, even haunts them, and my elaborations here, in a sense, chase after what they will have been meant to inaugurate. Afterness, as I wish to understand it, should be conceptualized first and foremost as a structural phenomenon, but its historical dimension should not be repressed or ignored. While the *structural specificity* of afterness will become clear, in ever-shifting modulations, over the course of the chapters that follow, an appreciation of its *historical inflection* requires a slightly different, more genealogically oriented account. For this reason, it is appropriate to explain, if only in a rather elliptical way, the general sense in which the historico-epistemic terms "modern" and "modernity" frame the structural problem of afterness.

To be sure, afterness as a category hardly can be confined to any single historical episteme or narrowly defined cultural "period." Its particular logic and structural reach are at once too heterogeneous and too historically persistent for such a delimitation. By the same token, the very notion of modernity, like all forms of periodization, is problematic not only because so-called periods always are retroactively constructed by the historiographer's gaze, but also because any such historical invention must of necessity remain both over- and underdetermined, at once including and excluding too much. In the case of modernity in particular, intellectual and cultural historians' various designations of the term compete. One of the most well-articulated characterizations of modernity is provided by the political theorist Marshall Berman in *All That Is Solid Melts into Air: The Experience of Modernity*:

> There is a mode of vital experience—experience of space and time, of the self and others, of life's possibilities and perils—that is shared . . . all over the world today. I will call this experience "modernity." To be modern is to find ourselves in an environment that promises us adventure, power, joy, growth, transformation of ourselves and the world—and, at the same time, that threatens to destroy everything we have, everything we know, everything we are. Modern environments and experiences cut across all boundaries of geography and ethnicity, of class and nationality, of religion and ideology. . . . But it is a paradoxical unity, a unity of disunity: it pours us all into a maelstrom of perpetual disintegration and renewal, of struggle and contradiction, of ambiguity and anguish. To be modern is to be part of a universe in which, as Marx said, "All that is solid melts into air."[1]

Berman ultimately anchors his thoughtful account of modernity, which emerges in constant dialogue with the work of Marx, first and foremost—and perhaps at times too single-mindedly—in the political economy of early capitalist development and the earliest versions of something like a world market in the sixteenth century. What is to be gained from this articulate account is not only a politically mediated insight into the dialectical workings of modernity but also an appreciation of a methodological difficulty. For, like any account of modernity, Berman's ultimately cannot fully embody the complexities and internal contradictions that any use of such a term must necessarily gloss over.

As Berman implicitly agrees, the sometimes overly triumphant claim that the inventions and allegedly progress-driven changes that took place between feudal or medieval cultural structures, on the one hand, and those associated with the emerging bourgeoisie in the eighteenth century, on the other, deserve to be subjected to a far-reaching semantic, political, and ideological critique.² Indeed, if "the modern" can be regarded as a cultural and historical category at all, it would have to be situated somewhere within the matrix of irreconcilable assumptions that range from French poet Arthur Rimbaud's deceptively simple statement in *Une saison en enfer* (*A Season in Hell*, 1873) that "il faut être absolument moderne," via the more recent influential meditations on the so-called postmodern condition by Lyotard and Fredric Jameson, all the way to Bruno Latour's sentiment, *We Have Never Been Modern*.³ Yet my wager here is that modernity, if this category retains any use value or conceptual specificity at all, could be thought as the philosophical and cultural-historical episteme in which the experience of afterness acquires an unprecedented urgency, even an obsessive quality that inflects philosophical and aesthetic discourse in decisive ways. Viewed from the standpoint of its imbrication with afterness, the term "modernity" might best be conceived along the lines of what Derrida once termed a *paleonomy*—that is, the "maintenance of an old name in order to launch a new concept."⁴

The philosophy and culture of modernity, on the most general level, are conceived here as problems that follow from Kant's so-called Copernican turn in thinking in the *Critique of Pure Reason* (1781), where he proposes that consciousness and its cognitive faculties be called on to provide an account of the ways in which the world of phenomena becomes the object of a consciousness's mental representation that cannot be fully understood as such. Critical philosophy, as Kant conceived it, thus was required to distance itself from precritical modes of dogmatism and skepticism in order to confront reason as a form of the radical self-critique of reason. As the Kant of the *Critique of Pure Reason* explains, philosophy "demands that reason should take on anew the most difficult of its tasks, namely that of self-knowledge, and to institute a court of justice [*einen Gerichtshof einzusetzen*], by which reason may secure its rightful claims . . . and this court is none other that the critique of pure reason itself." He further explains that, by this, he does not "understand a critique of books and systems, but a critique of the faculty of reason in general, in respect of all the cognitions after which reason might strive independently of all experience, and hence the decision about the possibility or impossibility of metaphysics in general." Such a thinking can be set on its way only "after discovering the point where reason has misunderstood itself."⁵ In this self-critique of reason, the object world can be thought but ultimately not cognized (*erkannt*), which is to say that "things-in-themselves" are unknowable to us except as cognitive appearances, mental presentations that answer to the precepts of mind and intellect rather than to those of the world of things. These presentations may or may not correspond to the actuality of an object realm. Kantian philosophy therefore investigates the a priori conditions of cognition and experience—that is, the cognitive structures, suppositional necessities, and forms of judgment whose analysis is required even before their actual encounter with this or that idea, thought, or experience. Kant calls this form of inquiry *transcendental* philosophy, setting it apart from the sensuous philosophy of such early thinkers as Epicurus, empiricists such as Locke, and skeptics such as Hume. If, for Kant, a critique of pure reason always is a transcendental critique that is not *based on* experience but rather investigates the *conditions of possibility* of experience *prior to* any actual experience, then this critique can be said to withdraw the world from the modern subject, a subject that has become rich in *Geist* but, in a certain sense, "poor in world." It is with this fundamental "inward" turn that the subject of modernity is confronted not only with the requirements of its own possible freedom (since, for Kant, the project of critical philosophy is inseparable from the experience of freedom) but also with the sense of its inability to inhabit the object world fully and transparently. The world has become, quite radically, a question of interpretation—and of interpreting even the question of the question of interpretation—so that this world's truth has become the erratic movement of an ever-shifting hermeneutic investment.

The modern, post-Kantian subject acutely feels that it lives *after* the inherited certainties of traditional metaphysics, even—and especially—when it strives to cope with this felt experience of afterness by erecting magnificent systems of conceptual containment, as in the Idealism of Kant's successors: Fichte, Schelling, and Hegel. Being, in the world of modernity, is haunted by a fissure in the concept of origin, structured instead by forceful experiences of finitude, loss, mourning, and irrecuperable memory. The experience of modernity is the experience of afterness, of tradition fading away, of modes of life disappearing for good—whether it be the falling away of traditional metaphysics in the wake of critical philosophy, the Marxian notion that early capital has transformed the entire mode of human existence in a way that necessitates a "ruthless critique of everything that is," Baudelaire's melancholic evocations of life in the modern metropolis, the devastation of an entire generation with previously unheard-of technological devices during World War I, or the state-sponsored industrial killing associated with the

Shoah. The sense of an irretrievable passing, an absolute mourning without measure, is staged with remarkable literary subtlety in such paradigmatic modern novels as Thomas Mann's *Magic Mountain* (1924), a text interrupted by, and rewritten following, the trauma of World War I, and Robert Musil's *The Man Without Qualities* (1930–1942), with its evocation of the dying days of the Austro-Hungarian Empire. Even the various historical avant-gardes of early-twentieth-century European art hardly can be thought and understood without the concept of a philosophical and aesthetic imbrication with a felt afterness. The experience of afterness in modernity encompasses not only the notion that something has been outlived or survived by something else, but also the realization that what has been outlived or survived no longer belongs to the structural possibility of experience of that which is to come. It is no accident, then, that the German word *modern* has two different meanings, as has often been pointed out (by, among others, Friedrich Engels): when stressed on the second syllable, it is congruent with the English adjective "modern"; but when stressed on the first syllable, it becomes a verb meaning "to decay" and "to rot." Just as in the case of Hans Castorp—the quintessentially *modern* protagonist of Mann's *Magic Mountain*, who falls ill with tuberculosis while visiting a sanatorium where he ultimately is forced to remain for seven years, "decaying" as it were—the double valence of the German *modern* encrypts the dialectic of the modern experience.

While the experience of afterness in modernity, as a capacious philosophical, cultural, and aesthetic category, touches all the Western traditions in one way or another, it inflects the German intellectual tradition with particular force. Already one of Kant's earliest readers, the playwright and author Heinrich von Kleist, experienced Kant's Copernican turn as a fundamental trauma. The afterness of this trauma precipitated what has come to be known as his "Kant crisis." In a famous letter to Wilhelmine von Zenge dated March 22, 1801, Kleist writes that he "recently became familiar with the newer so-called Kantian philosophy," the reading of which had "painfully shaken [*schmerzhaft erschüttert*]" him. He explains:

> If all humans, instead of eyes, had green glasses, they would have to conclude that the objects which they perceive through them *are* green— and they would never be able to decide if their eye shows them the things as they are or if it adds something that does not belong to the things but to the eye. So it is with the understanding [*dem Verstande*]. We cannot decide if what we call truth is truly truth or if it only appears

as such to us. If the latter is the case, then the truth that we gather here *is* no longer after our death—and all striving to acquire property that also follows us to the grave is in vain. . . . My only, my highest goal has sunk, and I now have no more.

For, since this conviction, namely, that there is no truth to be found here, stepped before my soul, I have not touched a book. I have been pacing in my room; I have sat at the open window; I have run outside; an inner unease has recently driven me to tobacco stores and coffee houses; I have been attending plays and concerts looking for distraction; in order to sedate myself I even committed a stupidity that Carl may wish to tell about rather than I myself; and yet, the only thought that worked on my soul during these outward commotions with burning anxiety was always only this one: your *only*, your *highest* goal has sunk.[6]

While it remains a matter of dispute whether Kleist's crisis was precipitated by an unusually rigorous reading of Kant or by a misreading—does Kant really abandon the concepts of truth and understanding in the ways that Kleist imagines here?—what is culturally significant about Kleist's reaction to Kant is that it stages the radically transformative nature of Kant's critical philosophy as it came to be inherited by German and European thinkers and writers in the mode of mourning and loss. Just as, from the perspective of the writer, there is a Kleist before and a Kleist after the experience of Kant, so there is a modernity before and after the intervention of Kant's critique. It is perhaps this critical perspective on the before and the after that propels Hölderlin, in a remarkable and difficult passage from a 1799 letter to his brother, to write that "Kant is the Moses of our nation [*der Moses unserer Nation*] who leads it from its Egyptian exhaustion into the free, solitary desert of speculation."[7]

But it was not only the poets of the age who responded to the fundamental challenge of Kant's critique. It was, above all, the German Idealists—Fichte, Schelling, and Hegel—who saw themselves, in more ways than one, as living and writing in the afterness of Kant, seeking to develop speculative systems that would take up and, in significant ways, work to recuperate the subject of modernity. They all implicitly shared Hegel's sense of a post-Kantian modernity, a thinking that is both an afterness and a beginning. As Hegel argues in *The Phenomenology of Spirit*, it "is not difficult to see that ours is a birth-time and a period of transition to a new era. Spirit has broken with the world it has hitherto inhabited and imagined, and is of a mind to submerge it in the past, and in the labor of its own transformation." He continues: "The frivolity and boredom which unsettle the established order, the vague foreboding of something unknown, these are the heralds of approaching change," a change that "illuminates the features of the new world."[8] This new world, this birth time of a new era, is the image of modernity itself, which now must consider itself rigorously in terms of the fundamental afterness it has entered.

In response to this gradual yet irreversible birth of modernity, in which, as Hegel puts it, "the Spirit in its formation matures slowly and quietly into its new shape, dissolving bit by bit the structure of the previous world,"[9] Fichte developed a system of transcendental philosophy he termed *Wissenschaftslehre*, in which a renewed emphasis on the distinction between the "I" and the "Non-I" was to address the challenges of reason as the self-critique of reason. Schelling wished to articulate a philosophy of nature that would provide an account of nature and its necessary delimiting function in relation to *Geist*, transcending its Kantian limitations while serving as an important counterpart to the seemingly self-containing operations of the intellect as posited by Kant. Most importantly, Hegel's dialectical model of absolute knowledge, developed in the *Phenomenology* and elsewhere, worked to call into presence a system of cognition for which—through the movement of *Aufhebung* (a "sublation" that is at once a cancellation, a preservation, and an elevation)—everything is potentially a matter of recuperation and indirect, or *mediated*, rescue. A discarded, refuted, or lost object, idea, or experience always potentially can be retrieved in the service of an *Aufhebung* that feeds on what is lost or discarded in the relentless striving for ever-higher planes of cognition and the integration of knowledge. As Hegel famously puts it in the *Phenomenology*, the dialectical, mediating power of what is sublatable is founded on a concept of *Geist* in which "Spirit is this power only by looking the negative in the face, and tarrying with it [*dem Negativen ins Angesicht schaut, bei ihm verweilt*]."[10] To be sure, the Hegelian system understands the requirements of modern philosophy following Kant's Copernican turn "as the pathway of *doubt*, or more precisely as the way of despair [*der Weg der Verzweiflung*]," and there hardly could be any dialectical thought worthy of its name that was not founded on fundamental despair.[11] But, as Hegel argues, the "skepticism that ends up with the bare abstraction of nothingness or emptiness cannot get any further from there, but must wait to see whether something new comes along with it, in order to throw it too into the same empty abyss." He continues: "But when, on the other hand, the result is conceived as it is in truth, namely, as a *determinate* negation, a new form has thereby immediately arisen, and in the negation the transition is made through which the progress through the complete series of forms comes about of itself."[12] One of the elements that distinguishes a garden-variety form of negation from Hegel's determinate negation is precisely the notion that the determinate negation recuperates what is negated or lost in the form of a new form or a series of forms that are thereby brought about. They become legible as figures laying bare certain patterns of consciousness that interact with the idea and requirements of absolute knowledge. It is no accident, then, that Hegel ends his influential introduction to the *Phenomenology* by situating the recuperative force of *Aufhebung* that passes through determinate negation in an especially exposed and significant place in his text: "And finally, when consciousness itself grasps this as its own essence, it will signify the nature of absolute knowledge itself [*die Natur des absoluten Wissens selbst bezeichnen*]."[13]

For the Hegelian system that pivots on the regulative idea of absolute knowledge, there hardly can be a true form of absolute loss or an actual experience of the hauntings occasioned by an irrecuperable trauma—in short, nothing for which comfort could not be potentially adduced from elsewhere—but the life of afterness that Nietzsche imagines can never be one of redemption and *Aufhebung*. And, in fact, one might say that it is with Nietzsche's refusal of all *Aufhebung* and reconciliation in the wake of loss—in what Heidegger will later refer to as Nietzsche's final completion and simultaneous undoing of metaphysics—that the writers treated in this study linger, each in his own particular philosophical, cultural, and political idiom. In Nietzsche's genealogical model of thought, the experience of afterness assumes the name of *das Unzeitgemäße*, or "the untimely." Partially in response to what he regarded as a problematic self-understanding of German culture that he associated with his former idols Richard Wagner and Arthur Schopenhauer, Nietzsche formulates a notion of the untimely—in his *Untimely Meditations* (1873–1876) and elsewhere—as that which is at odds with its own times, refuses to play along, distancing itself from mediocrity, mass taste, and vulgar prejudice, in short, from a certain "herd mentality."

While Nietzsche implicitly agrees with Kant that the mind takes its laws neither from nature nor from the phenomenal world more generally but instead creates its own laws (that is, acts in accordance with the self-law-giving practices of *auto-nomia* rather than the state of *hetero-nomia*, which receives its laws from elsewhere), Nietzsche emphasizes, in part echoing Schopenhauer, the role that the Will plays in this self-constitution of the mind in relation to the world. Nietzsche's untimeliness understands itself as a form of afterness in which the metaphysics of presence, of being present, or of an alleged former presence gives way, as in his pre-Socratic "brother" Heraclitus, to the idea of a radical and perpetual becoming. This abiding interest not in what one is but in "how one becomes what one is" is made explicit as the subtitle of Nietzsche's autobiography *Ecce Homo*. For Nietzsche, "everything has become [*alles aber ist geworden*]," as he memorably states in *Human, All Too Human*, even afterness itself: "Everything has become; there are no eternal facts, just as there are no absolute truths. —Therefore, from now on historical philosophizing is necessary, and, with it, the virtue of modesty."[14] From the perspective in which things, persons, and ideas have neither a "natural" essence nor a stable meaning, but have temporally become, even human consciousness and the lure of *Geist*'s absolute knowledge are discovered to have had a variegated and contingent history, one that is anything but self-evident and, as such, could have been entirely *different*.

There is no such thing, for Nietzsche, as a timeless present or an unchangeable human nature—that is, a quintessential, transhistorically stable category of intellect, instinct, emotion, desire, and ideological orientation. Hence the need for "free spirits," philosophers of and in the future who may come to terms with the irrecoverable, nonsublatable element of being untimely and of having to fashion a thoroughly modern self that would cognize its own temporal disjunction as its particular (and interrogatable) form of self-consciousness. It is no accident, therefore, that Nietzsche, in his preface to *The Anti-Christ*, inscribes his own anticipated afterness in a birth that is always only yet to come and that, when reading his texts, will only ever have been: "Some are born posthumously."[15] From the perspective of this always already anticipated afterness that precedes any actual passing or departure, his philosophical treatise on Christian and Greek morality, *Beyond Good and Evil: Prelude to a Philosophy of the Future* (1886)—a philosophy preceded by a *Vorspiel*, that is, both a prelude and a foreplay—tellingly ends with a mournful poem entitled "Aus hohen Bergen: Nachgesang" (From High Mountains: Aftersong). One might say that the totality of Nietzsche's texts constitute neither an ultimately recuperative Hegelian *Aufhebung* nor a triumphant Wagnerian *Gesamtkunstwerk* but rather a kind of *Nachgesang*, an "aftersong," perhaps *the* aftersong of modernity itself.

What will have been at stake in the *Nachgesang* of Western, and especially German, writers and artists of modernity, then, is the structural, conceptual, historical, and aesthetic experience of a strange haunting, a ghostliness that cannot fully come to terms with the finitude of its body and *Geist*. There is no Cartesian self-presence, no mathematical analytic to rescue the self (even with the advent of a modern, postsecular religion of technological progress), no origin that is not haunted, no loss that can be reclaimed through sublation. The task and perspective of writing "after" the Copernican turn in the Western intellectual tradition, and after all that has passed (away) in its wake, is one in which what is at stake is no longer simply an afterness following this or that *before*, but the very idea of the *after*. Afterness as a constitutive form of modernity, one in which the belatedness of thought, the indebtedness of art, and various forms of language, memory, and the image conspire to yield a cultural paradigm in which there can be no realm of experience that would remain untouched by its movements of following or uninflected by the mediatedness and melancholia of its own radical finitude.

The Nietzschean tonalities inflecting the aftersong and afterness of modernity will come to signify, for Benjamin, the experience of the modern as such, from his dissertation on the German Romantics via his study of the allegorical structures of the *Trauerspiel*, or "mourning play," all the way to his readings of Baudelaire's Parisian modernity and the theory of the modern encrypted in *The Arcades Project*. For him, the afterness of modernity will not leave the very notion of experiencing that afterness, and, indeed, the afterness of the very idea of experience, untouched. The reality of modern experience, in Benjamin's perspective, is the experience of absolute loss. Here, Nietzsche's aftersong of modernity is heard only in the ever-changing varieties—and, to be sure, sometimes pleasurable modes—of *Erlebnis* (a superficial, transitory, thrilling mode of experience) rather than that of *Erfahrung* (a far-reaching transformative experience that situates the subject firmly in its own temporality). A Benjaminian formulation of this state of affairs is to be found in the *Trauerspiel* book—which, in spite of its "official" concern with German baroque mourning plays, actually represents Benjamin's not-so-secret history of modernity itself—encapsulates the predicament of the modern subject. "Every person," Benjamin writes, "every object, and every relation can mean absolutely anything else [*Jede Person, jedwedes Ding, jedes Verhältnis kann ein beliebiges anderes bedeuten*]. This possibility passes a devastating yet fair judgment on the profane world."[16] The experience of the profane world of modernity is one that must situate itself in the wake of vanished meaning, the afterness of the loss of stable sense. Yet, while for Nietzsche a certain Dionysian frenzy and sense of intoxicating, joyful liberation also attaches to this mode of loss, for Benjamin the modern poverty of experience inaugurates a persistent aura of melancholia. In many ways, we still talk about the experience of the afterness of modernity in the very terms Benjamin assigned to them throughout his oeuvre, including, among others, fragmentation, catastrophe, destruction, ruin, and mortification.[17]

In an attempt to update the canonical accounts of modernity or the "new age" (*die Neuzeit*) advanced by Reinhart Koselleck in *Vergangene Zukunft: Zur Semantik geschichtlicher Zeiten* (*Futures Past: On the Semantics of Historical Time*, 1979) and by Blumenberg in *Die Legitimität der Neuzeit* (*The Legitimacy of the Modern Age*, 1966), Habermas's *The Philosophical Discourse of Modernity* labors to situate the discourse of the modern age in a force field of historical tensions in which "modernity can and will no longer borrow the criteria by which it takes its orientation from the models supplied by another epoch; *it has to create its normativity out of itself.*"[18] While Habermas would implicitly agree with the Nietzschean and Benjaminian notion that modernity must confront its own mediatedness and finitude without recourse to a secure metaphysical grounding, he can only imagine a model of the modern that must generate *its own normativity*. The question for Habermas, then, is not whether or not the subject of modernity still can assume a normative metaphysical framework that will guide its actions in the post-Kantian world, but rather—taking the notion of normativity silently for granted—where this normativity is located. According to this model, after normativity comes normativity, so that normativity constitutes its own afterness without a real after. From this perspective, there hardly can be a concept of the modern that would not generate its own normativity through the communicative action and reason-based, transparent negotiation performed by a self-identical consciousness that possesses the ability to access itself and to employ language as an essentially unproblematic tool of straightforward representation and political intervention.

But the radically mediated and melancholic form of afterness that will have been at stake in the present study cannot be reduced to the Habermasian notion of modernity as an unfinished project that sometimes veers off course, but still, in principle, is capable of completion and redemption. The aporetic concept of afterness that lies at the core of our concerns refuses to be enframed by a pledge of allegiance to normativity and to the alleged transparency of presentation and communication that would characterize a more perfectible image of modernity. As the American philosopher Robert B. Pippin aptly observes in his reading of Habermas's understanding of Nietzsche, the "great problem of all post-Cartesian or modern philosophy"—that is, "how to justify the adoption of a new, rigorous method"—ultimately "became the perennial modern problem: some sort of comprehensive self-reassurance about the modern orientation itself; at once the academic problem of epistemological skepticism and the cultural and political problem of legitimate authority." Kant's "suspicions of dogmatism were turned against him, [and] his accounts of transcendental necessity, a fixed table of categories, [and] a 'natural' architectonic of reason etc." made apparent, at least in the eyes of some, how Kant's model of critique "had begun to devour itself." As Pippin adds: "Hence the nineteenth-century crisis with which Habermas begins his account: either a wholly new form of such reassurance—a Hegelian narrative of what sanctioning principles or justificatory criteria it has turned out we could not do without (and so, implicitly, an appeal to some social model of collective reassurance), or, apparently a spectacularly new beginning, an attempt to imagine a form of life *wholly* without reassurance."[19] What emerges, among other things, in this account of modernity without reassurance or consolation goes beyond a mere problematization of the wishful notion that modernity is incomplete—and, as such, a perfectible form of the *before*—to show us how, in the wake of modernity's challenges to the precritical dogmatism of methodological and interpretative certainty, self-consciousness is preempted by a radical form of writing, thinking, and living without consolation, reassurance, or recuperation: in short, without reserve. Thus the Nietzschean *Nachgesang* of modernity—in the work of Adorno, Arendt, Beckett, Benjamin, Bloch, Celan, Derrida, Deleuze, Kafka, Lyotard, and Schönberg, among so many others—can be thought as the soundtrack to this particular experience of unsublatable afterness.

2 *Afterness and Critique*
A Paradigmatic Case

Few, if any, concepts have enjoyed as much authority and sustained engagement over the past two hundred years of Western thought as the concept of critique or criticism (*Kritik*). Inasmuch as the gesture of critique presupposes a distancing of oneself from one's object of scrutiny, critique can be regarded as a textbook example of afterness. To be sure, there are forms of critique and criticism whose primary purpose is to call into consciousness, or build on, the objects to which their gestures fasten. One thinks here, for instance, of the more journalistically or pedagogically mediated forms of literary criticism, theater criticism, art criticism, film criticism, music criticism, and the like, whose main goal is to present a work to a larger educated audience. In the German intellectual tradition, one may think, in the eighteenth century, of Lessing's "Letters Concerning the Most Recent Literature," Klopstock's critical appreciation of Winkelmann's theory of ancient Greek aesthetics in relation to modern works of art, Wilhelm von Humboldt's reflections on Schiller's intellectual development, or Schlegel's engagement with Goethe's Bildungsroman *Wilhelm Meisters*

Lehrjahre; in the nineteenth century, one thinks of such texts as Hegel's articles—written in the late 1820s for the arts and culture sections of local Berlin newspapers—of Lessing's correspondence with his wife and of Schiller's tragedy *Wallenstein*, as well as of Heinrich Heine's popular essay on different ways of viewing history; and in the twentieth century, such pieces of criticism include Mann's reading of a scene by Wedekind, Georg Lukács's work on German Expressionism, or, more recently, Hans Magnus Enzensberger's broadly aimed essays of literary and cultural criticism.[1] But what I wish to focus on here is neither critique as a mode of exposition nor critique as a tacit means of furthering the object of criticism by standing on its shoulders; rather, what is at stake here is critique as an act of separation, negation, and succession. In this sense, critique presupposes the fundamental possibility of otherness and purports to argue from a position of afterness in relation to the criticized object, whether such afterness is construed as one of superiority or of temporal succession. After all, that which follows in the wake of critique not only marks a break with what preceded it but also tacitly perpetuates the very concepts and conditions it was believed to have left behind. The turn away and that which follows upon this turn necessarily reinforce and even retroactively construct that something or someone whose overcoming originally had enabled the movement of following.

It should be said at the outset that the impossibility of criticism and critique to separate themselves fully from what they set out to criticize and to overcome will be regarded here neither as a simple lack nor in a dismissive manner with regard to the very idea of critique. Rather, as the concept of afterness will allow us to see anew, the condition of possibility for criticism and critique emerges out of an inherent volatility in the gesture of the *krinein* itself—that is to say, something that makes the act of separating, deciding, and choosing both possible and precarious. The Blanchot of *Lautréamont and Sade* puts it well. For him, "criticism is lacking in almost any substance of its own. An idea that is itself but a shadow of a larger one. Here we should immediately add that such a disparaging view as this one does not fluster criticism. It openly welcomes it, as if, on the contrary, this very lack revealed its deepest truth."[2] Criticism and critique, which necessarily fasten on something that is not properly their own, coming into their own only in the felt contact with what they are not, separate from something precisely in order also to be sustained by it. The perpetual double gesture of departing from something while at the same time calling for sustenance from the terrain of its point of departure marks and re-marks the proper gesture of the *krinein*. In relation to the object that both sustains and resists them, critique and the act of criticism are inscribed in an afterness that makes them what they are while, at the same time, silently threatening to undo them from within.

In a lecture delivered in May 1978 to the Société française de philosophie, and posthumously published as "What Is Critique?," Foucault imagines critique "on the outer limits of philosophy, very close to it, up against it, at its expense, in the direction of a future philosophy and in lieu, perhaps, of all possible philosophy."[3] In order to grasp the concept of critique historically and systematically, he proposes to understand it as the label for a kind of bearing, an attitude. Foucault argues: "It seems to me that between the high Kantian enterprise and the little polemical professional activities that are called critique . . . there has been in the modern Western world (dating, more or less, empirically from the fifteenth to the sixteenth centuries) a certain way of thinking, speaking and acting, a certain relationship to what exists, to what one knows, to what one does, a relationship to society, to culture and also a relationship to others that we could call, let's say, the critical attitude."[4] He concedes that critiques, polemics, and other such attempts at delimitation have existed since long before the fifteenth and sixteenth centuries, and that the widely divergent critical impulses they express can be reduced only with difficulty to a common denominator, let alone a single all-embracing concept. Yet it is around this time in the history of the West that a revolutionary concern emerges ever-more clearly in the consciousness of those who engage in critique: "How not to be governed *like that*, by that, in the name of those principles, with such and such an objective in mind and by means of such procedures, not like that, not for that, not by them."[5] The critical attitude that Foucault interrogates is not just to be traced in its various genealogical strands, but demands that its own relational structure be examined as well. In the specific context of a thinking of afterness, which the French thinker does not address directly, it would be crucial to examine the relationality of critique, the fact that it is directed at something else, its other-directedness. Seen in this light, Foucault's following marginal comment assumes central importance: "After all, critique only exists in relation to something other than itself: it is an instrument, a means for a future or a truth that it will not know nor happen to be, it oversees a domain it would want to police and is unable to regulate."[6] Once critique is regarded in this way, as conditioned by its relation to something else, it becomes clear to what extent critique does not simply call another position into question from a fixed position of its own, but itself comes to unfold in the relation between the two positions. If critique always exists in relation to something else from which it must be minimally distinct, yet which it also cannot topple by installing itself in its place, then it must remain bound to the discourses and thought-figures of a relation that it both calls forth and determines. The question of critique thus always also entails the essential question of its relation to what is criticized, even and especially when critique, believing to have superseded the latter once and for all, proves unwilling or unable to reflect on its multiply mediated and ongoing relation to it.

In drawing on this complex phenomenon of the relational essence of critique to illuminate the logic of afterness, our aim cannot be to trace the history of the concept of critique in modernity from Kant, through Fichte's critical concept of abstract negation, Herder's idea of a metacritique, Schlegel's Early Romantic idea of critique as the progressive and radical mediator between philosophy and history in such canonical essays as "On the Essence of Critique," Hegel's developmental understanding of critique, Marx's articulation of critique as a radical unworking of all that presents itself to be natural and self-evident in a given system of dependencies ("a ruthless critique of everything that is," to use Marx's famous formulation), all the way to the Critical Theory of the Frankfurt School.[7] Likewise, the question of a strict conceptual delimitation of critique from related phenomena like the Nietzschean practice of genealogy or deconstruction will remain suspended.[8] I will instead restrict myself to a constellation of three proper names that play a paradigmatic role in the discourse of modernity, and that permit us to address some of the fundamental questions concerning the relationship between afterness and critique: Kant, Heidegger, and Adorno.[9]

In a central formulation in the *Critique of Pure Reason*, a formulation that in many respects still determines our discursive approach to the concept of critique, Kant writes: "Our age is the genuine age of criticism, to which everything must submit [*Unser Zeitalter ist das eigentliche Zeitalter der Kritik, der sich alles unterwerfen muß*]."[10] The concept of critique in its customary meaning is fraught with negative connotations. Critique implies that something is to be regarded as flawed or ameliorable; through the lens of critique, that which is criticized appears in the harsh light of an unfavorable judgment. Precisely by virtue of its negativity—which, in the radical and universally extended form given to it by Descartes, can even aim to establish a cognitive model for everything that exists—critique always takes an implied positivity as its point of departure. As long as the critical moment is conceived as being directed toward a determinate other, rather than as a purely formal corrosive principle, this positivity will necessarily draw on a standard of the essential and genuinely true against which what is criticized is measured and found wanting. As is well known, the word "critique" stems from the Greek verb *krinein*, meaning "to separate, differentiate, decide," or "to elect, to select." In ancient medical terminology, the cognate noun "crisis" designates the life-threatening climax or turning point in the course of an illness.[11]

This decisive and at the same time threatening aspect of critique has consequences for its epistemological claim, especially in the realm of aesthetics. In a theory of reading, that which the crisis of *krinein* separates can be conceptualized, among other modes, as the separation between textual performance and authorial intention—that is to say, as multiply mediated ways in which what language actually does cannot be contained by what it may have been meant to achieve. One sense of the crisis of *krinein* as it pertains to both of its two modern English descendants, "critique" and "criticism" (German has only one word, *Kritik*), therefore always names a peculiar disjunction. As de Man reminds us in "Criticism and Crisis," the "notion of crisis and that of criticism are very closely linked, so much so that one could state that all true criticism occurs in the mode of crisis. To speak of a crisis of criticism is then, to some degree, redundant." He adds: "In periods that are not periods of crisis, or in individuals bent on avoiding crisis at all cost, there can be all kinds of approaches to literature: historical, philological, psychological, etc., but there can be no criticism."[12] According to this model, *krinein* as the moment of crisis is the precondition for an investigation of the ways in which textual presentation is at odds with the mobilization of intention and, in this disjunction, acts as the very crux of what the difficult act of reading and making sense demands of an attentive, rigorous reader. This insight presents the radicalization, through an articulation of the rhetorical moment of critique and criticism, of what American New Critics William K. Wimsatt and Monroe Beardsley, writing in different circumstances, in 1946 first named the "intentional fallacy," the notion that meaning can be reduced to intention.[13]

To think the productive ways in which a sustained interrogation of crisis, critique, and criticism opens onto larger methodological issues requires the work of conceptual specification and distinction. In Benjamin's essay on Goethe's *Elective Affinities*, what distinguishes critique from the related form of commentary is, among other things, the fact that it is always oriented toward the truth content of the artwork: "Critique seeks the truth content [*Wahrheitsgehalt*] of a work of art; commentary, its material content [*Sachgehalt*]. The relation between the two is determined by that basic law of literature according to which the more significant the work, the more inconspicuously and intimately its truth content is bound up with its material content."[14] In this Benjaminian sense, critique, as the praxis of *krinein*, draws on the shifting and inconstant figures of separation that characterize truth content and material content. "If," Benjamin writes, "to use a simile, one views the growing work as a burning funeral pyre, then the commentator stands before it like a chemist, the critic like an alchemist. Whereas, for the former, wood and ash remain the sole objects of his analysis, for the latter only the flame itself preserves an enigma: that of what is alive. Thus, the critic inquires into the truth, whose living flame continues to burn over the heavy logs of what is past and the light ashes of what has been experienced."[15] According to this image, critique has its source in a flickering, dangerous flame in whose light what is to be separated is both seen for the first time and burned to ash. These cinders and ashen traces continue to testify to what was separated by critique, even if what has been separated in this way can be conceived only as absence, or as a presence that has fled into a vast, unapproachable distance.

Of crucial importance for our discussion is the fact that critique, unlike commentary, is always also marked, in the moment of decision and separation, by a will to put what it criticizes behind it, a will that presupposes the possibility of a clean break or scission. Critique therefore always implies an after, a kind of afterlife that aims to come into its own in the afterness of the critical act insofar as it seeks to define its own position by unfolding after, and in relation to, what it criticizes. An emphatic critique is thus in principle always an aftereffect. Yet the after-effectiveness of critique, so to speak, exposes it at the same time to a moment of uncertainty and deferred meaning, since it remains to be asked to what extent critique does not simply put what it criticizes behind it, but continues to be codetermined by it. Seen from this perspective, critique still finds itself in the thrall, and in the debt, of what it criticizes.

Before recalling Kant's fundamental articulation of critique, it will be helpful to examine an often-overlooked passage in the *Critique of the Power of Judgment* that concerns the temporally mediated connection between two different configurations of language and thought. A discussion of this passage will serve to set the stage for an interrogation of the twin themes of afterness and critique that are of interest to us here.

In the context of his deduction of pure aesthetic judgments toward the end of paragraph 32, Kant elaborates the "first peculiarity of the judgment of taste" in relation to the distinction between *Nachahmung* (copy or imitation) and *Nachfolge* (succession or following). Kant writes that "*Nachfolge*, which refers to a process, not *Nachahmung*, is the right term for all influence which products of an exemplary author or creator [*Urheber*] can exert upon others."[16] This means, according to Kant, that the essence of *Nachfolge* concerns itself with "taking from the same source from which the other himself took" while "learning from one's *predecessor* [*Vorgänger*]" merely "a way of behaving or relating [*sich dabei zu benehmen*]."[17] As opposed to imitating one's *Vor-gänger* in a process of *Nach-ahmung*, a truly transformative and challenging influence can be exerted by the tradition only through *Nach-folge*, in a manner that will not simply submit to "prescriptions [*Vor-schriften*]" but participates in the "advance [*Fortgang*] of culture" through a highly mediated relationship to the so-called original or predecessor.[18] To the extent that the one who creates in the wake or afterness of his predecessor is involved in learning how to translate (that is, learning to be faithful to an original—and only thus really learning from it) and simultaneously to betray it by departing from it (that is, accepting as an inheritance only certain *modes of behaving*, certain ways of *relating* to something, rather than appropriating the content or vainly reduplicating the singularities of an other's work), Kant's *Nachfolge* is predicated upon an open and constantly shifting relation to the legacy of the other, a coming to terms with an inheritance that demands fidelity, even, and especially, while forbidding it. Kant's model gives us the transformative relations among *Nach-folge*, *Nach-ahmung*, *Vor-schrift*, and *Fort-gang* to think. For him, the relations and translational acts implied in, and called for by, these concepts are inseparable both from an engagement with the norms and conventional expectations of the notion of relation and from an interrogation of the temporal-historical structure of aesthetic experience itself. Ultimately, there can be no rigorous concept of critique that would not also attempt to work through the requirements of these relational concepts of following and succession.

The radicality of Kant's concept of critique, however, does not just lie in the fact that his transcendental method accords it a functional value that was without precedent in what Kant himself had already referred to as an age of criticism. The true radicality of his concept of critique lies instead in its extension to the self-critique of reason. Reason, that is, must also submit itself to the demands of critique if it is to arrive at self-knowledge. It must learn, as Rodolphe Gasché reminds us, not only to think its criteria and boundaries through the aspect of critique, but to establish critique as the gold standard of its own chief enterprise.[19] Critique is therefore at the same time to be a critical theory of itself, a type of contemplation that turns away from all dogmas and forms of mere skepticism to make the radicality of self-reflection the principle of every critical movement of thought.

In paragraph 21 of the second chapter of *Die Frage nach dem Ding* (*The Question Concerning the Thing* or *The [Status of the] Question After the Thing*), a text based on a lecture held in Freiburg during the winter semester of 1935/1936, Heidegger pursues the question, "What is the meaning of critique in Kant?" He writes: "We are accustomed to hearing something overwhelmingly negative whenever this word is mentioned. For us, to criticize means to find fault, to tally mistakes, to point out shortcomings, and to dismiss what is thereby found wanting. We must try to distance ourselves from this customary and misleading meaning when faced with the title *Critique of Pure Reason*."[20] Heidegger continues: "Critique, far from being something negative, designates the most positive positivity, the positing of what must be put in place before everything else as the determining and decisive agency. Critique is thus decision in this prepositional sense. Only in consequence of this, because to criticize means to select and to bring out what is special, uncommon, and at the same time measure-giving, is it also to reject what is common and disproportionate."[21] He argues that the general meaning of the word "critique" gradually takes shape in the second half of the eighteenth century in discussions of art, the analysis of artistic forms, and the promulgation of rules and decrees. "But the word," Heidegger adds, "receives a fuller meaning through Kant's work."[22] It is incumbent on thought, according to this view, to understand this fuller meaning. "If critique has this positive meaning," he remarks, "then the *Critique of Pure Reason* will not simply dismiss and rebuke pure reason, 'criticize' it, but will instead first set out to circumscribe its decisive, peculiar, and hence proper being. This act of circumscription is not primarily one of preventative foreclosure [*Abgrenzung gegen*], but rather one of enclosure [*Eingrenzung*], in the sense that it demonstrates the inner articulation of pure reason."[23] From this situation, the conclusion could be drawn that critique is not simply "censorship." Referring to Leibniz and Baumgarten, Heidegger adds that one would be equally mistaken to regard "the architectonics, the architectural plan of the essential structure of pure reason," as "mere 'display.'"[24] From the perspective of fundamental ontology, a concept of critique interpreted in this way would help to determine the essence of reason itself.

This determination would need to be thought in relation to the opposing figures of foreclosure and enclosure, *Ab-grenzung* and *Ein-grenzung*. If the self-reflexive gesture of critique is one of *Eingrenzung* rather than of *Abgrenzung*, as Heidegger claims almost in passing, then *Abgrenzung* could be seen as a defensive ploy, a self-defensive measure directed by critical thought against an other that threatens to hinder its movement from outside, as it were. The *Eingrenzung* performed by critique, by contrast, remains in principle open to the influence of that other, whether that influence is friendly or hostile, since unlike *Abgrenzung* it does not seek to expel it as a persistent danger. The *Eingrenzung* of critique is far more preoccupied with its own procedures, cognitive schemata, and unexpressed assumptions; indeed, it seeks its most radical fulfillment in the interminable determination of its own assumptions and in their critique. In this sense, critique wants nothing more than to criticize itself; that is to say, it would first come to itself by interrogating and hence potentially taking leave of itself. The after of such *Eingrenzung*, in contrast to *Abgrenzung*, would at the same time also have to be conceived as a before, a state in which agreement on its own assumptions and inferential models remains still to come.

As Heidegger emphasizes in his late lecture "The End of Philosophy and the Task of Thinking," the thinking of such an after as a before would define the task that remains to be confronted by thinking *after* a metaphysically oriented philosophy. Here, as in the lecture on Kant's concept of critique, critique is ascribed the role of the most positive positivity in its function as a harbinger of futurity. The title of the lecture, according to Heidegger, "designates the attempt at a reflection that persists in questioning. Questions are paths toward an answer. If the answer could be given it would consist in a transformation of thinking, not in a propositional statement about a matter at stake."[25] Insofar as the lecture undertakes a renewed attempt to think through the thematics of *Being and Time* "in a more primordial fashion," it embodies a form of critique that faces the future in orienting itself toward the after. He explains: "This means subjecting the point of departure of the question in *Being and Time* to an immanent criticism. Thus it must become clear to what extent the *critical* question, of what the matter of thinking is, necessarily and continually belongs to thinking."[26] To think after philosophy—here equated with metaphysics and assumed to have arrived at its end—would be to reflect on the critical questioning that pertains to a thinking of the future. The still outstanding thinking that emerges in the aftermath of philosophy would have to set out on previously untrodden paths and foster forms of contemplative vigilance and attentiveness with regard to what had hitherto remained unthought in the metaphysics of Occidental philosophy. "The task of thinking," according to Heidegger, "would then be the surrender of previous thinking to the determination of the matter of thinking."[27] This tentative path of thinking *after* philosophy would have to orient itself toward a critical education, a reflection on the yet-unthought that presupposes a prior end while still always having to appropriate that end as its own before.[28]

In touching on the critical potential of this conceptual interlinking of before and after, we arrive at the third and final element in the constellation of critique and afterness to be outlined here: Adorno's negative dialectics. In his essay "Critique," published two months before his death, Adorno feels compelled to return to the central importance of that term both to his own project and to modern intellectual experience. "He who equates the modern concept of reason," we read there, "with critique is scarcely exaggerating."[29] Adorno proceeds to trace certain political aspects of the concept from Kant's refutation of Leibniz and Wolff in his three *Critiques* through Hegel and Marx to the postwar West German mobilizations of the term. Yet he is careful not to relinquish the concept of critique to a mere oppositional stance that, on a subterranean level, is still tacitly connected to what it wishes to overcome. Adorno therefore concludes "Critique" as follows:

> Those talking most about the positive are in agreement with destructive power. The collective compulsion for a positivity that allows its immediate translation into practice has in the meantime gripped precisely those people who believe themselves to stand in the starkest opposition to society. This is not the least way in which their actionism fits so smoothly into society's prevailing trend. This should be opposed by the idea, in a variation of a famous proposition of Spinoza, that the false, once determinatively cognized and made precise, is already an index of what is right and better.[30]

There is a mode of critique that becomes affirmative precisely in the moment when it finds, or assigns itself, its own comfortable place as the oppositional element in a given political structure, a structure that is then free to co-opt critique and to mobilize it for the purposes of perpetuating the dominant forces. For Adorno, critique would therefore always also have to be the self-critique of critique in which no predetermined—and therefore merely calculable and instrumentalizable—position can be assigned to it.

Adorno, for his part, develops a model of critique that consciously takes its own reflected nonsimultaneity, and hence the afterness that is inscribed in it, as its starting point. The first sentence of *Negative Dialectics* proclaims: "Philosophy, which once seemed passé, remains alive because the moment of its realization was missed."[31] The missing of philosophy's realization is by no means merely a lack. On the contrary, it is on account of this missed opportunity that critical philosophy lives on at all, that it possesses an afterlife that first enables it to come into its own as a critical philosophy to come. In a certain sense, then, philosophy's realization would bring about an unwanted closure; once realized and no longer perpetually deferred and contemplated anew, philosophy would stand in its own way. In conjunction with the conceptualization of critique that Adorno proposes, philosophy can be understood as a form of afterness, an apparently obsolete endeavor that unexpectedly reveals itself as the condition of possibility for a revolutionary praxis.

What is said of art in *Aesthetic Theory*—that it always must embody "the memory of accumulated suffering"[32]—applies in equal measure to the concept of critique. Of course, critique consists of more than just finding fault with what exists and causes human suffering. It also draws from the impossibility of leading a true life in the false, while nonetheless having to recognize this impossibility as the condition of possibility for thinking freedom, and for potentially overcoming a superstition that is all the more insidious for being propagated precisely in the name of freedom and mobilized under the ideological banner of technology, cultural amusement, or scientific, goal-oriented, and calculative rationality. Alongside the better-known *Dialectic of Enlightenment* (1947), Horkheimer's essay for the *Journal for Social Research*, "Traditional and Critical Theory" (1937), is of fundamental importance for Adorno and the Frankfurt School's understanding of critique. In this essay, Horkheimer sets out to distinguish the forms of critique practiced by the theorists of the Frankfurt School from the classical, allegedly affirmative understanding of theory associated with the Cartesian method.[33] How this new form of critique is to operate in any given context, however, remains purposely unspecified, since critique must invent its method each time anew; it must constitute itself differently for each new object in order to demonstrate its adequacy to the uncircumventable singularity of that object, even if these singularities are connected with each other in their respective singularity and thus embody their own other(s).

It is against this conceptual background that Adorno develops a model of critique in *Negative Dialectics* that "runs the risk of total failure—this in reply to the absolute certainty that has traditionally been obtained by stealth."[34] Critique, in the sense of a negative dialectic, calls in Adorno's view for a form of thinking that thinks against itself as well, as earlier works such as *Minima Moralia* had already suggested. Thus we read in *Negative Dialectics*: "Thought as such, before all particular contents, is an act of negation, of resistance to that which is forced upon it. . . . Today, when ideologues tend more than ever to encourage thought to be positive, they cleverly note that positivity runs precisely counter to thought and that it takes friendly persuasion by social authority to accustom thought to positivity. The effort implied in the concept of thought itself, as the counterpart of passive contemplation, is negative already—revolt against being importuned to bow to every immediate thing."[35] Adorno draws the following conclusion from this state of affairs: "Critical germs are contained in judgment and inference, the thought forms which not even the critique of thought can do without: they are never definite without simultaneously excluding what they have failed to achieve, and whatever does not bear their stamp will be denied—although with questionable authority—by the truth they seek to organize."[36] If critique could think its own afterness—and hence its collusion with the object it purports to have left behind it—as a constitutive moment of itself, then the effort of negation that both drives critique and is driven by it would take its measure from that which, despite the peremptoriness with which it is dismissed by critical thought, always also countersigns the decisive movement of critique, and thus in a certain sense first makes critique possible. Critique's nonidentity would thus be irrevocably inscribed within it as the condition of its possibility *and* as a threat to its movement of severance.

In "Meditations on Metaphysics," the concluding section of *Negative Dialectics*, Adorno is therefore concerned with the extreme limit case that is metonymized under the name of "Auschwitz." He gives the first part of this section the heading *Nach Auschwitz*, or "After Auschwitz." Perhaps no other phrase has since penetrated so deeply into the historical, theoretical, and experiential consciousness of the West.[37] But what does this famous formulation actually name? First of all, "after Auschwitz" places the German translation of the name of a town in Poland, Oświęcim, into metonymic relation with a historical event and a limit phenomenon of the thinkable: the Nazi genocide. At the same time, the preposition *nach* illustrates the extent to which any thinking of this limit phenomenon must also describe a temporal relation that splits the experience of temporality into a before and an after. Adorno's *nach* furthermore articulates the spatial dimension of an otherwise temporal structure, inasmuch as the intended temporality of a preposition is linked to the spatial particularity of a place. Quite in keeping with the etymological origin of the word *nach*, temporal and spatial dimensions are intertwined here in such a way that both forms of proximity come to the fore. For just as the dialectic of enlightenment, in Adorno's view, by no means began with the historical Enlightenment of the eighteenth century, but always already inhered in the potential for dialectical reversal to which disenchanting thought, particularly of the philosophical and speculative kind, can succumb, so it can scarcely be asserted that the fundamental structures of the thought that failed to prevent Auschwitz have been superseded once and for all. In Adorno's account, *nach* and *nah*, "after" and "near," still stand close to each other—and not just in an etymological sense.

Starting from the epistemo-critical entanglement (but nonequivalence) of *nach* and *nah*, it would be possible to establish links to a range of moral-philosophical concerns that animate Adorno's concept of critique. For example, the reading of afterness we are proposing here could be understood as expanding on what Christoph Menke once described as Adorno's turning away from metaphysical optimism. "The optimism criticized by Adorno," Menke writes, "claimed that human action could guarantee a happy outcome. Adorno's 'materialistic,' experience-dependent metaphysics rejects this: the idea of a happy outcome only comes into play where the thought of success corresponds to the experience of happiness." He continues: "'After Auschwitz' is, for Adorno, the name for a situation in which the capacity for this metaphysical idea has been dealt a crippling blow, because the connection between what the experiencing subject does and what is done to it has been broken."[38] Whether the "positive center of Adorno's negative philosophy" recently investigated by Martin Seel can be attained by linking the question of afterness to problems of moral philosophy remains uncertain.[39] But it can hardly be denied that the ethical and political dimensions of afterness, particularly "after Auschwitz," codetermine the effectiveness of the critical-revolutionary impulse that emanates from Adorno's model of critique.

This model specifically is concerned with the "less cultural question of whether after Auschwitz you can go on living."[40] An answer to this question—a question that demands the indefinite deferral of any answer until due attention can be paid through its reflective deferral—depends on the impossibility of a bringing to presence: "And the guilt does not cease to reproduce itself, because not for an instant can it be made fully, presently conscious. This, nothing else, is what compels us to philosophize."[41] For a critical theory of the nonidentical to bring this guilt to consciousness, it would have to think the nonintegration of such a consciousness as a productive moment of critique. Adorno writes:

> This throws a glaring light on truth itself. In speculation we feel a certain duty to grant the position of a corrective to common sense, the opponent of speculation. Life feeds the horror of a premonition: what must come to be known may resemble the down-to-earth more than it resembles the sublime; it might be that this premonition will be confirmed even beyond the pedestrian realm, although the happiness of thought, the promise of its truth, lies in sublimity alone. If the pedestrian had the last word, if it were the truth, truth would be degraded.[42]

The critical program of thought that, according to this model, can never be made programmatic could then be expressed as follows: "If negative dialectics calls for the self-reflection of thinking, the tangible implication is that if thinking is to be true—if it is to be true today, in any case—it must also be a thinking against itself. If thought is not measured by the extremity that eludes the concept, it is from the outset in the nature of the musical accompaniment with which the SS liked to drown out the screams of its victims."[43] Critique after Auschwitz—which would have to be a thinking for, through, and against thinking—thus represents a possible response to the demand that the after of critique be conceived as the before of an always indeterminate future, one in which critique would have to come into its own as an ethico-political form without ever being identical to itself. Afterness can be understood here as the affirmation of a dismantling that does not merely destroy its object, but liberates what previously had remained unthought within that object precisely through the process of its dismantling. This never-ending gesture holds open a field of possibility yet to be colonized by any context of delusion. The wild thinking and unregimented experience that flourish there refuse to be tamed by mere repetition, by a comportment that never ventures beyond mere description, or by the apologia for what already exists. As the case of critique exemplifies, afterness points ahead through the movement of dismantling that is proper to it.

3 *Afterness and Aesthetics*
End Without End

The future thinking that Adorno's model of critique imagines resides in an irreducible tension. On the one hand, it must show itself responsible to absolute singularity and to the moment of departure from what has come before so that it may avoid the comfortable gestures of reassurance and self-inoculation, even in the moment of destruction. As he suggests in his 1965/1966 Frankfurt lecture course on the principles of a negative dialectic, "the moment in which nothing can happen to philosophical thought, that is, when it already resides in the realm of repetition [*Wiederholung*], of mere reproduction, in that moment philosophy has already missed its purpose or end [*Zweck*]."[1] On the other hand, thought, even when it proceeds from the specific and singular requirements of a particular object or idea and therefore is called upon always to reinvent itself, must take into account the multiple and elusive ways in which it comes *after* certain discourses, violences, ideologies, and historical aberrations. True thought in this emphatic sense therefore is always unexpectedly singular and at the same time a relentlessly inflected instantiation of *afterness*.

The thinking of afterness for which Adorno is best known unfolds in the space that he terms "after Auschwitz" to convey the idea that living in the aftermath of the Shoah requires a fundamental reorientation, even a new categorical imperative, that would allow thinking to come to terms with the unthinkable itself. The most famous condensation of his post-Auschwitz philosophy occurs in the programmatic and often misunderstood sentence from his essay "Cultural Criticism and Society" (1951): "To write poetry after Auschwitz is barbaric [*Nach Auschwitz ein Gedicht zu schreiben ist barbarisch*]."[2] The sentiment figures just as prominently in his main philosophical work, *Negative Dialectics*, whose final section, "Meditations on Metaphysics," commences, we recall, with a relentless meditation entitled "After Auschwitz." It is commonly assumed that these texts embody the most important ethico-political statements and figures of thought that Adorno contributes to a thinking of the afterness of modernity—that is to say, the dialectic of culture and barbarism that holds modernity in its grip. But it also is true that his philosophical project as a whole valorizes the thinking of a differently modulated afterness, one that strives to theorize the ways in which the aesthetic itself, experientially and cognitively, casts into sharp relief the possibilities that are encoded in artistic form. The work of art, for Adorno, is finite, living in and as finitude, while at the same time refusing to postulate an end: either an end of art or an end of reflection. On the contrary, the end without end unfolds as an afterness that always is in transition, *im Übergang*, to use his preferred phrase. This *Über-gang*, an über-transition and a walking across to the other shore, needs to be thought politically, as, for instance, in the final sentence of his essay "On the Question: What Is German?," which evokes the *Übergang zur Menschheit*, a "future transition into humanity," and aesthetically, as in his reflections on the music of Alban Berg, whom he calls *Meister des kleinsten Übergangs*, or "master of the smallest transition."[3] The afterness that Adorno's restless thought seeks to think always will have been a political and aesthetic category in which no end is what it seems. It is an afterness in and as transition.

To honor this abiding open-endedness even within what is finite, an aesthetic without end, we might begin by noting that readers of Adorno's texts, especially those devoted to philosophical aesthetics, cannot fail to be struck by their chiastic structure. The aesthetic theory that Adorno develops constitutes not only a theory of the aesthetic but also a theory that is itself aesthetic, hence a theory of literature that exhibits qualities associated with literary texts, and a theory of music that harbors within itself traces of musical composition. The rhetorically self-conscious tropes of his posthumous *Aesthetic Theory*, the stylized literary studies of his *Notes to Literature*, his musically inflected meditations on musicological questions about composers from Beethoven to Arnold Schönberg, and so many of his other texts perform this provocative inversion in a variety of registers and conceptual modulations. In *Aesthetic Theory*, for instance, Adorno insists that the aesthetic dimension of philosophy and the philosophical dimension of art are not merely dimensions among so many others: "Aesthetics is not applied philosophy but philosophical in itself."[4] What does it mean for an aesthetic theory itself to become aesthetic, for a literary theory itself to become literary, aside from the conceptual conflation of two otherwise independent spheres? This question is encrypted, in a different context, in Heidegger's intuition, expressed with regard to Hölderlin's hymns, that "thinking is almost like a poeticizing along [*das Denken ist fast wie ein Mitdichten*]."[5] Yet given the inherent epistemological difficulties, would such a self-conscious intervention not blatantly violate the requirement that theoretical thinking and writing—expected to be sober, vigilant, and rigorous—remain unaffected by the rhythms and rhetorical movements of its object, along the lines of a public sign displayed in Vienna opera houses around the turn of the twentieth century declaring: "*Mitsingen verboten!*" (No singing along!)?[6] Well aware of this problem, Adorno records, in his fragments on Beethoven, the cautious but resolute reminder from his friend Horkheimer that "philosophy should not be a symphony."[7] How can an aesthetic theory that thematizes, among other things, the dialectic of Enlightenment and the remote, yet thinkable, possibility of transgressing the requirements of the irrational and misguided mimetic structures that dominate a remainderlessly administered world justify the instrumentalization of the very structures that are the object of its critique to achieve this transgression without itself succumbing to those structures?

Contrary to the suggestion of some of his readers, the mature Adorno's interest in what he called a "*Verfransung*," an interpenetration of philosophy with modernist strategies of art, literature, and music that is characterized by a gradual dissolution of the generic and material boundaries that have defined Western avant-gardes at least since surrealism, cannot fully explain this chiastic structure.[8] After all, the self-conscious conceptual density and aberrant figural rigor of his language inform even minute details of individual sentences, such as when Adorno's diction, grammar, and syntax enact principles theorized in his meditations on what is German and on the philosophical significance of punctuation marks. The crystalline sentence fragments, apodictic metaphors, and notoriously deferred reflexive pronoun *sich* are only some of the best-known examples of this singular and idiosyncratic discourse.

To be sure, Adorno's experimental coarticulation of the philosophical and the artistic, of logic and rhetoric, is not unfamiliar to modernity's intellectual trajectory. Readers may think, for instance, of Schlegel's and Novalis's poetic investment of the philosophical fragment in Jena Romanticism, Nietzsche's aphoristically lyrical philosophy in such works as *Human, All Too Human*, or, more recently, Claude Lévi-Strauss's unconventional structuring of his main scholarly work to accord with the principles of musical form and Derrida's self-conscious use, in *Glas*, of interactive and competing columns of side-by-side text, one for literary readers, the other for philosophers. Each of these chiastic experiments of thought and form—of thought in and as form, and of form in and as thought—have provoked resistance from readers who, reenacting the primal scene in Plato's *Republic* when poetry is banished, are disturbed by such border transgressions. But in the case of Adorno, for reasons that have yet to be reconstructed, this readerly unease assumes special urgency. It is, after all, no secret in Adorno studies that the self-consciously aesthetic quality of his aesthetic philosophy always has troubled some of his readers—among them some of his most perspicacious explicators. The philosopher Rüdiger Bubner, a kind of unofficial representative of these perturbed readers, complains that in Adorno's work "all these complications would be avoidable if philosophy finally parted with the dream of being itself and yet something else." Demanding precisely the kind of philosophical self-identity that Adorno's project sought to dismantle, Bubner warns that aestheticizing theory places a theory of the aesthetic in danger of becoming "entangled in a semblance which is not the one of which it speaks" and that it would be well advised finally to disown "the attempt to allow theory to become aesthetic" which only can end badly, that is, "with the confusion of a semblance of theory with a work of art."[9] There is little use in constructing such readers as straw men for the cheap thrill of substituting a putatively erroneous reading with an ostensibly correct one, especially when the knotty relationship between the philosophical and the aesthetic in Adorno remains far from resolved. Yet from a broader perspective, it is nonetheless instructive not only to consider why Adorno's aesthetic project upsets even those readers whose erudition and analytical depth are beyond reproach, but also to consider why Adorno writes the way he does.

I wish to suggest that the chiastic structure of Adorno's aesthetic theory must not be thought in isolation from his conviction that "art stands in need of philosophy that interprets it in order to say that which it cannot say, whereas art only is able to say what it says by not saying it."[10] Adorno here puts his finger on the predicament at the core of the relation between speculative commentary and aesthetic production. On the one hand, art—at least the high modernist variety of Schönberg, Berg, and Beckett that Adorno so often championed—requires philosophical discourse to bring to the fore as a graspable, cognitive, and propositional structure the *Wahrheitsgehalt*, or the "speculative truth content," that, in the absence of critical commentary and elucidation, lies latent. On the other hand, the very thing that philosophy claims the artwork says, that on behalf of which philosophy acts as a kind of conceptual translator, can be said by the artwork only when it remains silent about this conceptual content. If the artwork actually said what it says in a transparent cognitive proposition, shorn of the mediations and aberrations of its imaginative flourishes and its singular expression of beauty and form, then it would cease to be an artwork. It would simply be a philosophical treatise on a conceptual content that now no longer could claim membership in the domain of art. Yet, if an artwork can be itself only by not saying what philosophy claims it says, if the cognitive propositional content on which philosophy focuses cannot be verified in the articulations and inscriptions of the artwork itself—lest it abdicate its status as a work of art—then how can one clarify and verify philosophy's claims about the content and meaning of artworks? And, by extension, why does art continue to stand in need of philosophy's translational services? These questions are inflected by Adorno's far-reaching insistence on what he calls his "model"—that is, the supposition "that artworks unfold in their philosophical interpretation."[11]

Adorno's conception of the vexed but necessary relation between philosophical commentary and the work of art is brought into further relief when we relate it to a specific rhetorical figure: allegory. As the literary critic J. Hillis Miller reminds us, allegory "means to say it otherwise in the marketplace, in public, as an exoteric expression of an esoteric wisdom. As in the case of parable, for example, the parables of Jesus in the Gospels, this is a way of revealing it and not revealing it. If you have the key to the allegory, then the esoteric wisdom has been expressed (otherwise), but then you would not have needed to have said it otherwise." And he continues: "If you do not have the key, then the allegory remains opaque. You are likely to take it literally, to think it means just what it says. If you understand it you do not need it. If you do not understand it you never will do so from anything on the surface. A paradox of unreadability is therefore built into the concept of allegory from the beginning."[12] If allegory resides in the space of an unreadability predicated on both its resistant opaqueness and the straightforward transparency that would make it superfluous, then the relays that Adorno forges between philosophical commentaries on artworks and the artworks themselves behave in a similar fashion.[13] If the meaning of an artwork remained sealed off from all logical comprehension, then no philosophy could ever truly speak to this meaning. But if the meaning of an artwork revealed itself readily, then no artwork would be needed—since its "content" could have been stated more easily in prosaic, discursive language that would require no philosophy to expound it.[14] The artwork requires the ceaseless and open-ended work of rigorous interpretation in order to become what it is.

The poetic work of Hölderlin, whose writings serve as a constant touchstone for Adorno's aesthetic meditations, provides a case in point for the predicament of allegorical or figurative reading. In "Parataxis," Adorno claims that while "Hölderlin's poetry, like all rigorous poetry, requires philosophy in order to bring to light its truth content, any recourse to a philosophy that merely appropriates the truth content in this or that manner is unusable."[15] While no poetic truth content can emerge in the absence of philosophy, it is equally the case that no philosophy can do justice to poetic truth while making claims to the stability of its meaning. In this context, we may recall the admonition that prefaces Hölderlin's epistolary novel *Hyperion* (1797–1799): "I would like to promise to this book the love of the Germans. But I am afraid that some will read it like a compendium, too much concerned with its *fabula docet*, while others will take it all too lightly, and both groups will fail to understand it. He who only smells my plant does not know it, and he who plucks it merely to learn from it does not know it either. The dissolution of dissonances in a certain character is neither a matter of mere reflection nor one of empty pleasure [*leere Lust*]."[16] It is therefore not enough to say that artworks afford pleasure, even though the most rigorous and beautiful ones certainly do, a point of which Adorno himself is keenly aware. As we learn in *Aesthetic Theory*, "whoever enjoys artworks concretistically is a philistine; expressions such as 'a feast for the ears [*Ohrenschmaus*]' give him away. Yet if the last traces of pleasure were extirpated, the question as to the purpose of artworks would be an embarrassment."[17] But, beyond the pleasure principle, what is at stake for Adorno's aesthetic theory in thinking through the relation between philosophical speculation and the work of art is the truth that expresses itself, in that very relation, not only otherwise but also as the singularity of a particular form that, while resistant to verification by logic alone, still offers a mode of complexly mediated insight that is unavailable to the conceptual terms of conventional speculative discourse. If this other kind of truth is merely an illusion, then it is an illusion that itself exhibits, as a negative capability, something other than mere garden-variety illusion, the very illusion of the illusionless. This is why for Adorno, "truth has art as the illusion of the illusionless."[18]

Insofar as truth "has" art in this way, the relationship between the philosophical and the aesthetic cannot but have epistemo-political implications. As Christoph Menke and others have persuasively demonstrated, Adorno's so-called aesthetic negativity cannot be reduced to the kind of neo-Marxian interventionist aesthetic that his friend Herbert Marcuse advocated any more than it can be assimilated into a purely aestheticist impulse that would elide the artwork's politically charged relation to the material situatedness that first sponsored it. As a determinate and necessary negation of any attempt at hermeneutic understanding, Adorno's project stresses the processual character of the aesthetic by casting aesthetic negativity as a perpetual provocation to all normative discourses of reason and transparent understanding.[19]

Yet if it is true, as Adorno and Horkheimer argue in *Dialectic of Enlightenment*, that the advent of the modern form of rationality has banished from the admissible realm of reason any form of cognition that does not conform to a series of narrowly defined scientific assumptions, then the artwork, if it is to offer any truth at all, even the truth of its untruth, is compelled to reconceptualize the relation between logic and rhetoric, science and art, theory and praxis. To put it in the terms of Simon Jarvis, Adorno, in his desire to exhibit art's cognitive truth-content, conceives of "art as having a cognitive content with a non-propositional character."[20] Here, I wish to explicate these propositions in relation to the singular idiom of Adorno's actual language and, in so doing, to examine the particular ways in which Adorno's praxis as a writer responds to a desire to remain faithful to the difficulty of the uneasy and nonpropositional elective affinity between philosophy and art. Specifically, I attempt to read the notorious one-page thought-image "Zum Ende," entry 153 in *Minima Moralia: Reflections from Damaged Life*, in light of these concerns. It is not only because "Zum Ende" constitutes the final entry in *Minima Moralia* that it is the allegorical sum and summary of all of Adorno's previous thought-images and their speculative concerns; rather, as an aberrant aesthetico-methodological commentary, it also is the instantiation and radicalization of the kind of thinking, mediated by a consideration of the relation between philosophy and art, that Adorno calls for and himself performs throughout his writings. Although often cited, "Zum Ende" has received relatively little sustained commentary because of the overly charged relays that crisscross it. Even an anthology entirely devoted to readings of individual thought-images from *Minima Moralia*—by such formidable literary critics and philosophers as Bernhard Böschenstein, Hans Ulrich Gumbrecht, Wolf Lepenies, Gerhard Neumann, and Slavoj Žižek—brackets "Zum Ende" as though it were the absent center that needed to be honored by remaining silent about it.[21] Adorno's sentences read:

Zum Ende.—Philosophie, wie sie im Angesicht der Verzweiflung einzig noch zu verantworten ist, wäre der Versuch, alle Dinge so zu betrachten, wie sie vom Standpunkt der Erlösung aus sich darstellten. Erkenntnis hat kein Licht, als das von der Erlösung her auf die Welt scheint: alles andere erschöpft sich in der Nachkonstruktion und bleibt ein Stück Technik. Perspektiven müßten hergestellt werden, in denen die Welt ähnlich sich versetzt, verfremdet, ihre Risse und Schründe offenbart, wie sie einmal als bedürftig und enstellt im Messianischen Lichte daliegen wird. Ohne Willkür und Gewalt, ganz aus der Fühlung mit den Gegenständen heraus solche Perspektiven zu gewinnen, darauf allein kommt es dem Denken an. Es ist das Allereinfachste, weil der Zustand unabweisbar nach solcher Erkenntnis ruft, ja weil die vollendete Negativität, einmal ganz ins Auge gefaßt, zur Spiegelschrift ihres Gegenteils zusammenschießt. Aber es ist auch das ganz Unmögliche, weil es einen Standort voraussetzt, der dem Bannkreis des Daseins, wäre es auch nur um ein Winziges, entrückt ist, während doch jede mögliche Erkenntnis nicht bloß dem was ist erst abgetrotzt werden muß, um verbindlich zu geraten, sondern eben darum selber auch mit der gleichen Entstelltheit und Bedürftigkeit geschlagen ist, der sie zu entrinnen vorhat. Je leidenschaftlicher der Gedanke gegen sein Bedingtsein sich abdichtet um des Unbedingten willen, um so bewußtloser, und damit verhängnisvoller, fällt er der Welt zu. Selbst seine eigene Unmöglichkeit muß er noch begreifen um der Möglichkeit willen. Gegenüber der Forderung, die damit an ihn ergeht, ist aber die Frage nach der Wirklichkeit oder Unwirklichkeit der Erlösung selber fast gleichgültig.

[*Toward the End.*—The only kind of philosophy for which, in the face of despair, responsibility could be assumed, would be the attempt to contemplate all things the way that they would present themselves from the standpoint of redemption. Cognition has no light other than the one that shines onto the world from redemption: everything else exhausts itself in reconstruction and remains a piece of technique. Perspectives would have to be manufactured in which the world similarly displaces and estranges itself, revealing its tears and cracks, as it at some point will lie there, needy and disfigured, in the Messianic light. To gain such perspectives without arbitrariness and violence, wholly from one's contact with the objects—this alone is what matters to thinking. This is the easiest of all because the condition irrefutably calls for such cognition, indeed, because completed negativity, once fully captured by the eye, shoots together to form the mirror-writing of its opposite. But it also is the entirely impossible, because it presupposes a standpoint removed, even if only by the most minuscule degree, from the sphere of the spell of being, whereas every possible cognition, in order to become binding, not only must first be wrested from what is, but, for this very reason, is itself struck with the same disfiguration and neediness from which it intends to escape. The more passionately thought seals itself off from its conditionality for the sake of the unconditional, the more unconsciously and, therefore, the more disastrously, it falls toward the world. It must grasp even its own impossibility for the sake of the possible. But, faced with the demand that thereby is issued to it, the question concerning the reality or unreality of redemption is itself almost irrelevant.][22]

Given its position at the end of *Minima Moralia*, "Zum Ende" seems to be appropriately titled. Yet the preposition "Zum" is of importance here, an importance elided by the published English translation, which simply gives us "Finale," as though Adorno had written "Ende," rather than "Zum Ende." "Zum" here can mean either "toward," describing a movement toward the end, or "on the occasion of," placing the text that follows in the position of delivering a commentary on something *other* than itself, namely, the end. A third possibility is that "Zum" here means "with regard to," in which case the reflections that follow could also be understood as commenting on the philosophical question of "Ende" as "Zweck," the end as goal—that is, in terms of the problematized means–end relationship at the core of Walter Benjamin's essay "Critique of Violence" (1921), an issue in which Benjamin was still deeply immersed when Adorno first met him in Frankfurt in 1923.[23] While Adorno's language leaves us suspended in the realm of undecidability between these three readings, what unites them is that in each case they are *something other* than the end itself. The relationship of the title to that which it names, the end, is not one of identity but one of alterity and even radical *nonidentity*, a category so crucial to Adorno's *Negative Dialectics*. In this way, what seemingly had announced itself as the end is rather one more deferral, one more erratic suspension, in nonidentity, of the finality that would foreclose any future thought or inspired act of reading.

For the narrating poetic voice of *Minima Moralia*—can we be absolutely certain that this is in fact the author's voice, rather than an invented and highly stylized poetico-philosophical narrator's voice whose model is the ironic gesture of Nietzsche's confession that "my books are one thing, I am another"?—the kind of philosophy that could still be practiced responsibly in the face of despair would attempt to read the inhabitants of the object world "the way they would present themselves from the standpoint of redemption." This gesture implies a doubly figurative or allegorical stance. First, philosophy is called on to regard things in terms of another, as what they are not. To enter a responsible relation to the object world—that is, to do justice to the objects—also is to depart from their unmediated manifestation; to remain faithful and responsible to them, we must break with them and see them *otherwise*. Second, the standpoint from which they are to be regarded, that of redemption, has itself not yet been attained, as the conditional mood of Adorno's grammar indicates (*"sich darstellten"*)—after all, the standpoint of redemption is a homeland to which no one has ever been. This means that philosophy is called on to assume a perspective on the object world that not only departs from the objects' manifestations as phenomena, but also stands in a figurative or allegorical relation to the perspective that is to be substituted for the perspective of the object world as it conventionally presents itself. Adorno's sentence thus encrypts the radically figurative and doubly allegorical relationship that philosophy is asked to assume vis-à-vis the world in which it occurs.

Our understanding of the speaking and thinking otherwise that constitutes Adorno's allegorical relation to the world in which thought occurs is intensified when, in the sentence that follows, we are told that "cognition has no light other than the one that shines onto the world from redemption." That Adorno is not at all triumphalist about the weak possibility of that redemption is suggested by the fact that redemption itself does not shine a light on the world (as the published English translation misleadingly states: "shed on the world by redemption") but, rather, it is only from the province of redemption that a light is cast, a light that has no agency other than its own self-reflexivity—"*kein Licht, als das von der Erlösung her auf die Welt scheint.*" It is as if the metaphor that seems to depict redemption as a light shining onto the world also undid itself by depicting that light as emanating from *the site of* redemption rather than identifying the light with redemption itself. This double gesture in which a promise simultaneously is extended and withdrawn can be read as an instance of the nonidentical, a reading that adds a new interpretive dimension to Adorno's conviction in *Negative Dialectics* that "what would be different has not yet begun."[24]

But how, one might well ask, can Adorno claim that this is the *only* light that cognition has at its disposal ("*kein Licht, als das von der Erlösung*") in its efforts to achieve knowledge and insight? Could one not imagine other forms of cognition that would be independent of such a highly mediated shining? Moreover, does not this general truth claim also undermine the singularity and idiom of the individual act of cognition that may fasten on this or that object and that may be facilitated by variegated modes and conditions of possibility? In the same vein, the part of the sentence following the colon extends this general truth claim when it states that "*alles andere,*" "everything else," exhausts itself and remains insufficient. Adorno here wishes to emphasize the universal applicability of this kind of thinking about philosophy in a time of despair. If, for him, everything else exhausts itself in reconstruction (*Nachkonstruktion*) and remains merely technique or technics (*Technik*), his sentence gives us other, alternative forms of thinking and writing to think. When viewed in the larger context of Adorno's work, his word *Nachkonstruktion* is negatively charged in that it conjures a form of mimesis that he generally abhorred: the direct, reflective, and reproductive kind. As he argues throughout *Aesthetic Theory*, what he wishes for in the work of art as well as in philosophy is in fact a different kind of mimesis: a mimesis of what does not yet exist, the negative traces of a futurity that can be neither predicted nor programmed in advance but that nevertheless inscribe themselves into the artwork, and into the philosophy that enters a relation with that artwork, as a nonidentical and negatively charged otherness. It is here that the difference between afterness and mere *Nachkonstruktion* becomes visible.

The philosophy at stake here sponsors perspectives "in which the world similarly displaces itself, estranges itself [*sich versetzt, entfremdet*]." Notably, it is the perspectives themselves that cause this displacement and estrangement; they enable, as a condition of possibility, a movement that the world itself performs, as emphasized in Adorno's notorious use of the reflexive *sich*. If, however, with the aid of these new perspectives the world is capable of displacing and estranging *itself*, presumably with an eye toward the kind of allegorical philosophical thinking that is yet to come, then that capability always already must have been latent in the world. In this sense, an allegorical thinking of the future is not an external intervention, mobilized by some autonomous standard of measurement or insight independent of that world, but an activation or liberation of what always already was at work, silently and invisibly, within the figures of the world itself. This figurative thinking thus works to actualize and radicalize, through a close and caring reading, the hidden movements and structures that become visible, if only in the blink of an eye, when the world has entered a course of displacement and estrangement that thinks and says things *otherwise*.

Clearly, when under the gaze of the allegorical perspective the world performs the defamiliarizing gestures of self-displacement and self-estrangement—that is, reveals itself, in the messianic light, as "*bedürftig*" (needy) and "*enstellt*" (disfigured)—it also reveals, in its need for redemption, the condition of possibility for the issuance of any messianic intervention. Adorno likewise extends his emphasis on an engagement with the internal logic and structure of the object, a gesture that refrains from externally mobilized interventions—which, for him, only can lead to "*Willkür*" (arbitrariness) and "*Gewalt*" (violence)—by stressing a "*Fühlung mit den Gegenständen*," a "felt contact with the objects." Yet why does he emphasize that "*darauf allein kommt es dem Denken an*" (this alone is what matters to thinking)? Here it is instructive to return to the published English translation, which gives us "this alone is the task of thinking," as if Adorno had written "*das allein ist die Aufgabe des Denkens*." The difference here could not be more crucial: Adorno's text implicitly refuses to assign a task to thought not simply because *Aufgabe* in German means both a "task" and a "final giving up," but also because the very idea of a task inscribes the radical kind of thinking that he imagines into the language and logic of instrumental reason, the target of much of *Dialectic of Enlightenment*. The new thinking here is not to be instrumentalized as a task whose aim is to locate objects and to assume contact with them according to an entirely rational, preplanned program, because such a program would only repeat one more time the rational structure of a too-narrowly-conceived notion of reason that already has led to such disastrous consequences as the current needy and disfigured state of the world (Adorno writes these lines in 1946/1947, amid the debris and trauma left behind by German Fascism). Rather than enlist a thinking to come that places itself in the service of instrumental reason, even with the best of intentions, Adorno initializes a thinking that is on the way *elsewhere*, its restless strivings born of an inner dynamic rather than in response to the assignments issued by a task whose aim it does not yet know.

The actualization of this movement of thought, however, never can be taken for granted or perfunctorily installed as an administrable program, even as it remains both necessary and *das Allereinfachste*, or "the simplest thing of all." This is so because the precondition for the *vollendete Negativität*, or "perfected negativity," to delineate, explosively, the *Spiegelschrift ihres Gegenteils*, the "mirror-writing of its opposite," never can be fully present: just as negativity never can be fully perfected or completed (*vollendet*), it never can be *ganz ins Auge gefaßt*, or "fully captured or completely faced." Thus while Adorno's metaphors give the impression of supplying the figures of a possible redemption, even the redemption that is lodged in negativity, his diction also withdraws that promise by retreating from a full actualization of the goal toward which it strives. It is no accident that this retreat is linked performatively to language, since it is the allegorical or figurative domain of language itself that draws the contours of redemption while at the same time undoing its triumphant endorsement. It is for this reason, too, that the metaphor of *Spiegelschrift*, or "mirror-writing"—erroneously rendered as "mirror-image" in the standard English translation, as though Adorno had written "*Spiegelbild ihres Gegenteils*"—is significant here. *Spiegelschrift* retains an emphasis on the idea that what is visible is not what is immediately accessible, a gesture that decouples perception from cognition. To read *Spiegelschrift* as *Spiegelbild* implicitly surrenders the status of the negatively contoured representation to the domain of an image in which visibility so often is mistaken for comprehensibility.

Further complicating the promise of, and retreat from, redemption in allegorical language, Adorno concedes that what he had called "the simplest thing of all" is also, dialectically, *das ganz Unmögliche*, or "the wholly impossible." This impossibility stems from the fact that the thought that thinks otherwise—that is, strives toward the *other* perspective that the text has worked to define—is itself lodged in the space in which the transformation of that very perspective is articulated and therefore also emerges as needy and disfigured. Adorno's sentence here stages the ways in which what hopes to depart from a given situation or problematic also is conditioned by it and that, by extension, a transgressive breaking-away from something on the way to something else always also is in part a tacit perpetuation of the same. The afterness of the after, we might say, remains in what Adorno here calls the "*Bannkreis des Daseins*," which is not merely the "scope of existence," as the published English translation claims, but also the tenacious spell and authoritative domain of existence from which thought had hoped to depart. Adorno here allegorizes a point made at greater length in the contemporaneous *Dialectic of Enlightenment*, that if an enlightened and putatively progressive thought fails to take account of its own residual attachment to that which it strives to overcome, if it fails to consider its own situatedness and conditionedness within the regressive forces it hopes to conquer, then this thought will, in a hardly perceptible dialectical reversal, revert to the very darkness that it had sought to illuminate. This fate is especially inescapable for the thought that "passionately" and relentlessly "seals itself off from its own conditionality" (*gegen seine Bedingtheit sich abdichtet*), with an eye toward escaping the unreliable and aleatory constraints of its multiple contingencies in favor of the universal transcendental aspirations of *das Unbedingte*, the unconditional unmarred by the conditions and contingencies of thought and experience. But for Adorno, this is a mistake, a dangerous aberration. The more thought strives to shuck the aleatory traces of its own contingency and conditionality, the more it returns to and reproduces the world's insufficiencies ("*fällt er der Welt zu*"), while believing itself to innovate and to transgress.

Adorno's maxim, situated somewhere on the far side of instrumental reason and the delusion of regarding afterness as a clean and absolute break, therefore is that thought should "grasp even its own impossibility for the sake of possibility." If there is to be possibility at all—and we never can be quite certain that there is—it first must travel through the aporia of the impossible. This is the future-directed negativity that Adorno, a few years later in "Cultural Criticism and Society," will designate as a movement of thought that follows the "logic of [an object's] aporias, the impasse contained within the task itself [*Logik seiner Aporien, der in der Aufgabe selber gelegenen Unlösbarkeit*]."[25] Indeed, a relentless thinking through of thought's impossibility is the condition of possibility for striving toward what is possible. Yet, if thought is impossible, how can it think its own impossibility with an eye toward the possible? Would this thinking and grasping of the impossible not be a sign that thought in fact is possible, as evidenced by its capacity to think something, namely, its own impossibility? Much hinges on Adorno's verb *muß* in "*muß er noch begreifen*" (it must at last grasp). What kind of command is being issued here? By whom? Situated where, if not precisely in the needy and disfigured world and therefore tinged by its shortcomings and aberrations? Is this *muß* a description of the current state of affairs, of what thought actually does—a possible reading, given the indicative present tense form—or is it the call from an unnamed otherness that a subject receives and henceforth is required to act on without quite knowing how—another possible reading, given that German often uses the present tense indicative to refer to an obligation or intention to be acted upon in the future?

The final sentence of Adorno's thought-image—or, in light of our discussion of the piece's title, perhaps we should say the sentence that unfolds on the occasion of or toward the end—suggests that we are to imagine a command being issued to thought from an unnamed elsewhere, an absent other: "But with regard to the demand that thus is issued toward thought [*die damit an ihn ergeht*], the question concerning the reality or unreality of redemption itself is almost irrelevant [*fast gleichgültig*]." Rather than assuming, as the published English translation does, that the difference between the reality and the unreality of redemption "hardly matters," Adorno suggests the opposite. Even though the demand that is issued to thought by an unnamed, absent otherness may be privileged over the unpredictable outcome of what it has set in motion—that is, the "that" of the demand is more strongly felt than its "what"—what remains at stake is still the thinking of a possible redemption, as the engine and arbiter of undeconstructable concepts such as freedom and justice, even if these have not been achieved and even if they remain the property of a negative otherness that is the homeland where no one has ever been.

If thought thinks its own impossibility in the name of a possibility that refuses to remain unthinkable even while presenting itself as impossible, then the movement of thought that enables this thinking is facilitated by the hypothetical idea of redemption. From the standpoint of the thought-enabling function of redemption, its actual manifestation or "reality" would not seem to matter: it works to set thought into motion, even when that thought seems to have been arrested for good. Almost. After all, Adorno refuses simply to write that the reality of redemption is irrelevant—he writes that it is *almost* irrelevant—*fast gleichgültig*. What literally is equally valid (*gleichgültig*) is cast into disequilibrium and asymmetry by the qualifying adverb. That this "almost" remains perpetually open, that it is never the last word but, literally and figuratively, the second-to-last word, not *das letzte Wort* but, as in *Minima Moralia*, precisely *das vorletzte Wort*—this names the fragile promise of any negative dialectics.

The language of this negative dialectics registers, in a diction at once poetic and philosophical, the injury but also the hope that resides in the very world in which it unfolds. The violence and injustice of this world cannot be thought in isolation from the rhetorical structure of any language that wishes to interact with them. "That the violence of the facts," Adorno writes in his Bar Harbor notebook, "has become such a horror, that any theory, even the true kind, looks like a ridicule of that horror—this is burned as a sign into the very organ of theory, language."[26] The language of theory therefore not only turns to the world of objects and ideas but also perpetually takes stock of the burned sign whose scar remains. Therefore, Adorno suggests in his "Theses on the Language of the Philosopher" that the philosopher's "decomposed language [*zerfallene Sprache*]" is compelled to construct a kind of writer whose "materials are the ruins of words to which history binds him."[27] For Adorno, as for Benjamin in his theses on the ruins of history, there can be no philosophical language that does not remain faithful to this difficulty. Here, the "intended comprehensibility of philosophical language today is to be uncovered in all aspects as a delusion. It is either banal, that is, naively assumes words to be pregiven and valid whose relation to the object matter, in truth, would be problematic; or it is untrue, in that it works to dissimulate this problematic, using the pathos of words that appear to have been extrapolated from the dynamics of history in order to bestow upon these words nonhistorical validity and at once comprehensibility."[28] The language of the writer who strives to remain aware of these difficulties therefore would follow the poetic and philosophical paths of a certain melancholia of negativity, a careful and caring probing, a provisional yet steadfast searching, a nonanthropocentric yet deeply responsible engagement with what remains nonidentical.

To say that Adorno's project of "philosophical modernism," which radicalizes the formal claims of Kant's third *Critique* and furthers the Jena Romantics' abiding insistence on the reflective judgments of art in the very space in which self-reflexive, fragmented writing embodies both philosophy and art,[29] is also to say that, for Adorno, no conjunction of philosophy and art even would be needed if it did not also, in the alterity of its own negativity, point to an elsewhere that has not abandoned a structure of promise, prayer, and the thinking of an unknown, and potentially worthwhile, futurity. What Adorno's project therefore shares with the Marxian transformation of Kantian aesthetics and of Hegelian dialectics is a certain oppositional spirit that allows aesthetic form to provide an elusive space in which the potential of the concept no longer is hampered by its rigid attachment to a purely logical system of reason that polices the legality and admissibility of a concept's movements and qualities.[30] As Adorno articulates this oppositional impulse in *Negative Dialectics*, the "utopia of cognition would be to use concepts to unseal the nonconceptual by means of concepts, without making it their equal."[31] The "almost" of thought, the otherness inscribed in works that, like "Zum Ende," embody both philosophical and aesthetic elements, both logic and rhetoric, is charged with the passionate insight through which we "strive, by way of the concept, to move beyond the concept."[32] While Adorno here echoes Heidegger's admonition against the pursuit of a thinking that "fails to recognize that there is a thinking more rigorous than the conceptual,"[33] he also departs from Heidegger in that he wishes to orient his remarks not with an eye toward the requirements of a new fundamental ontology but rather toward what within the artwork both embodies and radicalizes a thinking of nonidentity and of a negative dialectics that at any given moment deserves to be thought as the condition of possibility for a futurity that has not yet been foreclosed. To be sure, for Adorno the overconcretization of that futurity, what he prefers to call a mere *Auspinseln*, dooms even the dialectically charged artwork to endorse yet another humanism and to repeat the failure of what already is. But Adorno's faithfulness to a perpetual engagement with the radically opposed yet interdependent requirements of philosophy and art, enabled by the aesthetic form, continues to be a thorn (that is, a-*Dorn*) in the side of those ideologies of the end of history that have resigned themselves to mere mimesis and a tireless affirmation of self-identity. Today, a half century later, such ideologies amount to perpetuating, in mind and checkbook, geo-political empire building, the mindless diversions of our consciousness industry, daily worldwide ecocides, the suburban banalities of a globalized simulcast, and their attendant lack of affect. As a miniature artwork that possesses a negatively charged aesthetic cognitive content with a nonpropositional character, "Zum Ende" therefore only ever will have been a beginning. It will have been Adorno's afterness without end.

4 *Afterness and* Rettung
Can Anything Be Rescued by Defending It?

The question concerning the reality or unreality of redeeming and rescuing that we saw *Minima Moralia* cast into sharp speculative relief names one of the central preoccupations of our discussions of afterness so far. After all, the felt need to rescue something always implies an afterness. Wishing to rescue something—whether from disappearance, destruction, violation, or transformation—places the one who would rescue in a position after the fall, regardless of whether this fall has already occurred and now calls for decisive action or whether this fall has not yet come to pass but is regarded as likely or imminent. The critical situation in which what is at stake is the possibility of rescuing, saving, redeeming, or recouping—a state of affairs, an idea, an object, a person, even a fleeting intuition, the touch of an other, a mad moment of hope, or a dream—is always already situated in an actual or imagined postlapsarian force field. In the act of writing or creating, this postlapsarian force field will not leave the status and thrust of its own claims and intentions untouched. Indeed, thought that concerns itself with the possibility of rescuing something, through an affirmation in the broadest sense—

even through an affirmation of the elusive and of the unaffirmable—can hardly avoid giving an account of itself, and to itself, in the scene of rescuing that at first sight appears to be exclusively dominated by the demands of that which, or the one who, is in need of rescuing.

The stakes of this moment of rescuing as a form of afterness are alluded to in Hölderlin's hymn "Patmos" (1802–1803), where we find the following line: "But where there is danger, that which rescues grows also [*Wo aber Gefahr ist, wächst/Das Rettende auch*]."[1] Hölderlin's lyric voice constitutes neither a form of naive sentimentalism nor a wishful thinking; it is not a theodicy, in which the existence of a God is proved through an evocation of salvation in the face of danger; it does not wish to suggest that wherever danger is present there is automatic recourse, divine or not, to a remedy that would save one from the danger; nor can it be reduced to the proposition, now emphasizing the conditional or circumstantial dimension of the *auch*, that a rescuing grows *even there* where one would least expect it, in danger itself. Rather, Hölderlin's words would seem to suggest a certain vigilance with regard to the ever-shifting relation between danger and rescuing that refuses to be stabilized in advance. Language itself, and the archetextual writing in which this language is embedded, constitutes the scene in which the multiple affinities and repulsions between danger and rescuing ask to be negotiated as a form of afterness in critical thought.

Critical thought that concerns itself not only with its ostensible subject matter—its "aboutness," as it were—but also with the conditions of its own possibility cannot elude an examination of the ways in which it will not remain itself. Such critical thought addresses itself to a series of future possibilities in relation to this or that particular engagement of an object, a temporal perspective, or an abstract thought. What happens in such engagements to the subject matter at hand? In the case of a thinking that is concerned first and foremost with a traditional concept of critique, with the gesture of the Greek *krinein* that separates, weighs, and decides, the impetus may well be to undo what is, to change or to abolish a state of affairs believed to be false or otherwise untenable, until all that is solid, to use Marx's beautiful phrase, melts into air. Yet in those instances in which a mode of thinking is not primarily concerned with an immediate undoing of what is the case, or when the concept of critique that informs it is refunctionalized in order not only to negate but also to sustain, then the question arises as to what the relation might be between a restless, vigilant, rigorous thinking and the present and future states of that upon which its language trains its focus at any given moment. In other words, if the objective of such thinking were to *rescue* something without thereby becoming affirmative, to retain something that is about to disappear for good without thereby becoming an instrument of apologia for the status quo, then what kind of relationship can be imagined to connect the sphere of vigilant thought, along with the critical writing that it sponsors, to the nonaffirmative rescuing of its elusive and non-self-identical objects?

We may begin to think through such questions by revisiting certain dimensions of the exchanges between Benjamin and his younger friend Adorno. After all, in the multilayered conversations between Benjamin and Adorno, some of which are recorded in their extensive correspondence between 1928 and 1940, the elusive and vexing moment of "rescuing" plays a significant role. For instance, as Benjamin writes to Adorno in a letter from 1937 in the context of a critical evaluation of their mutual friend Siegfried Kracauer's recent sociological work on the composer Jacques Offenbach: "In that *Rettung* does not succeed, it emerges in disfigured form, as apologia [*Indem die Rettung mißglückt, kommt sie in enstellter Figur, nämlich als Apologie zum Vorschein*]."[2] The German word *Rettung* that Benjamin employs here—and that recurs throughout his entire corpus—can at times mean "rescue," "saving," "salvation," or "redemption." Indeed, the broad semantic realm of *Rettung* should be borne in mind when approaching this crucial dimension of Benjamin's work. The infinitive verb form, *retten*, can also mean "helping" and, in a reflexive construction such as *sich vor etwas retten*, "to escape from something"; *jemanden oder etwas retten*, in certain contexts, can signify "to liberate someone or something." *Sich vor etwas nicht mehr retten können* means "to be besieged or swamped by something." *Der Retter* can be the helper or rescuer but also the savior, as in Christ the Savior, and *das war seine letzte Rettung* means "that was his last hope or salvation." A *Rettungswagen* is an ambulance; a *Rettungsschwimmer*, a life guard; a *Rettungsboje*, a buoy. While its precise origin remains obscure, *retten* derives from the Old High German *hretten* and is genetically related to the Dutch *redden* and the Old Saxon *ahreddian* as well as the Old English *hreddan*, which can also mean "to remove from."[3] *Retten*, in this latter meaning, is related to the modern English "to rid." In certain forms of pre–Modern High German, an unusual and now long forgotten genitive construction, through which what is to be avoided or gotten rid of becomes the object of the construction that ostensibly signifies a rescuing, bespeaks this dimension of meaning: "so that no one's house will be destroyed, due to the rescuing or ridding of the fire [*ist daz keinem sîn hûs abgebrochen wirt durch rettunge des fiures*]." It is remarkable that this dimension of *retten* can signify *both* the rescuing *and* the ridding of something, as if in a dialectic that concerns itself with both sustenance and undoing, support and demolition. Perhaps, beyond the aleatory nature of historical contingency, there is something hidden deep within the etymology of *retten*, its *Wortgeschichte* (word history), that knows of the unruly dialectic with which the writings of Benjamin and Adorno wish to come to terms in their different ways. After all, "'construction' presupposes 'destruction,'" as Benjamin memorably glosses the method of his critical stance in *The Arcades Project*.[4]

It would be necessary, in the course of a multi-volume work, to trace and interrogate the specific and each-time-singular (Benjamin does not deliver consistent concepts) function of *Rettung* in some of the most salient preoccupations that suffuse his work, from the epistemo-critical prologue of the *Trauerspiel* book and the essay on Goethe's novel *Elective Affinities*, through the autobiographically suffused miniatures of *Berlin Childhood around 1900* and the planned book on Baudelaire, all the way to *The Arcades Project* and the "Theses on the Philosophy of History."[5] Among other things, Benjamin's ever-shifting preoccupation with *Rettung* would need to be understood also as the name of a figure of thought in which disseminations of the concept are inextricably intertwined in several fields: epistemology (especially as it became known to him through certain strains of the interpretation of Plato pursued by Hermann Cohen and other Marburg Neo-Kantians as well as through his philosophy teacher in Freiburg, Heinrich Rickert), theology (particularly as Benjamin encountered it in Jewish Messianism and through his exchanges with Gershom Scholem), and literary criticism (especially as he encountered it in Lessing as well as in the critiques of Lessing in Schlegel's Romanticist perspective and in Franz Mehring's Marxian reading).[6] But *Rettung* also deserves to be placed into syntactical relation with such canonical Benjaminian concepts or semiconcepts as profane illumination, weak messianic power, the experience of Now-Time, allegory, left-wing melancholia, progress, the dialectic of culture and barbarism, citability, criticism and commentary, violence, fate, the dialectical image, the petrified primordial landscape, the aestheticization of politics, the ruin, montage, myth and ritual, mimesis and language, deauratization, the angel of history, memory, apocatastasis, awakening, destruction, and mourning, among so many others. So much has been said about each of them, and yet so little. In each case, the intricate workings of a certain idea of *Rettung* could be shown to be operative in ever-shifting formulations and nuances and in ever-transforming modulations. Yet what concerns me here, within the limits of what can be said in a very compact space, is not a comprehensive history of *Rettung* but rather a focused engagement with some of the *structural* problems of the concept as it is mobilized in Benjamin's writings. In this way, I hope to make the old problem of *Rettung* appear interesting once again.

When Benjamin in his missive to Adorno worries about the ways in which a failed *Rettung* assumes the disfigured face of an apologia, he also articulates the stakes of the figure of *Rettung* with which his own writing wrestles. He can neither rid his writing of this dialectic nor rescue his writing from it. As a critical gesture of rescuing and saving, *retten* does not merely mean to affirm, in the sense of a temporally delayed, retroactive re-cognition that is the condition of possibility for every speech act, but also is the repetition and cementing of a given state of affairs. The *Retter*, as the one whose work hopes to achieve a rescue, thus always also runs the risk of becoming a tacit apologist for what is. While the potential for this dialectical possibility to become visible is always present, it exhibits its true face precisely in the moment when it falls short of its actual aims—that is, fails at *Rettung*. The failure of *Rettung*, then, can be both a failure and a success, a successful failure: it can fail to the extent that it proves incapable of rescuing, and it can succeed at the same time by making visible the normally concealed or dissimulated threat of apologistic affirmation that inheres in the gesture of *Rettung*.

In a June 1938 letter to Adorno from Paris, Benjamin returns to the question of *Rettung* at greater length, this time not with regard to Kracauer's work on Offenbach but rather in relation to Adorno's *Versuch über Wagner*. While he finds much in Adorno's work on the composer that is praiseworthy, he nevertheless suggests that "the historical-philosophical perspective of *Rettung* . . . is irreconcilable with the critical ones of progression and regression."[7] From this vantage point, the "use, without further qualification, of the categories of the progressive and the regressive, whose appropriateness to the central theses of your work I would be the last to infringe upon, makes the attempts at a *Rettung* of Wagner (on which I *at this point* would be the last to insist, especially after having read your text with its devastating analyses) exceedingly problematic."[8] For Benjamin, then, there is something structural at work within *Rettung* that prevents it from fully coinciding with the diagnosis of progress or regression, if these are to be understood as salient determinations within a binary opposition. *Rettung*, as this view implies, seems to harbor a dark underbelly even when it shines most brightly, even when its achievement of rescuing something—and, by rescuing something *in particular*, also affirming the general concept of rescuing *as such*—appears to be beyond doubt. Yet, from a Benjaminian perspective, *Rettung* never can be *merely* progressive *or* regressive; there is something within its deepest logic that renders it both and neither all at once.

What form would such a radically dialectical view of *Rettung* assume in the realm of writing and of aesthetic creation? Benjamin writes:

> Sie sind gewiß nicht willens, mir zu wiederspechen wenn ich sage, daß die Rettung als philosophische Tendenz eine schriftstellerische Form bedingt, die—um es unbeholfen zu sagen (weil ich es nicht besser formulieren kann)—mit der musikalischen eine besondere Verwandtschaft hat. Die Rettung ist eine zyklische Form, die polemische eine progressive. Mir stellen sich die zehn Kapitel des Wagners eher als eine progressive denn als ein Zyklus dar. . . . Das alles, wie gesagt, zeichnete sich wohl als Frage in einem unserer letzten Gespräche ab.

> [You will probably not want to contradict me if I say that *Rettung* as a philosophical tendency requires a form of writing that—to say it somewhat clumsily (because I do not know how to formulate it better)—has a special affinity with musical form. *Rettung* is a cyclical form, polemic a progressive one. The ten chapters of your "Wagner" present themselves to me more as progression than as cycle. . . . All of this, as I said, began to emerge in one of our last conversations.][9]

Benjamin finishes this thought by transitioning from Adorno's work to his own. He suggests that the "difficulties with my 'Baudelaire' are perhaps precisely the inverse" and that "the form of *Rettung* could, in relation to this object, itself become a problem."[10] Here, as everywhere in his work, Benjamin shows himself to be a thinker for whom the "what" of a thought cannot be considered in isolation from the "how" of its presentation, so that, for him, innovative thinking always also requires that the thinking confront the opportunities and aporias of its own textual form.[11] While he always privileges, by comparison with the musically minded Adorno, the language of the image, whether in figurative language or as instantiations of the *eidos*, over the language of music to capture certain philosophical and historico-political truth-contents, this is one of the few passages in his work that concedes to musical form a special cognitive value. What Benjamin finds in musical form and in the way in which this musical form can be made to structure critical writing is its relation to the idea of a cyclicality, a movement that renounces the linearity of progression and regression, instead returning, in specifiable, strategic intervals, to the expression of a certain form or motif. Benjamin may have had in mind, for instance, the cyclical dimension of a baroque fugue or of a Wagnerian leitmotif. He no doubt also appealed to Adorno's sense, consistent with the latter's musical training and with the high esteem in which he held the experimental work of such Second Viennese School composers as Schönberg, Webern, Berg (Adorno's composition teacher), and others, that serious philosophical works should have the structure of a complex musical composition rather than of teleological and purely instrumentalist argumentation.

In Convolute N 9, 2, of *The Arcades Project*, Benjamin picks up the idea of *Rettung*'s cyclicality, this time mobilizing nautical imagery: "On the concept of *Rettung*: the wind of the absolute in the sails of the concept. (The principle of wind is the cyclical.) The position of the sails is the relative."[12] Because the wind, even the wind of the absolute, is never a stable force, and cannot, like the weather itself, be predicted with reliable accuracy and linear constancy, what it propels forward can also suffer from its vagaries and vacillations. The cyclical wind of *Rettung* enables and stalls, liberates and entraps at the same time, not unlike the wind that gets caught in the wings of Benjamin's angel of history, who, because of the wind's force, is propelled forward while at the same time forcefully being prevented from closing his wings in order to tarry.

If Benjamin's association of *Rettung* with a cyclical form and of polemic with a progressive form can be maintained, *Rettung*, unlike the polemic, never can proceed along the fault lines of a linear, teleological, deductively structured unfolding. *Rettung*, for Benjamin, cannot progress, even when its aim is progress; it progresses toward the thinking of progress precisely by refusing progression. Its cyclicality calls on it to return to itself always one more time, involving itself in an infinite conversation about its own conditions of possibility, without allowing this conversation to sever its ties from its place of utterance and, ultimately, from the historical and political *Lebenswelt*, or "life world," to use Husserl's old phenomenological term, in which it is embedded. What Benjamin hopes to rescue in the critical gesture of rescuing is the way in which it also fails at rescuing. "What is decisive in *Rettung*," Benjamin writes, "is never the progressive; it can resemble the regressive as much as the goal [*Ziel*] resembles that which Kraus names origin

[*Ursprung*]."[13] *Rettung* here is to be thought as that which refuses to differentiate between progression and regression, just as in the "Theses on the Philosophy of History" and in the essay on Eduard Fuchs, there can be no document of culture that is not at the same time a document of barbarism.

If there is something at the core of the undecidability of *Rettung* that exceeds any normative inscription, then the particular challenge that it issues is not merely, as one of Benjamin's readers suggests, tied to the problem of how "to gain distance from what has been transmitted and how to establish a reasonable principle of selection [*ein vernünftiges Selektionsprinzip gewonnen werden soll*]."[14] From a more radical perspective, the central issue is not predominantly one of how to don the judge's robe most comfortably in order to decide at any given point between two options. That is to say, the problem is not in the first instance one of securing categorical criteria as to what is worthy of rescuing and what is not, which act of rescuing is merely conservative and apologetic and which act of rescuing is forward-looking and politically progressive. Rather, the problem, as Benjamin conceives of it, pertains to ways in which any act of *Rettung*, for structural reasons, cannot be thought in isolation from what within it is already at odds with it, silently works against it, even when faced with the demand for a stable act of deciding and separating that critique as the Greek *krinein* issues forth.

In his response to Benjamin's missive, Adorno writes from Bar Harbor, Maine, in early August 1938 that he is in agreement with Benjamin's assessment but emphasizes that *Versuch über Wagner* by no means wishes to base the "*Rettung* of Wagner," understood in the double sense of the genitive, solely on the moment of progress.[15] Rather, as Adorno reminds Benjamin, his study of Wagner attempts to articulate the moment of *Rettung* in relation to the dissonant movements of progression and regression, especially in the final chapter, which is more attuned to the cyclical form of *Rettung* that Benjamin claims should receive attention. But it is not until decades later, and long after his friend's suicide, that Adorno returns to the elusive question of *Rettung* that had concerned him in his exchanges with Benjamin, especially in such works as *Negative Dialectics*.

In 1972, Adorno's former student Habermas published an essay entitled "Bewußtmachende oder rettende Kritik—die Aktualität Walter Benjamins" (Walter Benjamin: Consciousness-Raising or Rescuing Critique).[16] This essay, the first in any language to thematize *Rettung* as a major element in Benjamin's corpus, assumed a significant place in the history of Benjamin scholarship and helped to shape a broader reception of Benjamin's writings for years to come, in both an approving sense, as in certain quarters of the so-called Second Generation of the Frankfurt School, and in a critical sense.[17] Habermas's reading of Benjamin's multiple engagements with *Rettung* focuses on their uneasy relation to historical materialism in such a way as to diagnose in Benjamin a tacit imbrication of enlightenment and mysticism. For all the Benjaminian intuitions that appear valuable to Habermas, what disturbs him in Benjamin's rescuing gestures is, in short, that "Benjamin did not succeed in his intention to unite enlightenment and mysticism because the theologian in him could not bring himself to make the messianic theory of experience serviceable for historical materialism," with the result that one finds in Benjaminian attempts at critical *Rettung* an "odd adaptation of Marxian critique of ideology" and the equally vexing difficulty of "a politicized art."[18] If, especially in his aesthetic theory, Benjamin conceives of rescuing critique as performing the "mortification of the artwork only to transpose what is worth knowing from the medium of the beautiful into that of the true and thereby to rescue [*retten*] it," then Habermas suspects a certain failure in Benjamin's thought.[19] "A criticism," Habermas claims, "that sets out to rescue semantic potential with a leap into past *Jetztzeiten* has a highly mediated position relative to political praxis. On this, Benjamin did not manage to achieve sufficient clarity."[20] A thinker as redoubtable as Habermas develops these claims in a circumspect and convincingly argued manner, based on an intimate familiarity with Benjamin's writings to the extent that they were available in the early 1970s—that is, prior to the publication of the *Gesammelte Schriften* by Benjamin's German editors, Rolf Tiedemann and Hermann Schweppenhäuser. But when Habermas ultimately accuses Benjamin of a certain conservatism that fails to follow the precepts of ideology critique, one gains the impression that something is missing in Habermas's otherwise erudite reading that cannot simply be reduced to missing texts. Rather, it may be, for lack of a better word, a "feeling," or at least a certain *Fingerspitzengefühl*, for Benjamin's project. For what if that which Habermas uneasily terms Benjamin's "conservative-revolutionary hermeneutics" were in reality the embodiment of resistance to an either–or taxonomy that makes room for successful or failed attempts at applying a theologically, aesthetically, and politically conditioned concept of *Rettung* to this or that moment of historical-materialist ideology critique aimed at yet another normative intervention into the structure of a so-called political reality, and instead wished to rethink the very notion of the political itself along the multiply mediated and differentiated encounters with a non-self-identical gesture of rescuing? That is to say, is it not possible that what Benjamin envisions in his revolutionarily charged commitment to *Rettung* even—and precisely—in the face of its failure is not coextensive with a new subjectivity based on communicative rationality and on a concept of action based on transparent negotiation, but rather works to perform a more radical interrogation of the ways in which the aporias of a rescuing critique itself make possible a rethinking of the ethico-political and aesthetically transformative stakes of *Rettung*? Perhaps it is along the lines of these open questions that Benjamin's unorthodox attempt to mobilize, as he explicitly writes in a preparatory note to the book on Baudelaire, "*Rettung* as a literary and a political category" becomes more comprehensible.[21]

To help us consider the distant possibility of this aesthetic and political heresy in Benjamin, we may turn once again to Adorno, whose main philosophical work, *Negative Dialectics*, represents, I wish to suggest, a sustained engagement not only with Hegel's method but also with Benjamin's uneasy relation to the demands of *Rettung*. While Benjamin makes several explicit appearances in *Negative Dialectics*, it is perhaps in a passage toward the end of the work, a passage that does not mention Benjamin by name, that Adorno's thoughts return most fully to the orbit of those that he had once considered together with his friend:

Nichts auf der Erde und nichts im leeren Himmel ist dadurch zu retten, daß man es verteidigt. Das "Ja aber" gegen das kritische Argument, das etwas sich nicht entreißen lassen möchte, hat bereits die Gestalt des stur auf Bestehendem Bestehens, sich Anklammerns, unversöhnlich mit der Idee des Rettens, in der der Krampf solcher prolongierten Selbsterhaltung sich löste. Nichts kann unverwandelt gerettet werden, nichts, das nicht das Tor seines Todes durchschritten hätte. Ist Rettung der innerste Impuls jeglichen Geistes, so ist keine Hoffnung als die der vorbehaltlosen Preisgabe: des zu Rettenden wie des Geistes, der hofft.

[Nothing on earth and nothing in the empty skies can be rescued by defending it. The "yes, but" against the critical argument, which refuses to let something be torn away from itself, already has the form of that which obstinately insists on what is, of a clinging-to, irreconcilable with the idea of rescuing in which the convulsion of such prolonged self-maintenance would dissolve. Nothing can be rescued unchanged, nothing that did not first pass through the gate of its own death. If rescuing is the innermost impulse of all intellect, then there is no hope but the one of unreserved surrender: of that which is to be rescued and of the intellect that hopes.]²²

The perspective that these apodictic meditations open up is striking. Yet at this point, the objection could be raised that the intellectual stance that they sponsor is a mode of mere passivity, even a certain defeatist quietism of thought that obstinately refuses to be translated into the rescuing gestures of intervention that Habermas and others will have called for.²³ After all, does not that which we consider worthy of continued existence, and which we have the passion and the will actively to sustain, require that we defend it? Is not the very concept of *Rettung* imbricated with the idea that something is defended, protected from its decline or disappearance through an active mobilization of will and a conscious act of intervention? Would not the failure to defend something that one wished to rescue amount to an admission of defeat or, worse, of a lack of engagement and effort, even an ethical lapse? Who in good faith could possibly claim to have an interest in rescuing, not to mention a rescuing critique, if he or she were not willing or able to defend? And yet, there is *nichts* (nothing), Adorno writes, "Nichts auf der Erde und nichts im leeren Himmel," which is "dadurch zu retten, daß man es verteidigt."

The activity of *retten* that is at stake here cannot be reduced to a theological one. This is why Adorno locates the scene of the inability of *Rettung* to be defended "on earth" (*auf der Erde*) and "in the empty skies" (*im leeren Himmel*)—that is to say, by and among humans and in a realm that is not occupied by a God or an equivalent transcendental signified. The qualifier "empty" (*leer*) is perhaps even more important in the original than it is in the English translation, since German has only one word, *Himmel*, to designate both sky and heaven; *leer* makes visible the invisibility of an absent God, and even of a *Deus absconditus*. The logic of the argument pivots on a structural rather than a theological condition for the following reason: if the activity that is required for the *Rettung* of something is one of defense, a refusal to release and to concede without reserve, then the very condition of possibility for something can also be said to be the condition of its nonpossibility. If a *Rettung* that is based on *Verteidigung* is at odds with what one had hoped to rescue; if the idea of *Rettung* already is incompatible with a certain refusal and with the demand for self-maintenance; and if the spirit, mind, intellect, or ghost (*Geist*) that wishes to maintain itself is called on to do so in a manner that is inconsistent with its own logic and orientation, then that which is to be rescued by *Rettung* can enact this feat only by disappearing. To preserve something, then, may also mean permitting it to become something else; this is why, as something that can do nothing else than to be transformed, that which is to be rescued must "first pass through the gate of its own death." It becomes what it is, can be rescued on its own terms, only when it is no longer itself, has passed on, as it were.[24]

Is there not something in every defense, in every rhetorical and philosophical attempt at *Rettung*, an elusive element that tacitly acknowledges, and in a certain sense *makes thinkable* for the first time, the very *possibility* of the actual and complete disappearance of something? Does the attempt at saving something through a radical and passionate defense of it not also unintentionally set the stage for its vanishing? Could the threat of *Rettung*, in the double sense of the genitive, not only be its potential failure—which, according to Benjamin's critique of Kracauer, at times works to turn *Rettung* into mere apologia—but also be the frightening gesture of putting the possibility of the disappearance of something squarely on the table with a force and a clarity that even those apparent or concealed forces that necessitated the rescuing could not surpass? For instance, Foucault's genealogical model analyzing war in terms of its discursive mobilization of "truth" as a political category of defense in military thinkers such as Carl von Clausewitz is also a way of thinking about the disappearance of any possible political justification for pursuing war as politics through other means.[25] And, in a very different conceptual register, the thoughtful commemoration of the gradual disappearance of odd items and quotidian objects from contemporary life in a quasi-Benjaminian way in the recent volume *Kleines Glossar des Verschwindens* (*Small Glossary of Disappearance*)—which includes thirty so-called obituaries for disappearing objects such as the ink blot, galoshes, the frost flower, the typewriter, and the handkerchief by well-known writers and critics such as Hans Ulrich Gumbrecht, Jochen Hörisch, Gerhard Neumann, and Harald Weinrich—may make their disappearance that much more easily accepted through evocative and forcefully stylized rhetoric.[26] It is perhaps in this sense, too, that Benjamin in "Pariser Passagen 1" (1927) records his general methodological investment neither in the actual appearance of objects nor in their final and irreversible disappearance, but rather in their transitional, nonpetrified state, what he calls "things in the moment of the 'being-no-longer' [*Dinge im Augenblick des Nicht-mehr-seins*]."[27]

The challenge that the image of *Rettung* in *Negative Dialectics* gives us to think, in which nothing *"ist dadurch zu retten, daß man es verteidigt,"* is one in which the inability to rescue something by defending it is not an obstacle to be overcome, an embarrassment that prevents the tenuous relation between *Rettung* and critique from becoming fortified as a stable rescuing mission. Rather, the dialectical reversibility of *Rettung*, the constitutive antagonism that is lodged in its core, is what necessitates restless vigilance in the thinking of what it is and what it still can hope to be. It fails to rescue *Rettung* through defense, even while it rescues and defends the productive failure of all *Rettung* through defense—the productive failure that makes vigilant, self-reflexive writing what it is in the first place. It is here, in the aporia of radical, self-reflexive thought itself, that something of thought's failed rescue mission may be said to be rescued in spite of itself.

Even in those moments when a tenuous *Rettung* appears to have been achieved, what is rescued will not remain the "same" object once and for all. Nothing that is rescued will simply remain itself; nothing that is rescued can avoid the transformations of time and space, the aleatory movements of language, and the unpredictable changes that future readings and interpretations will visit upon it. This reading of a non-self-identical *Rettung* in relation to a non-self-identical object world is consonant with the predicament of Benjamin's modernity in the *Trauerspiel* book where "[a]ny person, any object, any relationship can mean absolutely anything else."[28] Even what is rescued—having attracted the gesture of *Rettung* through its singularity and difference, that is, having been *singled out* for rescuing—survives as something *other* than merely itself; it will come to mean *something else*. *Rettung* therefore is but one of the names for the thinkability of an object's singularity as it presents itself—or, more precisely, as it will have presented itself in a future perfect that always only can be hinted at—in a series of future, and as yet uncontainable, iterations. What *Rettung* rescues, in this perspective, is precisely the knowledge that retains and respects the object's singularity as repeatable difference, as something that will not remain with itself in any transparent way.

In Convolute N 9, 4, Benjamin suggests a thinking of the ways in which *Rettung* itself could be rescued precisely by focusing the gesture of rescuing not merely on the conservation of what is but rather on that which, like the non-self-identical in *Rettung*, is non-self-identical in its objects. There, he writes:

> From what are the phenomena rescued [*Wovor werden die Phänomene gerettet*]? Not only, and not also from the disrepute and the disregard into which they have fallen, but from the catastrophe that is presented

very often by a certain means of their transmission [*Überlieferung*], their "appreciation as heritage."—They are rescued through the exhibition of the crack or fissure [*Sprung*] within them.—There is a transmission that is catastrophe.[29]

What *Rettung* rescues, then, is also the non-self-identity of the object world, the multiply mediated ways in which phenomena are not fully themselves, are not what they appear to be on the surface or to the judgment of a hasty reading. "Nothing that is so is so," as Shakespeare tells us in *Twelfth Night*. To rescue *Rettung* in the emphatic sense and to rescue a phenomenon means to allow its resistance to a unified meaning to emerge and to subsist, without attempting to normalize it or to explain it away from the vantage point of a putative metatheoretical perspective. The catastrophe of transmission is to be counterbalanced by remaining faithful to the irreducible yet normally hidden *Sprung*, the "crack or fissure," in the hull of the phenomenon under consideration, just as *Ursprung* needs to be rescued, at least for the Benjamin of the *Trauerspiel* book, not simply as an origin but as a primal crack or leap, an *Ur-sprung*.

Adorno once wrote that "in all his phases, Benjamin thought the demise of the subject and the *Rettung* of the human being as one thing [*den Untergang des Subjekts und die Rettung des Menschen zusammengedacht*]," locating a radically aporetic transformation in Benjamin's thinking whereby that which still deserves to be called human can survive only through the dismantling of the fiction of a self-present and self-identical consciousness.[30] If there is going to be *Rettung*, it is one based on destruction; if there is going to be destruction, it is one based on *Rettung*. Indeed, the aporetic movement of *Rettung* assumes a concrete form in two specific instances in Benjamin's corpus. The first can be observed in his evocation of the theological through the figure of blotting paper in *The Arcades Project*. The second can be found in his image of photography.

In *The Arcades Project*, Benjamin writes: "My thinking relates to theology the way that blotting paper [*Löschblatt*, literally "erasing sheet"] relates to ink. It is fully saturated with it. Yet, if the blotting paper had its way, nothing that was written would remain."[31] While an exhaustive explication of this allusion-rich passage exceeds the scope of this discussion, one nevertheless should take note of Benjamin's choice of blotting paper as a prime instantiation of the kind of *Rettung* that is at stake. It preserves—albeit in inverted form—the substance of that with which it comes into contact within itself, in essence rescuing that which it erases. To this day blotting paper is used by German schoolchildren to dry the ink of their fountain pens before the writing becomes smeared or sullies the hands or clothing of the writer. Benjamin's choice of this particular rhetorical image works to illustrate how theology is both erased and preserved in his work, an oeuvre that opposes a purely theological mode of argumentation while at the same time being saturated—informed, motivated, and ultimately sustained—by it. The particular kind of *Rettung* that Benjamin's thought performs could be seen, somewhat paradoxically, as a nontheological theology, a theology without theology—that is, a theology of the blotting paper.

The second example of an aporetic *Rettung* can be located in the general orbit of Benjamin's variegated meditations on the photograph, meditations that inform not only those texts that he explicitly dedicates to photography, such as his essay "Little History of Photography" (1931), but also the full spectrum of texts, in a variety of registers, that traverse his corpus.[32] For Benjamin, the photograph works to rescue the object or human being as an image, preserving it from the relentless flow of time, which is interrupted by the click of the shutter release. An expression, a look, a mode of being-in-the-world in a particular time and space are torn out of temporality, fixed as a citable and shareable memory. But, with the passing of time, what the photograph has rescued no longer coincides with itself. The photographed face, body, scene, or object visibly ages, a process that is set in motion as soon as the picture is taken. The *Rettung* that the photograph performs, then, is always also an introjection of permanence into the category of change, but what preserves or rescues, as an image, also always becomes a memento mori, the image of a death to come.

From the perspective of the elusive yet abiding promise associated with *Rettung*'s failed rescue mission, the impulse associated with *Rettung* becomes readable in a new light. In Convolute N 11, 4, Benjamin writes that the "object of history is that upon which cognition is performed as the object's rescue [*Gegenstand der Geschichte ist dasjenige, an dem die Erkenntnis als dessen Rettung vollzogen wird*]."[33] The *Rettung* that Benjamin here evokes cannot be the mere rescuing of historical phenomena as stable categories of knowledge and experience. Rather, considering the manifold implications of the view that nothing really can be rescued by defending it, the *Rettung* that can be performed according to Benjamin's paleonomic historical materialism is one whose productive promise is tied to its ability to account, theoretically and politically, for the singular movements of its incapacity to live up to its own demands. Thinking *Rettung*, then, would require coming to terms with the possibility of failing at something for which there can be no a priori conditions of success. Because even a presumably successful rescuing is still haunted by the specters of its own internal contradictions, whatever critical promise *Rettung* may still harbor for us is inseparable from the gesture in thinking that radically opens itself to the permanent possibility of its most brilliant failure. To evoke Benjamin's image from his essay on Goethe's *Elective Affinities*, *Rettung* too could be said to belong to the "enigma of the flame itself"—that is, to "the truth whose living flame continues to burn over the heavy logs of what is past and the light ashes of what has been experienced."[34] Here, in the illumination provided by the self-consuming flame, truth-content becomes visible not as an object but as a dynamic and transformative afterness that is tied to the interpretive act, an act that leaves neither its object nor the rescuing subject unaltered.

5 Afterness and Translation
The Politics of Carrying Across

> We do not yet really know what a translation is.
> —Friedrich Schlegel, "Philosophy of Philology"

> Tell me what you think of translation, and I will tell you who you are.
> —Martin Heidegger, *Hölderlin's Hymn "The Ister"*

In an essay accompanying the recently published transcript of Heidegger's seminar on Schiller's *Letters on the Aesthetic Education of Mankind* (1794) held at the University of Freiburg during the winter semester 1936/1937, the German philosopher Odo Marquard claims that much of Heidegger's interest in philosophical aesthetics should be understood chiefly as a form of ideological disappointment and intellectual displacement. To understand the context of Marquard's claim, it is important to recall that the seminar on Schiller took place a relatively short time after Heidegger, in the autumn of 1933, had rejected offers of professorships from the major metropolitan universities of Berlin and Munich—appointments that carried the expectation of an overtly "political" agenda—to remain in his provincial Freiburg, at a time when he is believed to have been growing increasingly disenchanted with the German National Socialist movement. In October 1933, Heidegger, as rector (chancellor) of the University of Freiburg, had appointed his colleague Wilhelm von Möllendorf as dean of the School of Medicine in spite of the fact that Möllendorf had been forced to step down from his position as rector by the National Socialists because of his social-democratic allegiances. When, in February 1934, the party's Ministry of Culture pressured Heidegger to remove Möllendorf as dean of the School of Medicine and to remove Erik Wolff (a Jew) from his position as dean of the Law School, Heidegger resigned from the rectorship.[1] Although Heidegger had held a summer camp in 1933 aimed at strengthening the commitment of lecturers and assistant professors to a National Socialist agenda for remodeling the German university system, a year later the leadership of the party felt that the philosopher's ideological attachment to the movement could not be trusted. National Socialist plans to exploit the international reputation and standing of Heidegger, by then long famous for his *Being and Time* (1927), by making him the director of a new National Socialist academy charged with forming and fortifying the ideological spirit of Germany's future elite academics were cancelled. Walter Gross, director of the party's "Office of Racial Policies," warned Hitler's chief racial ideologue Alfred Rosenberg—author of *The Myth of the Twentieth Century* (1930), an influential book that propagated the replacement of Christianity with a new Arian "religion of the blood"—that Heidegger could not be entrusted with such an important task.[2] Heidegger, who had at one time sympathized with National Socialist ideas, now was spied on by Nazi students who infiltrated his Freiburg lectures and seminars and who reported on his teaching to the party's officials. In an unpublished notebook entry from April 1934 concerning his resignation from the rectorship, Heidegger writes that he "could no longer responsibly serve" in that office, decrying the National Socialists' "mediocrity and noise." His "entire rectorship" was further doomed under "the great error [*großen Irrtum*]" of wanting, Heidegger notes, "to bring to the dispositions and perspectives of the 'colleagues' questions from which they, for their own sake—as well as at their peril—best remain precluded."[3] Save for a few isolated remarks and exchanges—such as a 1948 letter to his former student Marcuse, a letter to Karl Jaspers in which he famously referred to his involvement as *eine Dummheit* (a stupidity), and a posthumously published interview with the German magazine *Der Spiegel*—after the war Heidegger chose not to address his political involvements in 1933 and 1934 in any sustained manner. This refusal has led a broad spectrum of readers—among them Otto Pöggeler, Dominique Janicaud, David Farrell Krell, Berel Lang, and Jean-François Lyotard—to theorize the philosophical and ethico-political implications of his "silence."[4]

Although Marquard does not furnish these details, this is the political background before which he makes the assertion that in Heidegger, as in Schiller, "erstwhile revolutionary sympathies survive the political failure of the revolution aesthetically." He argues that in the Schiller seminar we witness Heidegger's attempt "to substitute a failed revolutionary politics with successful art: the fundamental step into art is the vehicle for the soft belly landing of burst revolutionary hopes."[5] Marquard goes on to suggest that following Heidegger's disenchantment with National Socialist politics, the philosopher allowed art to assume the proper place of revolutionary hope. Bracketing a renewed discussion of the specifically philosophical stakes of Heidegger's so-called *Kehre*, or "turn," in the 1930s, Marquard argues that Heidegger's dashed hopes for an antibourgeois revolution that the German Fascist movement initially had seemed to promise can explain his aesthetic engagements in the mid-1930s, including, presumably, the 1935/1936 lectures on "The Origin of the Work of Art"; the series of lectures and seminars on Friedrich Hölderlin beginning in the winter semester 1934/1935; the 1936 speech "Hölderlin and the Essence of Poetry"; the 1936/1937 lecture course "Nietzsche: The Will to Power as Art"; and, prominently, the 1936/1937 seminar on Schiller's aesthetics.[6] Whatever its merits and shortcomings, Marquard's argument is perfectly clear regarding the question of what Heidegger's engagement with the philosophy of art signifies.

Marquard implicitly distances himself from Philippe Lacoue-Labarthe's argument that Heidegger's "national aestheticism" is a formation of political involvement that is structured, even haunted, by an abiding attachment to *techné* and its myths. This latent affinity, according to Lacoue-Labarthe's reading, cannot be circumvented by any modern political philosophy or state apparatus. Rather, he suggests that both philosophy and the state must negotiate this affinity precisely in order not to be blindsided by it.[7] Neither would Marquard follow the road that led Derrida to meditate on the role that the discursive formation of *Geist* and the attendant "question of the question" play in Heidegger's period of engagement with German National Socialism.[8] Instead, by rehearsing a long-standing argument concerning the relationship between modern German intellectual production and the empirical world of the political—one that has, among other incarnations, suggested that there are so many eighteenth- and nineteenth-century German dramas about the French Revolution, by Schiller and others, precisely because Germany did not experience an empirical revolution of its own—Marquard detects in Heidegger's engagement with the work of art a displacement and a compensation, essentially the work of psycho-political aberration and unacknowledged intellectual *ressentiment*.

Much would need to be scrutinized with regard to this claim, including, among many other things, the full intricacies of Heidegger's political involvements and unforgivable silences, the by-no-means self-evident relationship between his life and his work, the status of art and the aesthetic in his pre-1930s work, the very idea of intellectual compensation in a work of art, and the relation of art to fundamental ontology.[9] But what interests me here is the way in which the transformative art that Marquard ascribes to Heidegger in the context of his seminar on Schiller can be thought as a figure of *translation*. One way of reading Marquard's interpretation of Heidegger's aesthetic gestures, and in particular of the latter's understanding of Schiller, is to view it in terms of *a translation of the source material of revolutionary commitments into the target language of aesthetic theory*. In this alleged act of translation, the target language of the aesthetic is confined to live in the *afterness* of an original impulse, one that dictates the movements and investments of the translation in an unacknowledged or a dissimulated but consequently all the more powerful way. According to this model, there can be no translation of an original into another discourse that does not always also repeat the afterness of its after in relation to the now sublated and reinscribed conceptual structure and marching plan of the source. Here, then, it will be especially instructive to ask what Heidegger's philosophy itself may have to say about the act and concept of translation, especially during the years of the alleged revolutionary disenchantment that Marquard claims are so formative for the trajectory of Heidegger's post-*Kehre* thinking, and specifically in the context of Heidegger's attempted "translation" of Schiller into future-oriented concepts and discourses of thinking that can no longer be contained by conventional metaphysics and institutionalized philosophy. If, as we found in our discussions of Adorno and Benjamin in chapters 3 and 4, there can hardly be a *Rettung* that would remain self-identical and recuperative, Heidegger's "translation" of Schiller unfolds on the far side of this knowledge, proceeding from the position of a thinking that no longer takes the recuperation of its object for granted.

We should note that Heidegger's seminar itself today lives on in the ghostly form of a "translation" of sorts, albeit not in the conventional sense that takes place between languages. The *Übungen für Anfänger*, or "exercises for beginners," as Heidegger termed his course, happened to be recorded by the Freiburg physician Wilhelm Hallwachs, who, although he was already a practicing doctor, audited and took copious notes on many of Heidegger's seminars and lectures between 1930 and 1938.[10] We have 366 octavo pages of Hallwachs's transcriptions and notations relating to the Schiller seminar, with his protocols spanning the entire semester's work, from November 4, 1936, through February 17, 1937. Despite the fact that after six years of taking Heidegger's courses Hallwachs could be said to have been an experienced Heidegger note taker by the beginning of the Schiller seminar and the fact that Heidegger was known at the beginning of each seminar session to review and correct the minutes, prepared by students, of previous sessions, the published text cannot be considered authorized by Heidegger himself. Instead, it embodies what in German is called a reliable *Mitschrift*, literally a "writing-along," a transcription that bears witness, in a rigorous yet necessarily interpretive gesture, to what Heidegger said in seminar, including his emphases, gestures, and accentuations. Hallwachs's "translations" of Heidegger allow the philosopher's intensive engagement with Schiller's aesthetics to survive and have an afterlife or afterness in the language of the other, which is especially noteworthy considering that Heidegger rarely ever mentions Schiller and his particular brand of German Idealism in his extensive corpus. As a translation of a certain scene of translation, the seminar protocols of the "exercises for beginners" can be said to embody, even in their unauthorized version, a most appropriate venue for a negotiation of Heidegger's engagement with the concept of translation as it relates to his idiosyncratic reading of Schiller's aesthetic theory.

At this point, the objection could be raised that it would be peculiar to argue that translational considerations subtend Heidegger's engagement with Schiller's aesthetic letters, given that Heidegger never translates Schiller in the conventional sense from one language into another, and that Schiller's letters themselves do not seem to address the question of translation in any direct manner. Indeed, except for brief passages here and there as well as occasional allusions in his correspondence with contemporaries such as Christian Gottfried Körner, Schiller rarely addresses the problem of translation in his extensive corpus directly. Readers concerned with eighteenth-century theories of translation—that is, the discourse of translation at a time when, historically, philosophies of language first came into their own as recognizably "modern" concerns—seldom turn to Schiller, preferring contemporaries such as Goethe, Schleiermacher, and Wilhelm von Humboldt, who all wrote extensively on the topic. And yet, when viewed from the larger perspective of Heidegger's fundamental engagement with an expanded concept of translation, Schiller's aesthetic letters and Heidegger's seminar on them are mutually illuminating in unexpected ways. In fact, by thinking of "translation" figuratively, we find ourselves closer to the force field of differences and displacements that make translation what it is; when we are *thinking*, we are always "closer" to translation than we might think. Translation is always already figurative, on its way elsewhere, in the language of thought—indeed, as such, it is the figure par excellence of afterness.

The difficulties of "translating" Heidegger's German, which so often unfolds at the intersection of a self-conscious etymology, a reactivation of word roots and references, and the trance-like tone and style of a system of signs that keeps returning to itself, are well known. When translating Heideggerian words such as *Dasein, Erörterung, Enthüllung*, and *das Seiende* into any other language, the translator, pushed to the limits of the thinkable and the sayable, is likely to revert to the practice of keeping Heidegger's German words alive even in the translation. Here, one is reminded of James Joyce's answer to a question regarding the use of foreign words in his texts: "Aren't there enough words for you in English?" To which he replied, "Yes, there are enough, but they aren't the right ones."[11] In fact, the recent testimonies gathered by the Romanian Society for Phenomenology regarding the "practical" challenges of translating Heidegger—by those who have translated him into such languages as Bulgarian, Czech, Dutch, English, Finnish, French, Greek, Hungarian, Italian, Japanese, Korean, Portuguese, Romanian, Slovenian, Spanish, Swedish, and Turkish—eloquently illustrate this point.[12] What is less fully appreciated, however, is that the question of the afterness of translation occupies a central position in Heidegger's own conceptual orbit. Even though there is no single work in which he systematically collects all his thoughts on the problem of translation, the philosopher explicitly thematizes translation in many of his essays and lecture courses. We could say that there is no single Heideggerean text exclusively devoted to the question of translation in part because the question already is everywhere in evidence, permeating everything; it is being "translated" into myriad contexts at any given moment in the 102 volumes of his *Gesamtausgabe* (collected works), of which over 70 have now been published. To read a single sentence by Heidegger requires us to contemplate the question of translation whether we are "translating" it in any conventional sense or not.

For Heidegger's project, the stakes of translation and mistranslation are high. To the extent that any act of understanding is always also an act of interpretation and, therefore, of translation, the act and concept of translating are inseparable from the movement of thinking itself. One way of understanding Heidegger's work as a whole is to read it as a perpetual engagement with acts of translation—philosophical, linguistic, and experiential. These encompass the translation of traditional Western metaphysics into the task of a thinking yet to come; the translation of Greek thought back into itself; the translational relations among thinking (*denken*), thanking (*danken*), and poeticizing (*dichten*); the relations among building, dwelling, departing, and arriving; the innumerable questions raised by the philosophical need to translate specific Greek terms against the grain; and, finally, the constant requirement of engaging the production of meaning in terms of a simultaneous lack and excess of signification, one that fundamentally imbricates understanding with translating, even in one's mother tongue. It is no accident that in several languages translation and interpretation are semantically contiguous, as they are in English when we speak of a simultaneous interpreter at a United Nations convention or when we are in need of an interpreter when we wish to speak to authorities in a country whose language is unknown to us. The language of music, too, requires an "interpreter" when it is to be performed; it demands to be "interpreted" as though by an act of translation. It is with these concerns in mind that Heidegger states in "What Is Called Thinking?": "But every translation is already interpretation [*Auslegung*]. Every translation must first have addressed itself to what has been said, to the state of affairs [*Sachverhalt*] that was articulated within it or came to language within it [*in ihm zur Sprache kommenden*]."[13] To interpret and to translate is to allow something to take form in and as language, to let something be in and as signification. This letting-be-as-language for Heidegger is the process of interpretation as *Aus-legung*, a Germanic word meaning literally a "laying-out" that he privileges over the Latin term, just as common in German, *Interpretation*. A laying-out is the process of perpetual interpretive unfolding, a perpetual laying bare of the ways in which language means and makes its claims on us.

In his 1942/1943 lecture course on Parmenides, which is dedicated less to the pre-Socratic thinker per se than to the general attempt to translate the Greek word *aletheia* not in the conventional sense as *Wahrheit*, or "truth," but as *Unverborgenheit*, or "unconcealment," and thus to situate Greek thought in a fundamental relation to the thinking of Being, Heidegger writes: "One often assumes that 'translating' is a carrying across from one language to another, from a foreign language into one's native language, and vice versa.

But we do not see that we are constantly translating our own language, our mother tongue, into itself. Speaking and saying is a translating whose essence cannot be reduced to the notion that the translating and the translated word belong to different languages." He continues: "In every conversation and self-conversation a primordial translating rules [*waltet ein ursprüngliches Übersetzen*]."[14] This primordial translating, a translating without reserve, cannot be a matter of paraphrase, a way of finding synonyms or alternative formulations for what allegedly remains the same "content." On the contrary, the perpetual act of a primordial translation names us, with regard to our being-in-the-world, as those linguistic selves who are always only *on the way* toward thinking and the understanding that it promises.

It is this originary but always refractory act of translation, lodged in the core of any act of making sense, that leads students of Heidegger as different as Gadamer and Derrida to remind us that there can be no interpretive understanding without an engagement with translation. Gadamer in his essay "Lesen ist wie Übersetzen" (Reading Is Like Translating) shows that the act of reading itself is an act of translation.[15] And, in the words of Derrida, the "origin of philosophy is translation or the thesis of translatability," the notion that something can be interpreted, presented, and understood in terms of something else.[16] We could say that what a rigorous engagement with the scene of translation reveals is that the difficulty and question of a translation unfolds always already in the afterness of the ways in which the original text cannot be translated into itself—that is, into itself as the bearer of a unified meaning that is shared by, and transparently accessible to, its native or near-native speakers, listeners, readers, and writers. To read Heidegger's seminar on Schiller's aesthetics therefore is to be confronted with the problem of the possibility and impossibility of translating German into German, of translating a Schillerian text that itself performs a series of conceptual translations into the discourse of the concerns of fundamental ontology. This gesture is mindful of Heidegger's enigmatic statement in his lectures on Hölderlin's poem "The Ister" that "we ourselves must, with regard to ourselves, henceforth think in a more German way than all previous Germans [*wir selbst müssen in bezug auf uns selbst künftig deutscher denken als alle bisherigen Deutschen*]."[17] Although it seems to be carried by a certain nationalistic tone, Heidegger's statement can be reduced neither to simple nationalism nor to the expression of an alleged linguistic supremacy. To think in a more German way than all previous Germans would also entail departing from a concept of Germanness and the Germans in order to travel back into it there where it no longer is self-identical, no longer the transparent mode of communication one can take for granted, in a way already un-German, but un-German precisely in a German way.

We may frame our engagement with Heidegger's Schiller seminar by noting the philosopher's stated interest in "translating" Schiller's aesthetic theory into those concerns that occupy us here and now and that, as a matter of learning how to think, bespeak a certain futurity that is yet to be thought. He emphasizes in the seminar that its purpose is neither "to find the appropriate place of Schiller in intellectual history" nor to read his texts with a "general historical intention that aims to know what happened *back then*, but rather to ask for ourselves and that means for the *future* [*sondern wir fragen für uns und d.h. für die* Zukunft]."[18] The translational gesture that asking for ourselves—"*wir fragen für uns*"—implies does not mean shunning historical knowledge or genealogical insight for the sake of an aggressive and ill-informed presentism that knows no historical awareness. Rather, it implies a perpetual futurity, a contrary-to-factness that will not remain contained simply by what merely is or claims to have been.

This future-directed translational act, for Heidegger, must traverse any rigorous reading of Schiller's aesthetic letters, beginning with their very title. In the first seminar session, on November 4, 1936, Heidegger reminds us that our understanding of Schiller's aesthetic letters might commence with a translation of the preposition *über* in *Briefe über die ästhetische Erziehung des Menschen*. "*Was kann das sein?*" (What could this mean?), Heidegger asks, suggesting that it could signify "*Erziehung durch die Ästhetik*" (education *through* aesthetics), "*Erziehung zur Ästhetik*" (education toward aesthetics), or "*die Erziehung selbst ist ästhetisch*" (education itself is aesthetic), but ultimately arguing that none of these are meant. Rather, Schiller's task is to emphasize the title's phrase *des Menschen*, not of any individual human, or even of humanity, but, in Schiller's preferred terminology, the *Zustand*, the state or condition, of being human: "The humanness of the human is not a general humanity (all humans), but the Being-Human [*Die Menschheit des Menschen heißt nicht die allgemeine Menschheit (alle Menschen), sondern das Mensch-sein*]"— so that Schiller's question, "Where does the human step when he steps out of nature? [*Wohin tritt der Mensch, wenn er aus der Natur heraustritt?*]," a form of *über-setzen*, of "translating or carrying across," from the state of nature into art and history, touches the aesthetic and political essence of what it is to be human in a Schillerean sense.[19]

What is cast into sharp relief as one of the subterranean leitmotifs in Heidegger's seminar is the way in which Schiller's aesthetic theory itself can be thought in terms of a series of translational efforts. These include, among others, the translation of Kant's binarisms of the intelligible world and the empirical world, and of reason and sensuousness, into the binarisms of necessity and freedom, imagination and cognition, arbitrariness and law, as well as nature and culture. They also include the translation of beauty into freedom; of *Formtrieb*, "form drive," and *sinnlicher Trieb*, "sensuous drive," into *Spieltrieb*, "play drive"; of metaphysical into transcendental method; and of an aesthetic education into a desirable political form. While the attractiveness of Schiller's aesthetics hardly can be thought outside of these translational efforts, the translations nevertheless have occasioned a series of questions and criticisms, including the accusation of having misunderstood and mistranslated Kantian aesthetics as well as de Man's diagnosis of what he, in "Kant and Schiller," terms Schiller's "aesthetic ideology." This ideology, with its emphasis on the political investments of an aesthetic education, names the confusion of an aesthetic reality with an empirical reality, the rhetoric of semblance with the putative commitments of a state form.[20]

Before returning to the translational rhythms of the Schiller seminar, it is necessary to take another step back, a Heideggerean *Schritt zurück*, in order to comprehend the significance of the translational movements thematized in Heidegger's understanding of Schiller in the larger context of his philosophical concerns with expanded concepts of translation and translatability.

Translation and translatability are inscribed in Heidegger's general emphasis on language as the space in which the relationship of Being, being-in-the-world, experience, and thinking are to be negotiated. "Questioning is building a path," he suggests in his well-known 1953 Munich lecture "Die Frage nach der Technik" (usually translated as "The Question Concerning Technology" but also fully readable as "The Question After Technology," that is, the status of the question following the advent of the modern technological ideologies and enframements). In that lecture, the "path is a path of thinking. All paths of thinking lead, more or less noticeably, in an unusual manner through language [*Alle Denkwege führen, mehr oder weniger vernehmbar, auf eine ungewöhnliche Weise durch die Sprache*]."[21] A perpetual and caring engagement with this unusual manner of traveling within and through language is the task of thinking that always still remains to be learned. It is in language that the path becomes visible as a path. This path both leads the way and remains strangely and always again unusual, singular, *ungewöhnlich*. It is *in* language that the path of thinking itself becomes visible or audible *as* language, and there can be no true path of thinking—however provisional and tentative, however at risk of becoming a mere *Holzweg*, or "wrong way"—that does not lead through language as the ex-perience, the moving through and across, of thought itself. Language is the medium of thought as well as the medium of questioning. Thoughts and questions are not merely expressed by language as a medium, as though thinking and questioning preexisted language, waiting merely to be ex-pressed by it. Rather, language is always already the unspoken condition of possibility, the a priori space of potentiality in which something may become intelligible *as* something in the first place. As such, language, we might say, is the proper space of the *as*, the *as-ness* of all experience and thought.

If Heidegger's linguistically oriented critique of metaphysics is in large part founded on the question to what extent metaphysics is a form of *Seinsvergessenheit*, the "state of having forgotten Being," in which an answer wishes to exert continued dominance over the question, then his emphasis on keeping language open as a form of perpetual questioning, of deepening the question rather than allowing the answer to erase it, becomes more understandable.[22] These are concerns that Heidegger pursues throughout the trajectory of his work, for instance in his notes taken between 1936 and 1946—during the time of his Schiller seminar—that first were published in 1951 as "Überwindung der Metaphysik" (Overcoming Metaphysics).[23] The crux of Heidegger's concerns in this regard is that thinking language, and translation as the privileged mode of linguistic experience, requires, beyond interpretation in the narrower sense, a kind of *Destruktion* in which the unsaid, the unthought, the hidden, the repressed, the forgotten, and the opaque that language inscribes in the experience of being are invited to reemerge and speak. To employ an image offered by a recent commentator, this linguistic *Destruktion* of metaphysics is necessary for Heidegger's project because it allows texts to say what they cannot say of their own, just as the overgrown, submerged walls of an old building or ruin first must be cleared of multiple sedimented layers of debris before they can become visible.[24]

In "The Origin of the Work of Art," Heidegger emphasizes the ways in which a certain mistranslation, an inability to open to the aporetic demands that the simultaneous necessity and impossibility of translation places upon us, lies at the core of Western thought. There, he argues that the translation of the Greek names into the Latin language is not at all the inconsequential process it is considered to this day. Rather, beneath the seemingly literal and thus preserving translation hides a translation or carrying-across [*Über-setzen*] of Greek experience into a different way of thinking. Roman thought takes over the Greek words without the equi-primordial experience [*ohne die gleichursprüngliche Erfahrung*] of what they say, without the Greek word. The groundlessness [*Bodenlosigkeit*] of Western thought begins with this translation or carrying-across.[25]

Pointing to the process of appropriation by which Greek words and concepts such as *hupokeimenon* became *subiectum*, *hupostasis* was turned into *substantia*, and *sumbebekos* was rendered *accidens*, Heidegger suggests that a certain view of the world of things has, in the moment of mistranslation or misguided appropriation, resulted in an inappropriate or blindly proprietorial relationship to the object world. Here, a "simple propositional statement consists of the subject, which is the Latin translation, and this means reinterpretation, of *hupekeimenon* and the predicate, in which the thing's traits are stated of it."[26] For Heidegger, the task of thinking is not to undo the basic relational structure that is thus called forth, but to defamiliarize and then to interrogate the ways in which the epistemo-linguistic structure suggested by the translation from Greek to Latin is not a reproduction of what is found in the inner structure and proper logic of the thing but rather may be a function of the projection with which this relational structure is imposed on the object. By extension, this structure is imposed on our modes of relating to the object world in particular ways. Another way of putting this is to say that both the structural and the temporal appropriations that a translation or mistranslation cause stand in relation to the object world that constantly demands to be rethought and adjusted. Here, our relation to the object world is, through the translational act that sponsors it, an aftereffect, a moment of afterness that touches us in the form of a dissimulation, that is, as an allegedly natural and self-evident mode of relating.

Yet for Heidegger, the diagnosis of mistranslation from the conceptual orbit of the Greeks to that of the Romans, which, for him, is the basis for the groundlessness of Western thought, does not simply imply a call to return to the Greeks or to the Greek language, even if such a return were possible. The movement of his thought is not one of nostalgia or retroactive recuperation from the perspective of a postlapsarian afterness. As Gasché reminds us, for Heidegger "it is at most a question of returning—if it can be called a return—to something already at work in it, cracking it apart, which it renders only imperfectly." This imperfection implies that the "distorting translation of Greek concepts into the Latin tongue derives from an 'unthought' of the Greek language itself (that which, for example, makes possible the advent of modern technique as well as the *Ge-stell* [frame], insofar as it is an unthought of Greek thought concerning the notion of thesis)."[27] We could say that the originary fissure even—and especially—within what one calls the mother tongue therefore does not signal an aberration from a gold standard of unified, self-present meaning but rather names the very logic that, even within our "own" language, remains concealed and unthought. The mistranslation of certain Greek concepts into Latin is therefore at the same time a correct translation: even while mistranslating Greek words and concepts for which Latin was in some sense not prepared, the mistranslation translates successfully a disjuncture or inner doubleness that is lodged in the split core of language itself. From this perspective, every translation is therefore both a failure and a triumph, a triumphant failure and a failed triumph. There cannot but be translation, and there cannot but be mistranslation. Translation, to the extent that it marks an absolute necessity and an impossibility, fails successfully when it translates the unthought of a language as the unthought of language itself.

To say that translation translates the unthought of a language as the unthought of language itself is to emphasize an experiential and cognitive relation to the cracks and fissures that render even one's mother tongue unfamiliar and the language one possesses an object of dispossession or expropriation. As Heidegger writes in *Über den Anfang* (*On the Beginning*, 1941), the experience of "ex-propriation lets 'stand' in the Being-less [*die Ent-eignung läßt im Seinlosen 'stehen'*]," so that "expropriation only is in the event." Here, the "expropriation of the event [*Enteignung des Ereignisses*]" can be thought as "departure" and "even the leave-taking [*Verabschiedung*] of the expropriation."[28] Seen from the perspective of translation, the moment of having departed from one language but not yet having arrived in the other language, searching and groping for sense even when language itself has, in a way, been left behind and not yet recuperated, is the primal scene in which language itself speaks, that is, speaks precisely in the moment of its elusiveness or even absence, that is, in the expropriation that is the event of speaking.

In a passage from "The Essence of Language," Heidegger elaborates this relation between the moment in which language itself speaks by failing and our uncanny experience of language as language:

> Only because in everyday speaking language does *not* bring itself to language but holds back, are we able simply to go ahead and speak a language, and so to deal with something and negotiate something by speaking.
>
> But when does language speak itself as language [*Wo aber kommt die Sprache selber als Sprache zum Wort*]? Curiously enough, when we cannot find the right word for something that concerns us, carries us away, oppresses or encourages us. Then we leave unspoken what we have in mind and, without rightly giving it thought, undergo moments in which language itself has distantly and fleetingly touched us with its essence [*in denen uns die Sprache selber mit ihrem Wesen fernher und flüchtig gestreift hat*].²⁹

If we know language best when we are at a loss for words, if we can experience language most fully when it betrays us, if we "have" language most fully when we lose it, and if language, as the German idiomatic expression has it, "comes to the word" (*kommt zu Wort*) precisely when it remains silent, then the scene of translation is always also a stammering, a consternation. This scene of translation involves, as in Benjamin's theory of translation in "The Task of the Translator" (Die Aufgabe des Übersetzers), an *Aufgabe* that is both a task and a giving up as well as a sending of something on its way—as in *einen Brief aufgeben*, to "mail a letter." As such, translation provides us with the experience of language as language par excellence. But, for Heidegger, when we have left one language and have not yet arrived in the other—whether in the making of sense within one's own language or in the heightened intensity of translation—we are not simply lost in the space between two languages, but in fact are experiencing the ghostly unthought fissure, the originary leap or crack (*Ur-sprung*) of that which, before any language, makes language language and which touches us every now and then, in the fleeting, prayer-like moment of attention, only ever so lightly and almost imperceptibly across the spectral span of an unbridgeable distance.

To be touched ever so fleetingly by the distant reverberations of the essence of language as that which is the most ordinary, quotidian occurrence yet eternally removed is to learn to listen to the way in which language speaks—of and through itself, but also in our stead. In his discussion of Trakl's poem "Ein Winterabend," which also is a poetic miniature encryption of a philosophy of language, Heidegger writes:

> Der Mensch spricht nur, indem er der Sprache entspricht.
> Die Sprache spricht.
> Ihr Sprechen spricht für uns im Gesprochenen.
>
> [Man speaks only as he responds to language.
> Language speaks.
> Its speaking speaks for us in the spoken.][30]

Heidegger characterizes the language that traversed the speaking subject as coming from an elsewhere. What can be called "the activity of the subject (speaking) is conditioned by something else—something more 'middle voice' than a passivity," as David Wood has noted of Heidegger's general understanding of language.[31] Always something other than a passivity, the language that speaks calls on thought to inscribe the subject in a network of relations in which multiple dependencies and mediations are constantly negotiated. The difficulty of translating *"entspricht"* here bespeaks the conceptual point that Heidegger attempts to put forward. The English translator renders it quite correctly as "responds to." But several additional layers of signification are operative here, as *entspechen* also can mean "to correspond to" (as in the dative construction *etwas oder jemandem entsprechen*); it can mean to "speak out of" (*ent-sprechen* as *aus etwas heraus sprechen*); and it could signify, if we apply some conceptual and contextual pressure on the verb's prefix, to "speak away from," to "move away from by means of speaking" (*ent-sprechen* as [*sich*] *von etwas hinwegsprechen*). Finally, *entsprechen* is not too far removed from *entsagen* for us to hear the common echoes of speaking and saying, *sprechen* and *sagen*, as in the construction *einer Sache entsagen*, to "withdraw from or to renounce something." To speak, then, means to relate to language in all of these modalities, eschewing perhaps the ossified relational structures that the Latin appropriation of Greek concepts bespoke. *Entsprechen* thus requires its constant translation into all the meanings that remain operative each time it speaks forth, not only when we are translating it from German into another language, such as English, but also when we attempt to come to terms with the demands it makes on us in the context of its own, proper idiom—as when, for instance, we attempt to translate German into German in the context of a seminar on Schiller.

It is also through the mediation of these relational structures of *entsprechen* that language in turn can be said to speak for us (*"spricht für uns"*). It speaks "for us" in the sense that it is our tool, it performs its task for us, but it also speaks in our stead—that is, speaks in our place and precisely then when we no longer simply are its master or assume ourselves to be in full control of its workings, hermeneutic or otherwise. The *für uns* of language therefore names the doubling of an instrumentality that is also an expropriation, a seeming reinforcement of the speaking subject that is always also its beginning dissolution and necessary reinscription elsewhere. This is the gift, in both the English and the German sense of the word—a present and a poison—that language has in store *"für uns."*

To say, however, that language can be experienced as both translation and expropriation is not to reduce the workings of language to the private realm of subjective experience. On the contrary, for Heidegger there can be no thinking of the effects of translation that does not also confront the historicity of these effects—that is, their genealogical specificity and even necessity. For instance, in *Der Satz vom Grund* (*The Principle of Reason*), he differentiates between translation as interpretation, *Übersetzung* as *Übertragung*, and translation as a handing down or passing on, a form of inheritance in which *Übersetzung* becomes *Überlieferung* and thus, of necessity, a form of historicity. Translation for Heidegger deserves to be understood as belonging "to the innermost movement of history."[32] As John Sallis has pointed out, it is "because such translations inscribe responsively the saying within the sending of being . . . that they belong to the innermost movement of history, constituting nodal points, points of jointure, where tradition (handing down from the sending of being) takes place."[33] To send (*schicken*) language on its way through an engagement with its historical fate, its destiny or *Geschick*, is thus to inscribe the task of accepting or rejecting an inheritance into the scene of translational thought. As Heidegger explains in another passage of *Der Satz vom Grund*, a "translation [*Übersetzung*] becomes, where the speaking of basic words *translates* from one historical language into another, a handing-down [*Überlieferung*]."[34] As a form of handing down, *Überlieferung* can, "if it ossifies," become "a burden and an inhibition" in which tradition acts as an oppressive command issued forth from what has come before the afterness of the after. But it can also be a liberation, because "*Überlieferung*, as its name indicates, is a delivery [*Liefern*] in the sense of *liberare*, a setting free [*Befreiung*]."[35]

The undecidabilty of *Übersetzen* as a form of *Überlieferung* between the imposition of a burden and the setting free whose secret promise it holds demands that with each act of translation we reject the principle of immediate co-optation or appropriation and instead confront our relation to that historical handing anew, inventing it once again for this specific linguistic and material event. In order to learn how to relate in a free and open manner to what has been handed down to us by *Übersetzung* as *Überlieferung*, we must learn what inheriting a tradition, and inheriting *as translation*, might mean.

Bearing these considerations in mind, let us now return to the Schiller seminar. Confronting Schiller's attempted translation of Kantian aesthetic concepts, Heidegger suggests that Schiller's understanding of art and the beautiful is characterized by a rather elusive translational movement: "Although Schiller emphasizes that no step is possible without Kant, he nevertheless performs a turn [*eine Wendung*] in the direction of history. This step is, like all epoch-making steps, wholly inconspicuous [*ganz unauffällig*]."[36]

To characterize Schiller's philosophical steps—always inconspicuous, never fully visible, as determined translations of Kantian aesthetics, always dancing, always on the move elsewhere—is to engage with Schiller's understanding of *der ästhetische Zustand*, especially as it emerges in letter 19, to which Heidegger's seminar returns again and again. This letter is crucial because it stages the question as to how the aesthetic realizes itself in the Being-human (*Menschsein*); that is to say, its fundamental interest concerns the possibility of the Being-human as aesthetically and historically inflected. According to Heidegger's interpretation, Schiller views the Being-human in a way that considers how that which is necessary to determine this Being also, by itself, never quite is capable of determining the reality of Being-human. Schiller shows, according to this reading, that a *Wesensbeschreibung*, or "description of an essence," always also calls into being the *Wesensnotwendigkeit*, or "necessity of an essence," of an other. What makes the Being-human what it is always strives beyond itself toward an other on the basis of which there first can be a ground on which the Being-human can be such and such a being, *this* being. By way of this schemata of the Being-human, Schiller develops the necessity of the aesthetic *Zustand*. Heidegger is emphatic about this translation in and of Schiller's letters: "This is the skeleton of all the letters, everything else is variation [or, we might say, translation]: the schematization of the essence of the Being-human conditions the necessity of the aesthetic *Zustand* as a basic reality [*die Notwendigkeit des ästhetischen Zustandes als der Grundwirklichkeit*]."[37]

Let us turn, then, to two of the translational gestures that Heidegger argues are at work in Schiller's *Letters*: the movement from sensuousness (*Sinnlichkeit*) to the aesthetic *Zustand*, and the translation of a metaphysical mode of analysis into a transcendental one.

First, the *Zustand*. In the seminar of December 9, Heidegger specifies that the crux of Schiller's letters is to be found in the transitional or translational movement through which the human being leaves the realm of pure sensuousness to enter an aesthetic *Zustand* in which the possibility of acting in a free manner is lodged ("that the human being is carried across [*übergeführt wird*] from sensuousness into the aesthetic *Zustand* in order then to act in a free manner. This transition [*Übergang*] from the sensuous to the aesthetic *Zustand* is what is decisive").[38] But what is Schiller's aesthetic *Zustand* in this translational movement? According to Heidegger's explication, the aesthetic *Zustand* is not simply one *Zustand* among many others, but rather the very condition of possibility for the Being-human to emerge as a historical category: "not one *Zustand* among others but rather that which is to from a human being's *responsibility* in general [*was die Zuständlichkeit des Menschen überhaupt bilden soll*], to the extent that the human being is one that *acts historically* [*sofern der Mensch ein* geschichtlich handelnder *ist*]."[39] We might say that *Zustand*, in Heidegger's understanding, is a *Stehen-zu*, both a standing-toward and a form of affirmation or confirmation (*zu etwas stehen*), in which the possibility of being-open-to also enables the very idea of relating to oneself in a particular manner (*sich zu sich zu verhalten*). This possibility of relating to oneself as a manifestation of something or someone relating to something or someone also is the condition of possibility of relating to an other whose difference has not yet been foreclosed. As Heidegger argues:

> Ein Zustand im Sinne des sich-so-und-so-befindens, in-einem-Zustande-sein, gibt es nur da, wo etwas zu sich selbst *und* zu etwas anderem *stehen* kann. Dieses Zu-etwas-Stehen und dabei *in* diesem Zu-etwas-anderem-stehen, zu *sich selbst* stehen—das ist die *Zuständigkeit*. Was heißt dann der ästhetische Zustand? Er ist von hier aus gesehen der zuständige Zustand,—das Grundverhältnis, zu *etwas* zu stehen und dabei zu *sich selbst* in der Weise des Fühlens.

> [A *Zustand* in the sense of feeling such-and-such, of being-in-a-state, exists only there where something can relate or *stand* toward itself *and* toward something else. This relating-toward or standing-toward

something while standing within this relation toward or standing-toward something, to relate toward and to stand toward oneself—that is responsibility or jurisdiction [*Zuständigkeit*]. But what, then, is called the aesthetic *Zustand*? Seen from here, it is the responsible Zustand [*der zuständige Zustand*]—the basic relation of standing toward something and simultaneously to stand toward oneself in the manner of feeling.][40]

To the extent that Schiller's aesthetic model engages in a translational gesture that works to carry Being over from sensuality into an aesthetic *Zustand*, it opens a relational condition of possibility for the experience of freedom and its self-law-giving, "autonomous" properties.

Second, Schiller's transcendental method. From Heidegger's perspective, the possibility of thinking an object is predicated on givenness and determinative thinking. An object emerges only when something encounters or is encountered and when this encountering or encountered something is determined in thinking. It is here that the conditions of possibility of cognition (*Erkenntnis*) are met. Heidegger calls this a transcendental perspective. A metaphysical perspective might ask where these two elements came from, how they developed, and so on. A transcendental question does not ask how sensuousness came into being and why it is there but rather focuses on its elements (sensuousness and thinking) in order to determine them in their differential essence and then to pose the question to what extent cognition (in Schiller's case, the cognition of the Being-human) is possible and in what way the two elements participate in this process.

Schiller's aesthetic translation, in the *Letters*, of a metaphysical into a transcendental perspective is indebted to Kant, who laid the groundwork for the transcendental method. As Kant states in the *Critique of Pure Reason*, "I call all cognition *transcendental* which does not focus solely on the objects but is concerned, rather, with our a priori concepts of objects in general. Such a system of concepts could be called transcendental philosophy."[41] In the transcendental perspective, "transcendental" is the name of a mode of cognition (*Erkenntnisart*), for a way of proceeding or a method. By contrast to the transcendental, "transcendent" signifies something that exceeds sensuousness itself, such as God. If, for Heidegger, Schiller adopts the Kantian translation from metaphysical into transcendental logic, the latter is called transcendental because it is *übergehend*, or "transitional," in a movement of carrying across;

as such, it captures that dimension of cognition which within it is grasped *in the terms of* something, in terms of a way of relating, and it captures any transitional movements within the sphere of cognition: "And it is called transcendental (transitional) because it captures this transition as such, captures this transition as transition [*Und sie heißt transzendental (übergehend), weil sie diesen Übergang als solchen festhält, diesen Übergang als Übergang festhält*]."42 The stakes of this *Über-gang*, which is always also an *Über-tragen* and *Übersetzen*, for Schiller are so high because it signifies the step into the aesthetic core of humanness itself. In Schiller's aesthetics, the human being, Heidegger explains, "comes into its own only by detaching itself in a certain way from sensuousness, but when the human being makes the transition [*übergeht*] from sensuousness toward the 'I think,' from a being-lost within the senses toward himself, then he leaves sensuousness behind and holds himself to himself, *but* we are now dealing with the actual human being, the human being who comprises, and takes over, the two elements in their unity." He continues: "This is why, if he wishes to make the transition [*übergehen will*] toward himself as himself, precisely then he *must take a step back* [*gerade dann muß er einen Schritt zurück tun*]. To preserve sensuousness as such, the step back into it must once again be taken. Yet is a *step* back, that is, not forlornness but true appropriation. This step back is *art* [*Dieser Schritt zurück ist die* Kunst]."43 Taking a step back here is not to be understood historically or temporally, as though it meant returning to a previous point in time or to an epoch long passed, but rather it is to be understood as a deliberate movement along the path of a more primordial thinking.44

In the case of translation, this temporal-historical structure unfolds in a kind of afterlife or afterness of language, in close proximity to what Benjamin in "The Task of the Translator" thinks of as a *Fortleben* (living on), an *Überleben* (surviving), and a *Nachreifen* (an "after-ripening," or a gradual ripening of language post factum).45 The survival of language in and as interpretation and translation causes it to be non-self-identical, forever at odds with itself even when it is "first" uttered and disseminated—but can this "first" ever be a real "first"? Yet this internal self-division, in which language comes into its own only when it has already departed from itself, when it is on a *different* historical, political, or epistemological path, also embodies the condition of possibility for language to have a future, to be essentially promissory and future-directed. In the double essay "Living On / Border Lines," Derrida writes that "*Übersetzung* and 'translation' overcome, equivocally, in the course of an equivocal combat, the loss of an object. A text lives only if it lives *on* [*sur-vit*], and it lives *on* only if it is *at once* translatable and untranslatable." This is so, he reminds us, because "totally translatable, it disappears as a text, as writing, as a body of language [*langue*]. Totally untranslatable, even within what is believed to be one language, it dies immediately. Thus triumphant translation is neither the life nor the death of the text, only or already its living on, its life after life, its life after death. The same thing will be said of what I call writing, mark, trace, and so on. It neither lives nor dies; it lives *on*."[46] We encounter a text, even the one that we ourselves speak or write, as a form of afterness. To have a future, it must not be fully understandable—that is, translatable—lest it disappear like an empty shell with the final exhaustion of its accessed meaning. To the extent that it resists full—but *not all*—understanding and translation, it still has a chance of being interpreted in a future time that cannot be foreseen or programmed. Never present to itself, language and translation—that is, the idea of translatability—unfold together in the future perfect, the grammatical tense that resists being anchored in either the present, the past, or the future. We can only ever say that translation *will have been*, not now, not yesterday, not tomorrow, but in a future perfect that cannot yet have been assigned a fixed temporal space. The language of translation therefore always also is a matter of historical inheritance, the experience of *a language that will have been*. This experience marks the uncontainable historicity of translation.

An important element in this historicity of translation is the afterness of the original itself. The originality of the "original" is neither natural nor self-evident; it is always constructed long after the fact, according to the logic of signs and traces that cannot fully stem from itself. We do not speak of an original before it has been translated—that is, has become something that it is not. For instance, we would not speak of Schiller's "original" *Aesthetic Education* prior to the book's translation into another language, such as the now standard English version by Elizabeth M. Wilkinson and L. A. Willoughby. Never simply itself, the "original" requires the historicity of translation in order to become, always retroactively, what it is. The "original" text is dependent on its supplement, its translation—that is, on an other, a certain non-self-identity—to be self-identical. The historicity of translation shows that, as a form of afterness, originality is always *derived*—and therefore always already unoriginal.

From another perspective, to say that translation always involves a form of historical inheritance, a fate or demand, is also to allow for the possibility of historical transmission to go awry, for translation to break down, unless the model for interpretive translation—and there can be no other— is one of mere *Nachahmung* (imitation) and, by extension, of reliability, predictability, and stability, rather than of an as-of-yet unarticulated *Nachfolge*, and thus of uncontainable risk, chance, and contingency, to employ the Kantian distinction that we encountered in chapter 1. Therefore, both the felicity or fortuitousness and the apparent breakdown or failure of a translation stand in a charged and overdetermined relation to the original, such that a mistranslation is not simply an inferior aberration—to say nothing of the many instances in Heidegger's own idiosyncratic translations from the Greek that always have struck some classicists as inadmissible but that nevertheless, at least according to the logic of Heidegger's own thought, penetrate the *unsaid* and the *unthought* of the Greek word more deeply than a conventional translation would. Here, we may think, among so many other instances, of his critique in "The Question Concerning Technology" of the—to him—problematic Latin translation of the Greek *aletheia* as *veritas*, which reduces truth (*Wahrheit*) to correctness (*Richtigkeit*) and thereby contributes to a worldview in which mere calculating thinking (*berechnendes Denken*) is valorized at the expense of reflective thinking (*besinnendes Denken*), even though it is only in reflective thinking, not in the means–ends instrumentality of calculation, that thinking may come into its own.[47] To move away from the correctness model of truth that Latin enthroned, Heidegger proposes, as we recall, to translate *aletheia* as "unconcealment." We also recall his provocative translation of *deinon* as *das Unheimliche*, or "the uncanny"—and, by extension, of *deinotaton* as *das Unheimlichste*, or "the most uncanny—in his explication of the Greek conception of the human being in his lecture course *Introduction to Metaphysics* (1935).[48] The translations that Schiller's aesthetic letters perform would then always have to be measured against that possibility of aberration and the missed transmission.

If translation therefore always assumes the form of an inheritance, and the form even of a particular responsibility to the singularity of this or that inheritance, the question of the correctness of a translation is not a factual content decided on externally but rather touches the inner logic of the workings of language itself. In section 12 of his lectures on *Hölderlin's Hymn "The Ister,"* Heidegger suddenly interrupts his discussion of the Greek interpretation of human beings with a "Bemerkung zum Übersetzen," a "remark concerning translation":

Yet who decides, and how does one decide, concerning the correctness of a "translation"? We "obtain" our knowledge of the meaning of words in a foreign language from a *Wörterbuch*, a dictionary or "wordbook." Yet we too readily forget that the information in a dictionary must always be based on a preceding interpretation of linguistic contexts from which particular words and word usages are taken. In most cases a dictionary provides the correct information about the meaning of a word, yet this correctness does not yet guarantee us any insight into the truth of what the word means and can mean, given that we are asking about the essential realm named in the word [*sofern wir dem im Wort genannten Wesensbereich nachfragen*]. . . . Viewed with regard to the historical spirit of a language as a whole . . . every dictionary lacks any immediate or binding standards of measure.

Let us interrupt Heidegger's interruption here to make a few remarks. The *Wörterbuch* of which Heidegger speaks can—although it is useful—never fully grasp what is essential in a word—that is, the ways in which its *Wesensbereich* signifies with regard to the historicity of language itself. To engage the word means to engage itself and its historical formation, that is itself *in and as* a historical formation that, however, cannot in turn be ascertained in a transcription of a series of its allegedly synonymous meanings. That is to say, the *Wörterbuch* only can refer me to other words; it explains words by substituting other words, the meaning of which I will then look up elsewhere in the *Wörterbuch*, which in turn will refer me to yet others entries in the same "wordbook." But this system of differential self-relations may or may not yield the historicity of a linguistic spirit.

Let us return to Heidegger's passage:

Every interpretation [*Auslegung*], and everything that stands in its service, is a translating. In that case, translating does not only move between two different languages, but there is a translating within one and the same language. The interpretation of Hölderlin's hymns is a translating within our German language. The same holds true for an interpretation that has as its theme, for example, Kant's *Critique of Pure Reason*, or Hegel's *Phenomenology of Spirit*. In the cognition that we are here necessarily concerned with a translating, there lies the acknowledgement that such "works" are, in accordance with their essence, in need of translation [*übersetzungsbedürftig sind*]. Such need is not a lack, however, but rather the inner privilege of such works. In other words: It pertains to the essence of the language of a historical people to extend like a mountain range into the lowlands and flatlands and at the same time to have its occasional peaks towering above into an otherwise inaccessible altitude. In between are the "lower altitudes" and "levels." As translating, interpreting indeed makes something understandable—yet certainly not in the sense that common understanding conceives it. Staying within our image: The peak of a poetic or thoughtful work of language [*dichterischen oder denkerischen Sprachwerks*] must not be worn down through translation, nor the entire mountain range leveled out into the flatlands of superficiality. The converse is the case: Translation must set us upon the path of ascent toward the peak. Making something understandable should never mean assimilating a poetic or thoughtful work of language to just any act of meaning or to the horizon of understanding of such an act of meaning. Making something understandable means awakening our understanding to the fact that the blind obstinacy of habitual meanings must be shattered and abandoned if the truth of a work of art is to unveil itself.

This interim remark about the essence of translation is meant to recall that the difficulty of a translation is never merely a technical issue but concerns the relation of human beings to the essence of the word and to the dignity of language. Tell me what you think of translation, and I will tell you who you are [*Sage mir, was Du vom Übersetzen hälst, und ich sage Dir, wer Du bist*].[49]

Much deserves to be said about Heidegger's remark. Let me focus here only on the way in which the work of translation creates an opening for a disruption of encrusted modes of meaning and understanding. What translation gives us to think is the retreat of certain modes of meaning back into themselves, even when they appear to move elsewhere, that is, toward the shores of another language and the words of its historical experience. To understand something, then, is in a certain way to break with understanding, to reveal the fissures of the unthought that allows a language to appear as what it is when it is moving away from itself. A historically inflected language—and there hardly can be any other—thus shows itself, in translating itself into itself through translating itself into another—as a mode of departure, a historical departure that curves through the windy hills and valleys, the peaks and levels of thinking and poeticizing itself.

This historical path of translation cannot be reduced to a correspondence or adequation model—that is, to the detection of obvious deviations from a fidelity to the original—even as these questions of correctness on a fundamental level must never be abandoned. For instance, when I was involved in a translation of Benjamin's suggestive 1938 diary entries for the Harvard edition of his writings, questions of absolute fidelity to Benjamin's German naturally preoccupied me, especially as I was translating from my native German—but do Benjamin and I really share the "same" German?—into a language that is not my "own." Keeping in mind the Austrian writer Thomas Bernhard's caustic remark that a translation "is unrecognizable. A translated book is like a corpse that has been mutilated beyond recognition by a car" and Derrida's admonition that "one never writes either in one's own language or in a foreign language," linguistic difficulties imposed themselves from the very first sentence.[50] There, the task of the translator involves German constructions that are almost impossible to render in English, such as *Man erwies mir Freundlichkeiten*, which, after having gone through various English metamorphoses, finally appeared in print as the less-than-satisfactory "Friendly things came my way," a compromise with the ever-vigilant and less Teutonically minded copy editor at the press.[51] Certainly, then, questions of deviation and fidelity must remain central to the task of the translator. But it may be more fruitful to conceive of such deviations in terms of the difference between an error and a mistake.[52] A mistake is simply a clerical slip, an inadmissible moment of inattentiveness or lapse of reason or knowledge that prompts a translation to run awry. An error is more interesting: it may suggest an underlying economy of deviance, a thorough and perhaps ideologically filtered way of systematically misunderstanding. An illuminating example of a mere translation *mistake* occurs in the published conversation between Adorno and Ernst Bloch on the topic of the contradictoriness of utopian thinking. There, Bloch at one point uses the phrase *Es geht um die Wurst*, which in idiomatic German means, roughly, that the stakes are high, that one is dealing with an all-or-nothing situation, a go-for-broke game. The English version offers its readers this translation: "It's about the sausage," a literal rendition that in its treacherous faithfulness must remain incomprehensible to those who cannot hear the German idiom behind it.[53] But more interesting questions arise in cases where we are clearly dealing with deviations of a more systematic nature—that is, true *errors*. For instance, the following phrase can be found in the standard translation of Adorno's *Minima Moralia*: "Totalitarianism and homosexuality belong together."[54] But in Adorno's original German the sentence reads: "*Totalität und Homosexualität gehören zusammen*" (Totality and homosexuality belong together).[55] It would be instructive to pursue this interesting error, this shift from "totality" to "totalitarianism," as an epistemo-political model for the entire English translation of *Minima Moralia*, which is full of such instances.

Yet to acknowledge the serious role that both error and mistake play in their deviation also is to affirm that the path of thinking that Heidegger's engagement with translation will have opened up for us—a path that is always also and above all a thinking of the unthought of language itself—cannot simply make do with a mere model of nondeviation or fidelity. To think the unthought of language as a historical and epistemological problem with all the rigor it demands also means breaking with standard models of translation without simply becoming unfaithful to the languages in question. It is questionable whether Heidegger, who so often thought about the stakes of translating Hölderlin's German into German, would have approved of a 1997 experimental joint project between the German-language poet Schuldt and the American poet Robert Kelly that focused on Hölderlin's poem "Am Quell der Donau." Schuldt and Kelly's experimental translation of Hölderlin implicitly follows American lyric poet Louis Zukofsky's 1961 phonetic transliterations of Catullus's Latin works and the radical logic of what Austrian poet Ernst Jandl calls *Oberflächenübersetzung*, or "surface translation," in which the act of translation concentrates on the sonic patterns of words while disregarding their overt semantic or lexical content in a way that generates strange new image patterns and residual echoes of unexpected meaning.[56] Schuldt, who knows English, invited Kelly, who does not know German, to translate Hölderlin's poem phonetically—that is, based on what Kelly heard in his native English when he listened to Hölderlin's German. The two poets felt emboldened in part by the radically experimental nature of Hölderlin's eccentric German translations of Greek authors, translations that pushed German to and beyond the limits of what can be said and thought in that language. To be sure, Hölderlin's translations hardly can be said to embody phonetic or "surface" translations in Zukofsky's and Jandl's radical sense. And yet, the aporetic gesture of Hölderlin's self-imposed task pushed his language in unheard-of, extraterritorial directions, a task subtended by the desire not to make Greek speak German but to make German speak Greek and yet somehow itself as well. Kelly's phonetic English rendition of what he heard and saw in the strangeness that to him was Hölderlin was translated by Schuldt into German, this time preserving as far as possible the semantic content of Kelly's lines. These German lines by Schuldt were then transliterated again by Kelly into English, after which Schuldt once again translated Kelly's words semantically into German. The result was published in book form, with each line of each stanza reproduced fivefold: Hölderlin's original line, then Kelly's English, followed by Schuldt's German, followed by Kelly's English rendition of Schuldt's German rendition of Kelly's English rendition of Hölderlin's German line, followed once again by Schuldt's German version.[57] The five voices form a polyphony of the echoes of language, arbitrary and strangely rigorous at the same time, following poetry's speech into realms of translation that push beyond any conventional notion of speech and, indeed, beyond the very concept of translation itself—but precisely by "translating."

However Heidegger would have viewed such experimental "translations" of Hölderlin, the idea of pushing translation beyond translation by coaxing it into exhibiting a certain resistance to translation and self-translation found in language itself, the connection between a so-called original and the translation that follows it, the translation through which it lives on, also needs to be rethought, just as Schiller's translational relation to Kantian aesthetics must perpetually be opened to its own contingencies. Heidegger in his Darmstadt lecture "Building Dwelling Thinking" (1951) speaks of the bridge that connects in unexpected ways: the bridge "does not just connect banks that already exist. The banks emerge as banks only as the bridge crosses the stream. The bridge, by design, causes them to lie across from each other [*gegeneinander über liegen*]. One side is set off against the other by the bridge. Nor do the banks stretch along the stream as indifferent border strips of dry land. With the banks, the bridge brings to the stream the one and the other expanse of the landscape lying behind them. It brings stream and bank and land together into each other's neighborhood."[58] We hear in the language of the bridge the literalization of *Über-setzung*, the "trans-lation" that is a carrying or setting (*setzen*) across (*über*). After all, even in quotidian German *Übersetzen*, when the accent is placed on the verb stem, means "to translate"; when the accent is placed on the prefix, the same word means "to carry across, to ferry over." In his 1943/1944 engagement with Heraclitus, Heidegger alludes to this double imbrication: "In the case of translating words by Heraclitus, our difficulties are great. Here, Über*setzen* becomes *Über*setzen onto the other shore, which is hardly known and which lies beyond a broad stream. One easily is entangled in an odyssey, and more often than not it ends in shipwreck."[59] Thinking, and especially thinking in and as translation, exposes itself, to the extent that it unfolds as a linguistic carrying over, to the unknown other shore, the open space that it is striving toward but that it may not reach and whose laws and topographies it does not yet know. Thought is sent on its way here as a *Geschick*, at once a fate and a missive, in which the other shore remains other for the self, as its own otherness, to remain mindful of itself as the one who is still, and always, learning how to think with and as and through the other.[60] The other, that which is irreducibly strange, must remain recognizable as other and strange even within the self that has allowed itself to be carried across to the other's shore. We remain faithful to the language of the other by "saying the strange in our own way," as Günter Figal puts it, by allowing the self to move freely across to the other and back to the self in a double movement of alterity that will not leave either untouched—after all, what now is one's own, what's the other's, who is this known "I," who the strange "you"?[61] The carrying over, the *Herübersetzen*, which for Heidegger is the essence of translation, is one of the prime experiences in which, for a fleeting moment, the self recognizes itself as the otherness that it always already was, as a being on the way to language that dwells in the world only to the extent that it is related to the other—always this other, the one right here, to be sure, but also to all other others—in ways that are not fully transparent to it and that always require one more scene of translation, one more act of carrying over to the unknown.

The stakes of this scene of translation are high for Heidegger precisely to the extent that it touches the essence and future of Western thought. In his "Der Spruch des Anaximander" (The Saying of Anaximander, 1946), an attempt at "translating," a year after the end of World War II, a line by the pre-Socratic philosopher Anaximander in both the narrow and the broad sense that "translation" assumes in Heidegger's work, he suggests that "perhaps we will learn to think [*bedenken*] what can come to pass in translation [*was sich im Übersetzen ereignen kann*]. . . . Into what language does the West translate itself or cross over toward [*In welche Sprache setzt das Abend-Land über*]?"[62] To ask in a rigorous manner about the language and essence of Western thought from the perspective of a thinking that is still to come, we must be willing to be translated ourselves, carried elsewhere, toward an unexpected destination. As Heidegger argues in his lecture course on Parmenides:

> If we translate the Greek *aletheia* merely with the German *Unverborgenheit* [unconcealment], we are not yet translating. Translation only occurs when the translating word *Unverborgenheit* translates us and carries us over [uns *über*setzt] into the realm of experience and the mode of experience out of which the Greeks and, in the present case, the primordial thinker Parmenides, said the word *aletheia*.[63]

To translate, then, in a rigorous sense means to be translated and carried over to the shore of an experience that one has never had, an encounter with an otherness, even the otherness of language itself, that one did not know before; one allows oneself to be set on a journey—the *Fahrt* that inheres in *Er-fahrung*—toward the open, the other shore, the land that is not yet in sight.[64] Translation as being carried over to an unknown experience is a fundamental moment of *Ereignis* (event) as *Ent-eignis* (expropriation) in which nothing is at it appears.

Yet for Heidegger, the bridge that is translation does not simply put into relation two locations—topographies, languages—that are already fully there, present to themselves and simply waiting to be connected. We may think here of all the implications of Heidegger's preferred term *Erörterung*, which is usually translated as "elucidation," but in which we hear, when we read it as *Er-örterung*, the interpretive activity that seeks to establish the proper place or position (*Ort*) of something, whether it be a hut in the Black Forest or the *topos* of *Dasein* itself.[65] From the perspective of a topology of thought, to interpret and to elucidate therefore always also is to *situate*. To build a bridge is to call into being the very locations, connected by the bridge, *as* locations—*Bauen* and *Erörtern*, building and elucidating-situating belong together. If the experience of locations along the riverbank is a retroactive effect or invention of their other-directedness, then there can be no location as location that is not already on its way elsewhere. To think of translation as a bridge between texts, in the sense of a *Stiftung*, or "founding," is to acknowledge that the slippery bridge that is translation, whether it is crossed by Heidegger or by Schiller, neither simply marks nor re-marks but *constitutes* the very condition of possibility for linguistic interpretation.[66] Far from being a mere afterthought that follows the so-called original, the bridge of translation in its afterness writes into existence modes of signification that become visible as decidedly relational and non-self-identical phenomena. Any theory, practice, or politics of translation to come would have to begin with the bridge spawned by this afterness. It is with the experience of this bridge, too, that a rigorous evaluation of the political stakes of Heidegger's engagement with art and the aesthetic may begin in earnest.

6 Afterness and the Image (I)
Unsettling Photography

Having considered the relation between afterness and translation, we are now in a position to turn to a specific kind of "translation": photography—arguably the first "new" medium of modernity. As the British scholar Graham Clarke, echoing Hubert Damisch, suggests in his standard work on the cultural history and theory of the photograph, because the photograph interrupts time and removes its subject from history even as it records it for posterity, there is a sense in which every "photograph . . . has no before or after: it represents only the moment of its own making."[1] And yet, we could say that the photograph possesses an afterlife, a temporal structure of experience and ghostly reception that will not let it rest in its separation from the before or the after. Even the very first photographic image ever taken, Joseph Nicéphore Niépce's "View from a Window at Gras" (1826), a heliograph that required an exposure time of some eight hours, demands, in all its graininess and darkly spectral remove, that we come to terms with its "after" in the history of the medium. Indeed, the non-self-identity of the ghostly photographic image that announces itself as a relation without relation ultimately cannot be thought in isolation from the effect of a coming after, a certain afterness.

Encrypted in a series of relays and relations, promises and deferrals, the ontological status of the photograph itself deserves to be rethought. No longer simply a material entity—the product of a more or less mimetic process of recording and archiving the traces of an object's former presence—the photograph offers a model for conceptualizing thought itself. To the extent that this radical model of thinking exceeds the themes and motifs that structure the history of metaphysics—that is, to the extent that it holds open the possibility of the unexpected, the surprising, and the unprogrammable—the photograph rightly can be said to portray the reality of such thinking. Thought in this way, the photograph no longer can be viewed as merely an inscription with light by the pencil of nature, but rather ought to be seen as the point at which a multiplicity of uncontainable self-differentiation intersects in a purposeful, irreducible dance of light and darkness or, in the age of digital reproduction, in an inexhaustible proliferation of plus–minus information. Contrary to conventional notions of the image as ontological substance, as once canonized in such works as André Bazin's "The Ontology of the Photographic Image," the reality effect that the photograph occasions bespeaks not simply the absence of a former (and, in principle, re-presentable) visual presence but rather the reality of a thinking of alterity and even the alterity of thinking itself.[2] Having departed from the view (and worldview) of the photograph as an ontologically stable object, we are led by the photographic image into a distant land of alterity and dissimulation, an idiosyncratic strangeness that provides us with erratic glimpses of a thinking yet to come. This future thinking will have been more rigorous than the merely conceptual, even while it cannot do without concepts. It will have been more indebted to the aesthetic and presentational specificity of the image than conventional philosophizing has dared to acknowledge. The photograph not only *exhibits* the openness of thought itself; it *is* this openness.

But let us backtrack in order to consider the relation between afterness and photography more closely.

"And who took the photograph? Is it some sort of family occasion? Your father and brother appear to be in dark suits, with white ties, but the so-called brother-in-law is wearing a coloured one. Dearest, how powerful one is, face to face with a picture, and

how powerless in reality! I can easily imagine your whole family stepping aside and removing themselves, leaving you on your own, while I lean across the big table searching for your eyes, finding them, and dying of joy. Dearest, pictures are wonderful, pictures are indispensable, but they are torture as well."[3]

To confront the photograph, as Kafka just did—in the darkness or darkroom of the night from December 6 through 7, 1912—always also is to confront a moment of unsettling, a moment in which the photograph, in its refusal to yield its non-self-identity to our identity-seeking gaze, unsettles us by unsettling itself. I wish to set in motion a polylogue among Derrida and the figures whose proper names frame his own in the "group portrait" that this chapter records—Kafka to the left, the German photographer Stefan Moses to the right—a kind of unsettling freeze-frame of unsuspected family relations taken on a holiday or holy day of technical illumination. In the course of our engagement with Derrida and Moses, we will be interrupted periodically by incoming missives from Kafka, the great unknown theorist of photography, sent on their way between September 1912 and August 1913. Kafka's snapshot-like reflections on the difficulties and explosively charged minitragedies of promising, taking, sending, receiving, interpreting, and missing photographs in his love letters to Felice Bauer will illuminate our polylogue as embodiments of the interplay between the luminous (*photo*) and the trace (*graphy*).[4] Kafka's obsessive engagement with photography can be said to belong to a larger, heterogeneous orbit of literary meditations on photography, reflections that in the French modernist tradition encompass such texts as Baudelaire's "The Salon of 1859"; Proust's *The Guermantes Way* (1920), a volume of *In Search of Lost Time*; and Breton's surrealist novel *Nadja* (1928). In the German tradition, the literary discourse on photography extends from Weimar-era texts such as Mann's *The Magic Mountain* (1924) and Tucholsky and Heartfield's collaborative book of texts and photomontages, *Deutschland, Deutschland über alles!* (1929); through postwar projects such as Brecht's book of antiwar poems and photomontages, *War Primer* (1955); to the discussion of photography in Günter Grass's novel *The Tin Drum* (1959) and the recent hybrid novels of W. G. Sebald.

Let us begin with Derrida's polylogue about the photograph, which in turn will open onto a polylogue among Kafka, Derrida, and Moses. ("Polylogue" is the formal designation that Derrida first gives his 1978 engagement—in many voices and various personae at once—with Heidegger's and art historian Meyer Schapiro's competing readings of Van Gogh's painting *A Pair of*

Shoes [1885], depicting a pair of peasant shoes, in the section "Restitutions" of *The Truth in Painting*. Derrida will take up this fractured voice heard in his engagement with painting in his later reading of another visual medium, photography.) First, then, a series of open questions. What would it mean to think of the photograph neither in terms of reproduction nor with an eye to the reproducibility of that which is said to exist already, but rather in terms of a force field of relations that erratically thematize, always one more time, their own status as a relation, a relation that differs from and with itself even while suspending itself? In other words, what would it mean to alter our assumptions about the nature of the relation between the photograph and that which it appears to reproduce as well as the relation of the photograph to the very idea of relation itself? Learning how to read the ways in which the *téchne* of the photograph perpetually illuminates and obscures the relation of the relation to itself and to its referential function then would emerge as inseparable from the experience of learning to learn from the medial specificity of photography and from the idiomatic and unverifiable language of a given photograph. In contemporary work on photography, whether analog or digital, such issues are implicitly encoded—but rarely addressed directly—by writers such as Susan Sontag on the relation of photography to the pain of others; by philosophers of the image such as Vilém Flusser and his concern with a positively inflected "telematic" society; by historians of photography such as Geoffrey Batchen and his understandable preoccupations with the photograph's material and cultural inscriptions; and by theorists of photography such as Hubertus von Amelunxen and his ongoing investigations of how certain indexical and postindexical modes of seeing have rendered the late modern subject a "homo photographicus."[5]

What, then, would our stance be vis-à-vis the referential pull of these ontic commitments, given the impossibility of ever viewing photography as such and the concomitant necessity of only ever viewing a particular instance of photography, *this* photograph's *here and now* that arrives before my gaze as a translation of the specificity of a particular *there and then*. It seems that the photograph perpetually resists our Hegelian effort to see the universal of the absolute manifest itself in the singularity of the particular. We could say that, viewed from the perspective of these concerns, the photograph reformulates the three central preoccupations of philosophy according to Kant (What can I know? What should I do? What can I hope for?) as photography's abiding question: What can I relate to? Or, more precisely: What is my relation to relation?

As Derrida writes in *Right of Inspection*, his 1985 engagement with the images of a photo-novel by the Belgian photographer Marie-Françoise Plissart:

> In terms of the exteriority of the referent its being-in-the-past certainly cannot be eliminated. But when the referent itself consists of frames that are themselves framed, the index of the wholly other, however marked it may be, endlessly defers reference. The chimera becomes a possibility. If there is an art of photography (beyond that of determined genres, and thus in an almost transcendental space), it is found here. Not that it suspends reference, but that it indefinitely defers a certain type of reality, that of the *perceptible* referent. It gives the prerogative to the other, opens the infinite uncertainty of a relation to the completely other, a relation without relation.[6]

The relation without relation that one of Derrida's voices casts—in the polylogue that is his text—as the art of photography itself, the relation that, within the image, announces itself *as* relation but that never fully can guarantee the hermeneutic key to its internal and external networks of reference, gives rise to a multitude of senses and experiences that are mediated by the mise-en-scène of the relation itself. Therefore, one of the voices in Derrida's polylogue says: "You will never know, nor will you, all the stories, nor even the totality of one single story, I kept telling myself as I looked at these images." These lines open, and periodically return to punctuate, *Right of Inspection*. Here, the language of photography is inseparable from the experience of plurality and the plurality of experience. This double plurality encrypted in the photograph works to transform the aesthetic experience of time, language, gender, and genre, along with the very logic of a hermeneutics of seeing. Decoupling perception from cognition, Derrida's engagement with photography works to open the medium to its own alterity, to the ways in which photography exposes the non-self-identity and internal self-differentiation that, for him, ultimately condition any act of aesthetic experience and its ethico-political futurity. The concept of a photographic relation without relation illuminates syntactic linkages among some of the major claims of a Derridean aesthetics as it unfolds in the language of technically mediated images. From this perspective, *Right of Inspection* would need to be understood in the context of Derrida's other sustained engagements with photographic aesthetics—especially "The Deaths of Roland Barthes"; *Athens, Still Remains*; and his extended conversation with Amelunxen and Michael Wetzel, *Copy, Archive,*

Signature—as well as in terms of the supplementary status that photography assumes in relation to Derrida's major aesthetic claims about the visual arts and visual culture more generally, especially in *The Truth in Painting* and *Memoirs of the Blind: The Self-Portrait and Other Ruins*.[7]

The relation without relation that the photograph relates to us cannot be thought of in isolation from a certain adherence to the referent and the idea of referentiality, even though reference cannot remain immune from the unrelatedness of the relation. As Derrida reminds us in "The Deaths of Roland Barthes," the photographic referent "does not relate to a present or a real but, in an other way, to the other, and each time differently according to the type of 'image,' whether photographic or not."[8] Therefore, we are faced with the question of how to name the relation in and of the photograph without having to decide between referent and reference once and for all, always choosing both and neither as we engage the singular tenses, past and present, of the photograph. The having-been of what was photographed, then, opens a space that always unfolds *after* the event and with—that is, both in tandem with and according to—the reading of that event's history-marking occurrence.

Returning to an explication of the interruptive, other-directed *punctum* that Barthes contrasts with the intentional structure of the *studium* of the photograph, Derrida suggests a new term to name this photographic relation without relation that manifests itself, among other things, in the strategic refusal to decide between referent and reference. This is what we "might call the unicity of the *referential*," a word that allows us "not to have to choose between reference and referent: what adheres in the photograph is perhaps less the referent itself, in the present effectivity of its reality, than the implication in the reference of its having-been-unique."[9] One way to understand Derrida's logic of the *referential* is to imagine the uniqueness and singularity of the photographed not merely in the retroactive documentation of its existence that conceptualizes photography as the process of collecting archival evidence, but rather in the very relation that the photographic act allowed the various participants in the scene of photography (the subject, the photographer, the camera, the equipment, the light, and the perspective, among many others) to enter a singular and unique relation to one another. The photograph, then, would not be the record of any extraphotographic, autonomous singularity that had merely waited to be recorded. Rather, the photograph, in its legibility as a form of the *referential*, could be understood as an inscription with light of the uniqueness of a specific and now irretrievable relation, in a way that both emphasizes the specific relation—or set of relations—assumed during the scene of the photographic act and stages in a medium-specific way the general concept of relation itself.

The thinking of this double relation without relation that the photograph enacts in the space of the *referential*—the singular relation of the specific image and the general concept of relation—could be extended to include another doubling. If this double relation of the relation without relation is specific to the medium of photography, it also exceeds that medium's specificity in its staging of a certain extended reality of thought. As Derrida suggests, taking "all differences into account, we would not be reducing the specificity of . . . photography were we to find it pertinent elsewhere: I would say everywhere."[10] What photography teaches us about the *referential* is that the particular relation without relation that it captures is itself related to other relations without relation. That is to say, the relation without relation that photography relates is itself something of a photograph—and therefore a matter of technical reproducibility—a whole host of relations without relation. Seen from this perspective, the photograph performs in the singular time and space of its own idiom a relation without relation that saturates all relations and the presentational acts without which they would not exist.

Incoming missive: *"At the risk of ruining your Sunday, I am sending you my most recent photograph, and three copies at that, since I think I have discovered that in larger quantities it loses some of its horror. I don't know what to do, flashlights always give me a mad look—the face twisted, the eyes crossed and staring. Don't worry, dearest, I don't look like that, this picture doesn't count, it isn't one you should carry around with you. I'll send you another one soon. In reality I am at least twice as beautiful as in this picture. If that's not enough for you, dearest, then things are indeed serious. In that case, what am I to do? However, you do have a fairly true picture of me; the way I look in the little book* [Meditation] *is how I really look, at least that's how I looked a short while ago. And whether you like it or not, I belong to you. Franz."*[11]

The vexed question of the photographic self-portrait, as a special case in the register of the portrait, resides at the core of a project by Munich photographer Stefan Moses (born 1928), the great chronicler of German life, whose images not only have appeared regularly in such magazines as *Der Spiegel* and *Stern* but, since the 1950s, have introduced into German photography a singular precision, rigor, and soberly playful beauty. In 1963 he began facilitating a series of photographic self-portraits of well-known German writers, artists, philosophers, athletes, and public figures, including Adorno, Bloch,

Otto Hahn, Karl Jaspers, Walter Jens, Ernst Jünger, Erich Kästner, Alexander Mitscherlich, and Max Schmeling, among many others.[12] Moses traveled all over Germany with a kitschy chrome mirror on wheels, borrowed from the dressing room of a department store, to visit his subjects in their "own" environments and to encourage them to photograph themselves in front of the department store mirror with his camera. In the process, he too made a series of photographs of these sessions, delivering a perpetual metacommentary on, or portrait of, the very act of self-portraiture. Moses asked his subjects to linger with the scene of self-portraiture, to take their time, to find just the right moment—something akin perhaps to the Greek *kairos*—to release the shutter; his subjects would sometimes spend an entire morning or afternoon positioning and studying themselves in the chrome mirror to wait for just the right moment that would capture them, in a sudden flash of simultaneous illumination and blindness. No quickies, no half-hearted efforts, no cop-outs or crop-outs.

But what would be the right moment for a photographic self-portrait? What would make a self privilege this moment over that, this possibility of release over any number of others? We recall that de Man commences his *Allegories of Reading: Figural Language in Rousseau, Nietzsche, Rilke, and Proust* with an epigraph from Pascal: "If one reads too quickly or too slowly one understands nothing."[13] In a certain sense, even though this is not spelled out by de Man, his entire project can be understood as returning us again and again to the question of the right speed of reading. Yet, what would be the right speed? And what would be the right moment for me, as the photographer who is also the subject of the photograph, to release—that is, to let go and surrender to the luminous trace that is photo-graphy, light-writing? We could say that the task with which Moses's subjects are charged is one of finding, or, since it can hardly be coaxed, being open to, the simultaneity or interpenetration of two otherwise distinct genders that normally must not touch each other. In German, "moment" has two genders: it is sometimes *der Moment*, sometimes *das Moment*. As a masculine noun, *der Moment* designates a temporal condition, a point to be understood in relation to, and as the product of, time; as a neuter noun, *das Moment* refers to a conceptual position or philosophical perspective. The subjects who participate in Moses's theater of self-portraiture are called on to locate a *Zeit-raum*, or "temporal space," in which the apparent mutual exclusivity of these two genders—one of which, the neuter, already is something of a nongender—collapse. Where *der Moment* and *das Moment* become indistinguishable in a dance of light and shadow, illumination and blinding, the right moment, temporally and conceptually, demands to be recognized and affirmed by the release of a shutter, even if a shudder suddenly comes over us and even if we shudder to think what the potentially illicit bringing together of *der* and *das* eventually could mean for our captured bodies.

The otherness that traverses every photograph, the very alterity that makes photography what it is even when it seems to record the familiar and the self-same given, is the point at which its unsettlance is properly illuminated. "Photography," as Jean-Luc Nancy puts it, "is a monster with two subjects, with a double body (human) and a single, cavernous head whose eye blinks on and off. At this point, at this moment, in this place of the photograph in which time blinks and is distended as an immobile surface, the most exact and the most rigorous *nous autres* is produced."[14] He continues to suggest that "each one affirms its alterity while both together make the request for an identity distinct from every other, in whose distinction they are absorbed into one another, one by the other." Here, we are reminded of the ways in which it "is the identity of the photograph itself, openly non-identical to itself and thus strangely identical to the superimposition of the two others in it, the viewfinder and the viewed surprising one another," in a way in which we may observe the two "of them together, as a 'photograph,' pronouncing a kind of silent *nous autres*."[15] While in Nancy's specific example the *nous autres* unfolds between a portrait of James Joyce and the photographer Gisèle Freund, Moses's series of self- and other-portraits insists on the ways in which the other-directedness of the non-self-identical photograph is the very condition of possibility for the self-portraiture of a subject that is no longer at home with itself, has become fractured and displaced, inhabited by many others that make it what it is and what it presents to the click of the camera and its analog or digital afterness.

Moses calls his series "Selbst im Spiegel" (Self in the Mirror). Unlike his other sustained photographic series—such as "Deutsche" (Germans), with its self-conscious citation of August Sander's archetypal photographic portrait of the Weimar Republic; "Couples," with its gestural citation of such photographers as Freund and Germaine Krull; or his photographic mask project, which is indebted to the masks that play such an important role in the studios of artists such as Kirchner, Klee, Braque, and Picasso—"Selbst im Spiegel" situates Moses in relation not only to the myth of Narcissus and to Lacan's sublimely painful mirror stage but also, in the history of photography, to the work of Polish avant-garde artist Witkacy (Stanisław Ignacy Witkiewicz). Witkacy developed, at the beginning of the twentieth century, a technique for taking doubled and tripled photographic portraits through the strategic use of multiple mirrors, and his groundbreaking work was rediscovered by young photographers in Germany in the late 1950s.[16] The photographs that comprise "Selbst im Spiegel" coalesce around a series of aporias that exhibit each self (but who is this self?) in its *Geworfenheit*, its thrownness into a relation with itself as an other of which it cannot fully take account, a self that is as much invented as it is mimetically reproduced by the click of the camera, and a photograph that is as much an other-portrait—the empirical embodiment of a consciousness that encounters itself in the guise of a reflection whose difference from the self first gives the self to the self—as it is a self-portrait. Is the photographic self-portrait in the mirror therefore the image of an empirical referent or of the semblance (*Schein*) of that alleged presence? What the "Selbst im Spiegel" series finally gives us to think is the non-self-identity of the self itself, the dispersal and displacement that make the self what it is. The photographic self-portrait engages a certain relation without relation as the advent of the image. As Barthes once put it, "The photography is the advent of myself as other."[17]

If the aesthetic of the photographic self-portrait, in which the self-identity of the relation is suspended, presents an especially instructive instantiation of the relation without relation, we may turn to the most famous in Moses's series, the photograph of Adorno, to pursue this thought in relation to a particular image. The photograph, reproduced on several book covers—and especially on biographies of Adorno—has become an iconographic signifier in its cultural orbit. A close reading of this image will help us appreciate in a concrete and exemplary way some of the conceptual stakes with which we have been concerned.

Moses's famous photograph of Adorno in later life shows the philosopher perched on a small chair, the toes of his two feet timidly pointing inward, his facial expression stoic, his gaze averted, one hand covering his knee, the other holding a slim metal object (figure 1).[18] The image presents itself as an arrested mirror reflection, the scene of a photographic self-portrait by Adorno as witnessed and photographed by Moses. The shining reflection of Adorno cuts vertically through the dark room in which the standing mirror is positioned, framing an image of its subject within the larger picture. The camera,

FIGURE 1
Theodor W. Adorno, "Self in Mirror," 1964. (Image courtesy of Stefan Moses [Munich, Germany])

which is positioned behind him in the mirror reflection—inverting empirical space—is situated before us in the larger photographic surround. In this way, Moses shows us Adorno in a sharp displacement. The viewing subject is spatially positioned where the referential object must be for its image to be reflectable by the mirror's surface: the absent referent who bears the name Adorno is located outside the realm of the image, precisely where the viewer is now positioned. Subject and object do not merely trade places but also imbricate each other in a mutual mediation for this scene of vision to become possible. The self-portrait here becomes a kind of "other-portrait," in which the subject, who has not released the shutter himself but has his self-image taken by an other, portrays himself as an object or, more precisely, as the image of an object. The self-portrait's legibility is predicated on its multiple removal from the referent. After all, we are not looking at Adorno, at a picture of Adorno, or even at a picture of a picture of Adorno, but at a *scene* in which the very *act of creating* the picture of a picture of Adorno is self-reflexively arrested.

Moses's photograph of an Adornean self-portrait works to transform the self into the image of an object by uncovering the ways in which the self is always already an image. As Barthes writes of photographic portraiture, "Now, once I feel myself observed by the lens, everything changes: I constitute myself in the process of 'posing,' I instantaneously make another body for myself, I transform myself in advance into an image. This transformation is an active one: I feel that the Photograph creates my body or mortifies it, according to its caprice." If, as Barthes suggests, the photograph is "the advent of myself as other: a cunning dissociation of consciousness from identity," then the "madness of photography" can be said to have "transformed subject into object, and even, one might say, into a museum object." To the extent that I wish to coincide with myself as an image, "I do not stop imitating myself, and because of this, each time I am (or let myself be) photographed, I invariably suffer from a sensation of inauthenticity, sometimes of imposture (comparable to certain nightmares)."[19] The inauthenticity or imposture of the scene of photography is inseparable from death itself—for what does photography capture if not the prediction of its subject's finitude, the pronouncement that what once was no longer is (or no longer is exactly the way it is pictured in the image) and that its subject will at some point cease to be altogether? Yet, these questions become especially urgent in the scene of the photographic *self*-portrait. For it is here that I, as a self-portraying subject, actively countersign the displacements and the predictions of finitude that the photographic portrait works to encrypt.

The mourning that Moses's image of Adorno's photographic self-portrait stages is not only a function of its status as a memento mori, as Barthes famously suggests, but also a function of its status as the embodiment of an impossibility. The subject's gaze can never simply be itself; that is, its gaze cannot be available as an object to an other who is looking at it and, in the same moment, observe itself as a gaze that is being looked at. In a conversation about photography, Derrida remarks on the impossibility of this simultaneity. "One thinks," he says, "that the portrait captures the eyes, the gaze that is, among other things, that for which something like photography exists. The gaze is presumed to be what the subject himself cannot see in his own life. When one looks at oneself in a mirror, one sees oneself either as seen or as seeing but never as both at the same time." Derrida continues: "One believes that in principle the camera—photographic or cinematographic—should capture or hold a gaze which the looking eyes cannot see. I am seen as you see me speaking . . . but with a look that I, who am alive now in the present, cannot see. And therefore when I give someone my gaze, my look, the photographed double of my look, I give him something with which I see but which I myself cannot see. This is a situation of heteronomy: I give myself to the other precisely there where I cannot give myself to myself, cannot see myself seeing, in a way."[20] For Derrida, then, to the extent to which I give myself, so radically and irreducibly, to the other, and incapable of seeing or even verifying my own gaze as a gift, I expose myself to the expectations that the other imposes on me in an encounter with my image. In a gesture of deliverance, I as a photographed self offer myself to an uncontainable economy of subjects and objects, an economy that never can be identical with itself or with what is external to it.

If this image is Moses's perspective on Adorno's self-portrait, it is also a self-portrait of the self-portrait—that is, a photograph about photography. Here, subject and object, as well as the space that they inhabit, remain suspended in a dialectical play, a serious play that cannot be arrested by any synthesis. The image of Adorno that this scene of a self-portrait captures is caught in a moment of nonidentity, a rupture that can never be glossed over or repaired. As such, the scene of Adorno's self-portrait presents itself also as a self-portrait of the category of the nonidentical, what he calls *"das Nichtidentische,"* a fissured concept that centrally occupies his thinking at least from *Negative Dialectics* to the unfinished *Aesthetic Theory*. The nonidentical, for

Adorno, is the irreducible moment within philosophy that opens thought up to its perpetual self-differentiation, rather than providing a way into the absolute. As Adorno writes, a negative dialectic cannot be thought in isolation from decay: "Its logic is one of decay, of the badgered and reified form of the concepts which at first the cognizing subject encounters without mediation. Their identity with the subject is the untruth. With it the subjective preformation of the phenomenon slides in front of what is non-identical in it, in front of the *individuum ineffabile*."[21] The nonidentical exposes itself and its other, identity, to the nonidentity by which they are both touched but to which neither can be assimilated.

While Adorno's touchstone is Hegel, his own dialectic, as a *negative* dialectic, differs from Hegel's in that it refuses to yield the mediation of subject and object, or the identical and nonidentical, to a final moment of identity, a synthetic sublation within totality itself. His thought refuses to assimilate, into the absolute of identity, the irreducible difference that traverses even the concept of difference. While Hegel's dialectical model, in Adorno's reading, works to co-opt into its system even those moments of difference and objects of otherness that remain absolutely other to it, Adorno's thinking self-consciously wishes to remain responsible to what cannot be subsumed, even dialectically, under the concept, the system, the absolute, or totality itself.

In his study of Husserl, *On the Metacritique of Epistemology*, Adorno illustrates this point. There, he argues that both spirit (*Geist*) and the given (*das Gegebene*)—other names for subject and object—to the extent that they are mediated by each other, are equally unreliable as founding principles of a theory of knowledge: "Spirit is as inseparable from the given as the latter is from the former. Both are no first principles. That both are in essential ways mediated by each other makes both equally unusable as *ur*-principles. If one wished to recognize in such a being-mediated itself the *ur*-principle, then one would mistake a relational with a substantive concept and would posit as an origin the *flatus vocis*." He continues: "Mediatedness is no positive statement regarding Being, but rather a call for cognition not to rest with such positivity, that is, more precisely, a call to perform the dialectic concretely."[22] Motivated as much by epistemological considerations as by ethico-political ones, Adorno privileges a philosophy of negative dialectic that does not pretend to capture the truth more fully than other modes of thinking but that shows itself responsible to the ways in which its pretensions to truth are corrupted and infinitely mediated by a series of presentational dilemmas—such as mimesis itself—and politically inscribed wills to power. The truth of negative dialectic is thus the truth of its own impossibility. What remains promising in it is inseparable from the ways in which it does not cease to confront its own limitations. The responsibility of philosophical thought is thus to its own blind spots and contradictions—not to gloss them over but to expose their spectral workings in a world corrupted by falsity and totalitarian impulses. The nonidentical, for Adorno, ultimately names the condition of possibility for thought. The responsibilities and possibilities that the nonidentical opens up, as a form of negative dialectic that turns on its own blind spots, permeates Adorno's entire mature oeuvre.

If Moses's image of Adorno's self-portrait enacts certain dimensions of the nonidentical, it too will not remain identical in its nonidentity. The identity of its nonidentity is itself opened to nonidentity by the existence of a second photograph taken during the same session (figure 2). This second image also was created by Moses. In the second image, which at first glance appears rather similar to the first, nonidentity will not remain self-identical but instead returns with a difference. Here, in an additional layer of self-reflexive mediation, we witness the scene of a portrait of a self-portrait that explicitly comments on itself and its own imagistic gestures and inscriptions. While the posture of Adorno's image in the mirror is almost identical, his head appears slightly more tilted downward, and his facial expression looks more grim, with the corners of his mouth drooping slightly more. In this second photograph, we encounter an image of the referent whose name is Adorno, a referent who is in the process of turning himself into a self-portrait. Shot from behind what one hesitates to call Adorno's empirical head, the image self-consciously stages the scene of vision that had accompanied the first photograph as well, albeit there only on an implicit level. While the scene of Adorno's self-portrait is, in both versions, also about the very process of being looked at—caught—in the act of self-portraiture, the second version makes the dimension of spectatorship more explicit. Spectatorship "outside" the enclosed scene of self-portraiture is implied here by the light flooding in through the window on the left and illuminating the left side of Adorno's head—a sign of the public sphere intruding upon a private act—as well as by the focus on the medial or technical aspects of this photograph and, by extension, photography itself: the camera, the cable connecting the remote shutter release to the apparatus, and the leg of the tripod that cuts through Adorno's back to the left of the image. The mirror here appears smaller, displaced from the center of the image, because now the focus is shifting ever more toward the act itself, rather than toward its product. Most important,

FIGURE 2
Stefan Moses, Portrait of Adorno's self-portrait, 1964. (Image courtesy of Stefan Moses [Munich, Germany])

this portrait of a self-portrait is actually the portrait of a double self-portrait. It is the image not only of a self-portrait of Adorno, but also of the photographer, Moses, who is conducting the session and taking these images. After all, his left arm, from elbow to shutter-releasing fingertip, partially appears in the upper-right corner of the mirror. Reduced to his function, the photographer here appears as the disembodied hand that takes images, even images of images, without itself ever becoming a full image. This severed hand taking images, with its fingers performing the decisive action, figures for us, perhaps, as a harbinger—a Moses—of, very literally, the *digital* age, even though in the 1960s, digital cameras obviously had not been invented yet and the photographer used an analog apparatus.

As viewers, we are invited by Moses to watch Adorno photographing himself and watching himself being watched and photographed by a photographer whose acts of watching and photographing make this scene of watching and photographing available to yet another watching subject who is not in the scene but nevertheless is present and watching (we, the viewers). If the first image of the self-portrait allegorizes a displaced subject–object relation in which the infinite mediation that traverses this relation is staged as an embodied figure of nonidentity, then this second image of the self-portrait delivers an additional metacommentary on the mediatedness of this scene of nonidentity. It is a form of nonidentity that is capable of theorizing itself—staging precisely what for Adorno names the promise of a truly negative dialectic in philosophy, art, and politics. In so doing, Moses's images open up the scene of photographic self-portraiture as a space of ever-shifting relations, relations without relations, as well as implied or future relations.

To elaborate on this photographic non-self-identity that enacts the relation without relation, we may return from Moses's photographs to those of Plissart, which thematize in a variety of registers the implications of this non-self-identity. Thus one voice in Derrida's polylogue on Plissart's photographs reminds the other voices and us that "Benjamin emphasized that very same thing concerning the detail, namely that the *invention* of photography and the *advent* of psychoanalysis *concur*. Through a strange concurrence in the technical apparatus, more or less at the same moment, you can see Ps and Ph unite: a reading of the significant 'detail' in a blowup, in a process of increasing enlargement, of *découpage* or montage, a reinscription of metonymies, displacement, substitution, restaging, analysis of the figurative function of words in the silent *Darstellbarkeit*." Alluding to Benjamin's, and through him Kracauer's, analyses of the photographic image in "Little History of

Photography," Derrida can be read as delivering a metacommentary, from the perspective of the non-self-identity of the photographic relation, on the Benjaminian concept of the "optical unconscious," which differentiates between a readability of the ontic world by the naked eye and one that always already is mediated by the *téchne* of the nonhuman or posthuman apparatus. As such, the photographic machine and its products also join the psycho-prosthetic functions of the other technical devices and apparatuses that Derrida later addresses in the mnemonic terms of *Archive Fever*.[23]

If one of the voices in Derrida's polylogue therefore suggests that "you should speak of these photographs as of a thinking, as a pensiveness without a voice, whose only voice remains suspended," then it is the searching for a voice without or beyond the voice as presence—indeed, the present trace of an absence—that the photograph encodes. This present trace of an absence, even when it is not immediately recuperable in a dialectical sense as the absence that is merely a distant presence, as the singularity that is but a repeatable difference, would then not present the mere object of a thinking, but the image that gives us thinking itself to look at. Speaking of the photograph as a kind of thinking, a reflectiveness that always strives, as in Heidegger, to think what thinking might mean in the first place, means to think thinking not simply as an extension or amplification of what is thought but as a setting into relation of elements or nodal points that Adorno famously calls a constellation, a setting into relation that does not leave untouched the relation of the presence or absence of what is thought or given us to think photographically. The heterogeneous spectral images of former concentration camp sites by contemporary German photographer Dirk Reinartz, collected in his monograph *Totenstill*, provide a case in point.[24] The blurred photo-paintings of Gerhard Richter (the *other* one) and their oddly translational yet postmimetically mimetic relation to the photograph add another complex layer of mediation.

Incoming missive: "*I am enclosing a snapshot of myself when I was perhaps five years old; at the time the angry expression was put on as a joke, now I suspect it was secretly meant. But you must send it back, it is owned by my parents, who own everything, and want to be part of everything. (Today of all days I had to write about your mother!) When you've sent it back, I'll send you others, including a recent bad and silly one, which you may keep if you like. I can't have been five years old in this photograph, more likely two; but as a lover of children you will be the better judge. When children are around I prefer to close my eyes. Franz. This would be the most inappropriate moment to ask you to give or lend me a photograph of yourself. I just mention it.*"[25]

"Concurrence and recurrence, you say," Derrida writes, "but since what is lacking is the name or noun for it, the idiom, and the country, I see them chase *after* it. They both pursue and flee the name. They are *after it*. They come after it, in other words follow it, but, since they run behind it, in fleeing it you see them here *depart before it*, run to meet it, which amounts to the same thing." The temporal–spatial disjunction that Derrida puts his finger on, the afterness of the scene of photography, decouples perception from cognition, *Wahrnehmung* from *Erkenntnis*, so that something becomes what it is only from the perspective of what it will have been and what it will have ceased to be even before it has become itself. The image's afterness here is encrypted in its presence-toward-absence, which thereby also is disrupted. To become an image—that is, a true, melancholic image in the deep experiential sense of *Erfahrung*, rather than in the giddy experiential elation offered by a mere *Erlebnis*, the splinter in one's eye that Adorno memorably tells us is the best magnifying glass—also means to encode a future decay, a ruin or trace that is already silently at work in what is: not, however, in the Blochian sense of an aesthetic *Vorschein*, or "anticipatory illumination," but in and as a memento mori that every photograph also already embodies. "He is dead, and he is going to die," as Barthes writes of Civil War photographer Alexander Gardner's haunting "Portrait of Lewis Payne" (1865), of a handcuffed young inmate in a Washington, D.C., prison waiting to be hanged. As Barthes reminds us, "each photograph always contains this imperious sign of my future death."[26]

Incoming missive: *"That wonderful, excessively and undeservedly long letter! Dearest, you made me so happy. And with it the picture, strange at first, because of your unfamiliar posture and surroundings, but the longer one looks the more it falls into place, till now, in the light of the lamp on my desk—as in the sunlight of long ago—the dearest face becomes so lifelike that one longs to kiss the hand on the edge of the boat, and does. At that time you looked in better health than you do now; on the other hand—perhaps because of all that well-being—you look extremely sulky. What were you holding? A peculiar little bag? And who stuck the leaves in your belt? . . . And now you hold out hopes of more pictures. Dearest, you must keep this promise. One can't tell from the envelope, one rips it open as though it were just a letter . . . but then one finds a picture inside and you yourself slip out of it, as one fine day I will see you getting out of a railway carriage. . . . To rid you of all doubts (not for the sake of creating any doubts), I am sending you a flash photograph of myself. It is rather repulsive, but then it was meant not for you but for a power of attorney for the Institute."*[27]

The other-directed polylogue that is photography embodies a discourse that an aesthetics of light-writing, if there is one, can hardly do without. "Therefore," Derrida writes in *Right of Inspection*, "a primal scene exists before and after the fall. It belongs in any case to the time of writing on light, to the history of photography . . . let there be light, the story of the fall, the negative, Lucifer, angels of light and darkness—it's all there, no more, no less." It is as though photography were able to capture this primal scene, giving it to us to learn to read, appropriating for itself all the revolutionary force and refractory brilliance with which William Henry Fox Talbot, writing in the middle of the nineteenth century with his photographic "pencil of nature," developed the process of turning a positive into a negative before it reemerges as a positive.

Unexpectedly, the photograph, a relation without relation, an openness that nevertheless has a form, can be viewed as belonging to the aesthetic or artistic sphere of which Heidegger speaks in his 1935/1936 lecture "The Origin of the Work of Art." Heidegger's reflections are concerned "with the enigma of art, the enigma that art itself is. It is not a matter of solving the enigma. The task is to see the enigma [*Zur Aufgabe steht, das Rätsel zu sehen*]. One has called this reflection, almost from the inception of a separate reflection upon art and artists, aesthetic."[28] The thinking that aesthetic presentation can open up for us is thus not meant to explain and, by extension, to explain out of existence what in fact remains irreducible, singular, and resistant within the work. Rather, learning to think aesthetically, to think with and through the work of art, means learning to *see* what exactly the enigma or riddle is. Thinking means remaining open to what threatens to make thinking impossible. In other words, it requires a certain humility with respect to the hidden difficulties that gnaw at it—whether they be ossified modes of institutionalized philosophizing, encrusted worldviews that are taken to be self-evident, unexamined ideologies that mistake contingencies for universal truths, or other hidden assumptions that prevent us from seeing the full complexity of what is to be thought and of the task of thinking itself. We could say that the photograph offers us an unexpected mode of seeing that aids us in our task to learn to see the difficulty of thinking. *Zur Aufgabe steht, das Rätsel zu sehen*: The photograph constitutes a snapshot of our learning how to think and of the myriad difficulties that always conspire to prevent us from doing so. "What greater anxiety is there today than the anxiety before thinking? [*Welche Angst ist heute größer als die vor dem Denken?*]," Heidegger asks.[29] This anxiety is brought into the open by the photograph. The photograph neither celebrates nor eradicates this anxiety. Instead, the photograph gives this anxiety over to reflection by exposing it.

The other-directed polylogue called light-writing therefore can be thought of as taking place in the pictorial scene of what Heidegger calls a *Lichtung*, or "clearing": not an illumination per se, since the flash always also blinds, but the stage that provides just the right conditions—fleeting, finite, precarious, mortal—in which the intricate dance of light and darkness is given the opportunity to open onto a serious play of significations. The ecstasy and tragedy that Kafka, Derrida, and Moses frame are the blurred focal points of a snapshot that, in its theatricality and other-directedness, knows no common measure with the certainty of hermeneutic closure. In its elusive afterness, the photograph smiles, knowingly, even when it grimaces, and speaks of its pain and deferral even when it appears to be joyously and fully itself. As Kafka tells us, photographs are "wonderful," photographs are "indispensable, but they are torture as well [*aber eine Qual sind sie auch*]." Viewed from this perspective, a photographic afterness shares something of the experience that suffused Derrida's last words on October 8, 2004, relayed by his son Pierre at the grave and that now conspire to yield an image of Derrida, not a final or funeral image, to be sure, but another image, a final image without closure, an image of finality that is nevertheless always also just one image among so many others, an afterimage that is no longer and that is no longer simply one. Derrida said: "My friends, I thank you for coming. I thank you for the good fortune of your friendship. Don't cry. Smile, as I would have smiled at you. I bless you. I love you. Wherever I am, I am smiling at you."[30]

7 *Afterness and the Image (II)*
Image Withdrawal

All things exist in order to become images for us.
—Rainer Maria Rilke, Letter to Frieda von Bülow

One must obtain from oneself a silence of the Images. This does not mean that such a silence would be superior indifference, serenity, mastery: *Epoche*, suspension, remains a *pathos*: I would continue to be *moved* (by Images) but no longer *tormented*.
—Roland Barthes, "The Image"

As has become visible in our discussion of the photograph, the image is conceptualized here both as a physical object and as an intellectual figure—that is, as a portrayal of the process of speculative thinking itself. One might say, then, that the image viewed from such a dual perspective is one that manifests itself *after*—that is, both according to and following—the fundamental divide between perception and cognition. Our task, therefore, is to investigate what the specific afterness of an image thus conceived might entail.

After the image comes the image. The optical term *Nachbild*, or "afterimage," captures this movement, in which an image that has already taken leave of us, has moved on in the course of its journey elsewhere, continues to be visible in a spectral mode on our retina. The haunting shapes of the afterimage are simultaneously there and not there, visible as a haunting form that is in the process of dissolving and of being replaced by the forms of other images that are ready to impose themselves on the eye. An image that continues to appear, in both positive and negative valences, even after the eye is no longer being exposed to it, the afterimage is an illusion that is nevertheless real: in short, a real illusion. For instance, when looking into a photographic flash that simultaneously illuminates and blinds, the eye's optical makeup allows for the prolonged presence of something, the appearance of a bright spot, that already has become an absence. The "after" of the afterimage is the moment that rejects the demand to be simply a now or an after, refusing to choose between presence and absence, optical illusion and the weightiness of the real. This after of the afterimage situates itself on the limit, and as the limit, of the logic of afterness itself, de-limiting—as a sort of hyphen between limiting and delimiting—the structural logic by which the distinction between a before and an after is first made. The afterimage is what returns the after properly to itself, a spectral experience that imposes itself most insistently precisely in the moment when the after is both after and not yet quite after. Could it be, then, that the logic of the afterimage, situated somewhere in the empty space between visual illusion and the productive possibilities that come with witnessing the spectrality of an after that is not simply and not fully an after just yet, enables a more general meditation on the image that is in withdrawal? Retreating from the strictures of a purely binary model of before and after, vision and blindness, insight and delusion, is it possible to think the relation between image and thought in a way that would show itself responsible to the spectral dimensions of an image that is in retreat—from us as well as itself?

Given the omnipresence and uncanny "thereness" of the image, its aleatory dissemination across global media, techno-scientific inscriptions, and the remains of what the phenomenologists once simply called the *Lebenswelt*, or "life world," is it admissible even to consider the possibility of its withdrawal? In light of the sheer inexhaustible archives of the image, mnemonic and otherwise, past and future, who or what could ever withdraw? On the stages of our current so-called war theaters, Nietzsche's famous image of the moveable army of tropes and metonymies is accompanied by the widely felt necessity for troop withdrawal. Can the image withdraw or be withdrawn when what makes an image what it is seems to be intimately tied to its here-and-nowness, even in memory or the imagination? An image can withdraw from its viewer by retreating or re-treating what it was meant to depict, by the strategic withholding of the image of someone or something by someone or something. Without an image, or with an image that is on its way away from me, will there be a physio-psychological reaction or withdrawal syndrome as, for example, in the case of caffeine withdrawal? But encoded in "with-drawal" we also find the preposition "with"—suggesting the possibility that we also draw something with us, dragging it along. To what extent is a with-drawal also a drawing-with or carrying along?

Importantly, there are many things that the figure of an image in withdrawal, if it can be thought, would not enact. It would not attempt to articulate one more substitute for Winkelmann's canonical invention of modern art history in the eighteenth century in works such as *Geschichte der Kunst des Altertums* (1764), nor would it figure as one more curious latecomer to the logic and repertoire of "styles" as the Swiss art historian Heinrich Wölfflin imagined them in such works as *Kunstgeschichtliche Grundbegriffe* (1915). Likewise, it would not be simply another iteration of the Kantian sublime, which, mediated by the conceptual negotiations of the condition of possibility of a priori transcendental judgments, names the unpresentable as such. It would neither pursue the epistemological and political stakes of the question as to whether or not there are some things or ideas that are unrepresentable, as Jacques Rancière does in his recent *The Future of the Image*, nor revisit the status of the image in terms of the question of Kant "after" Duchamp, to invoke Thierry de Duve's phrase, that is, broadly speaking, the status of aesthetic theory based on transcendental judgments in an age in which the artwork no longer can take recourse to its own claims as an autonomous—that is, "self-law-giving"—rather than a heteronymous structure, a structure that receives its laws from elsewhere, in and as contingency: the political, the social, the market of commodities and fetishisms, bourgeois ideologies of art, and the like.[1] Instead, image withdrawal would have to be thought as a fundamental and radical operation inscribed in a non-self-identical structure, a signification whose existence depends on being at odds not simply with an other but also with itself, in a fleeting but perpetual self-resistance.[2]

If the so-called visual culture of today is to be more than a hegemony of the image of presence, more than a mere replacement of the slow rhythm of the verbal and conceptual with fast-paced visual stimulation that is largely, but by no means always, designed to manufacture consent and to promote consumption, then this culture would have to be measured against Adorno's polemical remark that "no thought is immune to its communication" for "it already suffices to utter it in the wrong place and with false agreement to undermine its truth. I emerge from each visit to the cinema, in spite of all my vigilance, stupider and worse [*Aus jedem Besuch des Kinos komme ich bei aller Wachsamkeit dümmer und schlechter wieder heraus*]."[3] If, on the one hand, no thought is immune from its communication—a communication that, for Adorno, would be a first step toward the betrayal of its truth-contents, a surrendering of it to the mere commerce of an exchange of opinions and other delusions—and if, on the other, there can be, at least in theory, a kind of relentless, self-reflexive thought that will not yield itself, as it were, in advance, then the question arises if an image too could be more and less (in fact, according to this logic, more *because* less) present to communicate. A literate visual culture would then have to allow for the conceptual and aesthetic challenges of a certain withdrawal of the image, a kind of refusal that is at the same time the holding open of an unsaturated possibility.

There are images. There will have been images. Before the possibility of withdrawal, there must have been a giving. No withdrawal without a prior installation or placement. The German language would have us say: "*Es gibt Bilder*" and "*Es wird Bilder gegeben haben.*" It gives images, and images will have been given, but not necessarily to us in any immediate or transparent sense. There is the *es gibt*, a gesture of giving that is not merely the affirmation of an a priori state of existence—there *is*, there is something on which this declarative phrase now comments and which, in commenting, it works to affirm—but rather, a giving of unknown origin, always a giving and thus a receiving that come from elsewhere, an arrival from the provenance of something or someone committed elsewhere, an elsewhere that, however, in the act of its giving, will not reveal itself fully. What this giving of the *es gibt* gives us to think is the image of an arrival or a presence without ground, a giving that, in giving without being a mere given, gives us the very concept of giving and even of givenness to think. *Es gibt* therefore also resonates with the noun form of *geben*, *die Gabe*, or "the gift"—the gift that, in giving something, that is, causing the propositional utterance "*es gibt*" in the first place, gives us the image of figuration itself to think, in German *bildliche Sprache*. One might ask what happens to these multiple inscriptions of *bildliche Sprache* as well as, chiastically, *die Sprache der Bilder*, or "the language of images," when the presence of that which they produce in their inaugurating moment of the *es gibt* is no longer viewed as the presentation or re-presentation of something that is not coextensive with the gesture of the *es gibt*. One way of thinking about this problem is to pursue the image or afterimage of an image that becomes what it is—or better, to avoid the presentism of the "is," the affirmatively certain character of the "was," and the subtle triumphalism of the "will be," "will have become," the future perfect that from the perspective of the scene of speaking imagines what has not yet happened in terms of a past that is not yet in the past—an image, therefore, that will have become what it is only by entering a relation to what it appears to present or re-present that is not yet fully saturated by the certainties of depiction, illustration, or exemplarity. The image is given and can withdraw. What gives the image, then? Or, in the case of the image, what gives, as we say colloquially, what gives, what is going on? I wish to leave these questions of giving and withdrawing suspended and therefore alive and charged with possibility. This chapter will attempt to circle around some of these concerns in relation to four singular and enigmatic articulations of the status of the given image in withdrawal, made by four very different thinkers: the first, an apodictic remark made by Benjamin in "Die Moderne," section 3 of his text "Das Paris des Second Empire bei Baudelaire" (1938); the second, an observation offered by Heidegger in his lecture course on Heraclitus, held at Freiburg during the summer semesters of 1943 and 1944; the third, an apodictic reflection recorded in Blanchot's "Two Versions of the Imaginary," an essay collected in *The Space of Literature* (1955); and the fourth, a hint found in Deleuze's study *Difference and Repetition* (1968).

In his discussion of Baudelaire and the investments of modernity, Benjamin writes the following remarkable sentence: "That of which one knows that one soon no longer will have it in front of one, that becomes image [*Das, wovon man weiß, daß man es bald nicht mehr vor sich haben wird, das wird Bild*]."[4] Under Benjamin's melancholic gaze, the image becomes what it is only from the perspective of what it will have been and what it will have ceased to be even before it has become it. The image is oriented toward its imminent absence, its departure, its future decay. Its presence-toward-absence is precisely what allows it to become a Benjaminian image in the first place—a mnemonic image *avant la lettre*, perhaps, the image of something in anticipation of its disappearance for good. The image for Benjamin—and here it would be necessary, if we had the time, to place this image of the image into syntactic relation with other images of the image that traverse Benjamin writings, such as the dialectical image, the filmic image of reproducibility, the image of the gesture, the photographic image, even the image of Proust and Kafka, the *Denkbild*, or "thought-image," and so on—the image for Benjamin encrypts the futurity of a decline or decay, a ruinous absence, the trace of a withdrawal that is already silently at work within it.

"That of which one knows that one soon no longer will have it in front of one, that becomes image [*das wird Bild*]": Benjamin imagines an image in withdrawal, an image that can become what it is to the extent that what it shows is depicted in terms of what it is not yet. The Benjamin of the Baudelaire material here convenes with the one on view in "Pariser Passagen 1"

(1927), the initial outlines and notes for *The Arcades Project*. There, he emphasizes his fundamental theoretical obsession with the appearance of things in the moment when they are about to disappear—that is, "things in the moment of the 'being-no-longer' [*Dinge im Augenblick des Nicht-mehr-seins*]. Arcades are such monuments of being-no-longer. . . . And nothing of them lasts except the name: *passages*."[5] We can place into syntactic relation the image that is about to disappear for good—*das wird Bild*—with the *Augen-blick*, the "moment" or, literally, the "blink of the eye," in which nothing remains what it is "*im Augenblick des Nicht-mehr-seins.*" This obsession with disappearance and melancholic decay also can be seen in the emphasis that Benjamin places on the figure of the ruin across the wide spectrum of his meditations, such as, for instance, in the *Trauerspiel* book, his study of the German baroque mourning play, in which he suggests that "allegories are in the realm of thoughts what ruins are in the realm of things [*Allegorien sind im Reiche der Gedanken was Ruinen im Reiche der Dinge*]."[6] To imagine the image of something in terms of its future decay, its status as a ruin—just as allegory, in its deferring temporality works to render what is figured always already slightly disfigured—is to capture an image in its withdrawal, the fragmented image of ruinous withdrawal. If, as Adorno once observed, Benjamin's constellation of images "throughout laments the irretrievability of what, once lost, congeals into an allegory of its own demise,"[7] this allegorical demise structures the ways in which Benjamin's restless thought encounters the world of objects and images in the first place, as though this world always already were conditioned by the movement of a constitutive withdrawal.

Yet, even this image of the ruin and fragmentation hardly would remain immune to political co-optation or "entirely useless for the purposes of fascism," as Benjamin famously puts it in his preface to the "Artwork" essay.[8] After all, even Hitler's architect Albert Speer developed what he called a "theory of the value of the ruin" (*Theorie vom Ruinenwert*) prior to World War II, in which he emphasized the importance of designing buildings that could be imagined in advance as beautiful ruins, architectural structures that, as future ruins, in hundreds of years still would impress with their beauty and fragmented grandeur.[9] Rather, Benjamin's image in withdrawal, the fragmented and ruinous trace, must show itself responsible, always one more time, to the ways in which nothing in its internal structure is guaranteed once and for all, nothing is permanently inscribed in the framework of this or that stable signification. This image in withdrawal takes risks and exposes itself radically and strategically to its own contingency. As Benjamin writes in theses

V and VI of his 1940 theses on the philosophy of history, while the "true image of the past *flits* by" and "the past can be seized only as an image that flashes up in the moment of its recognizability, never to be seen again," it is also the case that "only that historian will have the gift of fanning the spark of hope in the past who is firmly convinced that even the dead will not be safe from the enemy if he wins. And this enemy has not ceased to be victorious [*Und dieser Feind hat zu siegen nicht aufgehört*]."[10]

The true image of the past, and even the very concept of a true image, remains to be thought. The relation between the image and its explicit or hidden truth claims is always yet to be conceptualized. In his lectures on Heraclitus, Heidegger interrupts his discussion of the Greek philosopher to offer the following remark:

> All "essence" is in truth imageless [*Alles "Wesen" ist in Wahrheit bildlos*]. We consider this, unjustly, a lack. We forget that the imageless and unpresentable first gives all that which is image-like its ground and its necessity. Yet, what could a painter, who does not perpetually and first of all look farther and beyond that which colors and lines are able to give, paint? All that is presentable or concretizable as an image [*alles Anschauliche*] is, without the unpresentable or that which cannot be concretized as an image [*das Unanschauliche*] merely a pleasant stimulation of the eye [*nur ein Augenreiz*].[11]

Heidegger's highly nuanced passage is too rich and too carefully modulated for me to provide a responsible and inclusive exposition of all the issues it raises—this would require its own book. I will have to make do with an elliptical and rather selective gloss. To appreciate the significance of Heidegger's statement, we must hear in it echoes of several other Heideggerean tenets about the image. First, we recall that in his early lecture course on Plato's *Sophist* (held at Marburg in 1924/1925), Heidegger already problematizes the idea that an image, or *Bild*, provides privileged access to an act of cognition. Evoking the image-theoretical work of his teacher Husserl, Heidegger emphasizes that a theory of the image and its potential cognitive values cannot begin with what an image "shows" but rather must inquire into the essence of what makes an image what it is, its very *Bildlichkeit*.[12] Second, we recall that in "The Time of the World Picture" (Die Zeit des Weltbildes), Heidegger works to articulate a view of modernity that, with Descartes, issues forth from a world that has for the first time turned itself fully into an image, a

Welt-bild, an "image of the world," but by extension also into a particular worldview or ideology, a *Weltbild* that cannot exist in isolation from a particular *Weltanschauung*.[13] This worldview subjugates the world in the name of an image, and dominates and conquers according to mathematical principles of rationality, even in those realms of experience that ought not to be structured by calculative thinking but by reflection. Third, we also recall that for Heidegger there can be no event (*Ereignis*) in the true, radical sense—that is, an event that interrupts time by breaking out of any expected framework or temporal linearity, dividing time radically into a before and an after—that is not also an event of the act of seeing and, therefore, of seeing something, such as an image. He points out that the German word for "event," *Ereignis*, derives etymologically from *Er-äugnis*—that is, the first-person-singular indicative *er äugt* (he eyes, he sees)—so that the *-äugnis* of *Er-eignis* always carries within itself *das Auge*, or "the eye."[14] *Das Ereignis* would then be an event that is also always an eyeing of something, something to be perceived visually, interpreted along the lines of the gaze, but also to be born witness to.

In light of Heidegger's account, we also should recall that the notion of theory itself derives from the practice of witnessing a spectacle or an event in an official capacity. The Greek verb *theorein* which, as Wlad Godzich reminds us, means "to look at" and "to survey in contemplation," did not stand in mere opposition to *praxis*.[15] Rather, the logic of *theorein* developed into a system in which the Greeks designated certain individuals as a *theoros* (plural, *theoria*), whose gaze was privileged in the sense that they gathered on special occasions to bear witness to public events. Unlike others in the system—such as garden-variety citizens, women, children, and slaves—the *theoria* were endowed with the legal authority to testify to an event publicly and thereby to make it a fact. As a sphere of mediation, the *theoria* were empowered to transform mere perception into valid cognition in a way that joined the manufacturing of legally binding and epistemologically valid insight to the authority to relate in a particular and singular way to the image and the vision it occasioned. Through the *theoria*, the image of an event had to be borne witness to in order to become knowledge and a matter of essence, rather than mere sensual perception (*aisthesis*).

Yet in Heidegger's Heraclitus lecture, we learn that everything that can be called an essence, "*alles 'Wesen*,'" as he says, is properly *bildlos*, or "without image," *imageless*.[16] It is interesting to wonder why Heidegger here places *Wesen* in quotation marks, when that is not normally his practice when it comes to speaking of essence, one of the core interests of his fundamental ontology. It is as though these unexpected quotation marks introduced a moment of doubt or hesitation when speaking about the relationship between essence and the image, the image that for him remains imageless. By placing *Wesen* in quotation marks, it is as though Heidegger had given us an image of the imageless essence to think, precisely by turning the pictorial essence of the word "essence," the *Wesen* of the word *Wesen*, into an image of sorts, marked as different from the other, nonmarked words surrounding it, placing a kind of picture frame around *Wesen* as if to indicate that he is speaking in a quasi-Kantian as-if mode and that the imagelessness, *Bildlosigkeit*, of which he speaks somehow should be registered by removing the written image of a word from its straightforward, apparently transcribed appearance into a realm in which it is there and not there all at once, both uttered and withdrawn, given an image and refused that image at the same time—as if the thinking of the relation between essence and image deserved to be placed under erasure in a way not unrelated to the necessity he felt to write the word "is" and to cross it out at the same time, letting the crossed-out word stand in the printed text, but visible only under the mark of its own undoing. Is the essence of the image under erasure as well? Does it withdraw when it is drawn into presence?

The idea that all essence is imageless is not to be perceived as a mere lack, not a "*Mangel*," as Heidegger says in another sentence. There could be no image, and no thinking relation to that image, that is not fundamentally indebted to the imageless (*das Bildlose*) and what cannot be depicted (*das Unanschauliche*). If the imageless and the nonpresentable or nondepictable provide the *Grund* (that is, in German, reason, cause, basis, and physical ground or foundation, also in the sense of a foundational necessity) to an image, then the imageless character of its essence is neither a lack nor a threat but its negatively mediated condition of possibility.

The condition of possibility that this essence names is, for Heidegger, instantiated in the imagistic qualities of the artwork. In his 1954 meditation on Hölderlin's poetry, ". . . dichterisch wohnet der Mensch . . ." (. . . poetically the human being dwells . . .), he suggests the following:

> Der uns geläufige Name für Anblick und Aussehen von etwas lautet "Bild." Das Wesen des Bildes ist: etwas sehen zu lassen. Dagegen sind die Abbilder und Nachbilder bereits Abarten des eigentlichen Bildes, das als Anblick das Unsichtbare sehen läßt und es so in ein ihm Fremdes einbildet. Weil das Dichten jenes geheimnisvolle Maß nimmt, nämlich

am Angesicht des Himmels, deshalb spricht es in "Bildern." Darum sind die dichterischen Bilder Ein-Bildungen in einem ausgezeichneten Sinne: nicht bloße Phantasien und Illusionen, sondern Ein-Bildungen als erblickbare Einschlüsse des Fremden in den Anblick des Vertrauten.

[The name with which we are familiar for the sight and appearance of something is "image." The essence of the image is: to let something be seen. By contrast, copies (or depictions) and afterimages are already deviant variations of the actual image which as a sight lets the invisible be seen and in this matter imagines (or impresses) it into something that is alien to it. Because poeticizing takes the enigmatic measure, namely in the face of the heavens (or sky), therefore it speaks in "images." This is why poetic images are imaginings (or im-pressions) in a particular sense: not merely fantasies and illusions but imaginings (or im-pressions) as viewable lodgings of the alien in the sight of the familiar.][17]

The essence of the image is to let something be seen, and it stands in an enabling yet originary relation to those images and afterimages that follow it. But what the image, even the image in withdrawal, embeds within itself is something that is both itself (and that can therefore become visible in the first place) and an irreducible otherness, a strangeness (*Fremdes*) that resists depiction and that nevertheless can emerge as something visible in an image that is ostensibly of something else. We could say that the poetic or artistic image "images," as it were; that is, it imagines and renders into an image an otherness that is forever at odds with the quotidian order of the visible, an unthought or unseen otherness that in turn comes into its own as an image through an image that is not identical to itself. The essence of such an image is to be both utterly familiar, that is, readable, and at the same time deeply unsettling, that is, unthought and obscure.

By the same token, what *das Anschauliche*, understood as the imagable, the presentable, and the illustrative, back in Heidegger's Heraclitus passage gives us to view is not this or that imagable or presentable object but rather precisely the nonimagable qualities of the nonpresentable itself. To say, therefore, that all *Wesen*, placed in quotation marks, is in truth imageless is not a criticism of the abilities of the image or of imaging (which, at first glance, could be seen as mere delusions, seductive but misguided devices that will forever separate us from an ability to think in a more essential or, as Heidegger likes to say, more primordial manner). Rather, the imageless quality of essence enables the appearance of an image-like presentation that nevertheless does not depict the truth of any essence but rather the truth of its nonpresentability, of the ways in which what is essential refuses to be made to appear. I say "of the ways," plural, because it could now be assumed that this model strikes all images with the unbearable lightness of similarity. Yet, each image stages the ways in which the unpresentability of *das Unanschauliche* resists the *Anschaulichkeit* of presentation in *specific and singular* ways. For instance, *Mein Krieg* (1991), the film released in the English-speaking countries as *My Private War*, which puts into a constellation astonishing home-video footage shot by six German soldiers during World War II on the Russian front, stages a series of unpresentatable essences; it is in singular and idiomatic respects distinct from the ways in which the Chicago-based filmmaker Daniel Eisenberg confronts the multiply mediated layers of memory and presentation in relation to the city of Berlin in such experimental films as *Persistence* (1997) or how Italian filmmakers Yervant Gianikian and Angela Ricci Lucchi meditate on the relation between war and its effects on the human body in a disturbing, idiosyncratic film such as *Oh! Uomo* (2004).

If the imageless quality of essence will not leave the image itself unaffected, the image can be thought as a marker of the space in which disappearance is taking place. In "Two Versions of the Imaginary," his poetically inflected meditation on the image, Blanchot states: "But what is the image? When there is nothing, the image finds in this nothing its necessary condition, but there it disappears. The image needs the neutrality and the fading of the world; it wants everything to return to the indifferent deep where nothing is affirmed; it tends toward the intimacy of what still subsists in the world. This is its truth. But this truth exceeds it. What makes it possible is the limit where it ceases."[18] If the image, as it were, requires a certain nothingness as its condition of possibility and if it simultaneously disappears into the void of this nothingness, it is inscribed into a kind of groundless ground, a terrain in which it can neither affirm nor negate, neither articulate nor disarticulate. Blanchot suggests that this spectral quality of the image be thought along the lines of a certain intimacy, an intimacy that resides at the heart of the void. This intimacy, unfolding in the void that is inhabited by the image, also carries the truth of this image, but always in a manner that cannot be contained by the limits of the image—that is, its form and its presence as a mode of presentation. If, therefore, in a seemingly paradoxical formulation, the limit of the image is what makes it possible, if it comes into existence there where it is about to cease, Blanchot's understanding of the image convenes with aspects of Benjamin's and Heidegger's to the extent that the image performs its work most strikingly when it is in retreat, when its pretensions to representative power emerge as decisively inflected by a certain movement of withdrawal. This image withdrawal occurs always as a limit case, at the limits of thought and of the visible.

In this withdrawal of the image at the limit, the temporality of the relation between the image and that which it is commonly held to present is placed out of joint. "The image," as Blanchot reminds us, "according to the ordinary analysis is secondary to the object. It is what follows. We see, then we imagine. After the object comes the image. 'After' means that the thing must first take itself off a ways in order to be grasped."[19] He continues to suggest that "this remove is not a simple displacement of a movable object which would nevertheless remain the same. Here the distance is in the heart of the thing."[20] For Blanchot, once something has become an image, "it becomes that which no one can grasp, the unreal, the impossible. It is not the same thing at a distance but the thing as distance, present in its absence, graspable because ingraspable, appearing as disappeared."[21] The example that he provides is that of the corpse of a dead man that, still present for a while among the living, the survivors, both resembles itself uncannily, even elevates or redoubles the image of the one who has just passed on, and at the same time defies the need for resemblance and comprehension. The afterness of the image as the ungraspable returns us to the infinite distance that opens up between an image and what it appears to present; that is, it offers us a glimpse of distance *as* distance. What the image gives us to think in the moment in which we encounter its afterness as an experience of displacement is the fleeting touch of something unbridgeable, something that exceeds itself and its image when it emerges as the form of a recognizable, and potentially legible, structure. As that which follows, even as the very idea of following, the image is already ahead of itself, in a haunting afterness that will not remain at a standstill.

If the afterness of the image inhabits a certain caesura of time, if it must both catch up with itself and be ahead of itself, it conforms to the gesture of a withdrawal in the temporal and hermeneutic sense as well. As Blanchot suggests, "not only is the *image* of an object not the *sense* of this object, and not only is it of no avail in understanding the object, it tends to withdraw the object from understanding by maintaining it in the immobility of a resemblance which has nothing to resemble."[22] Saturated in this way as a form that promises both to exhibit and to mean, simultaneously to show something and to signify an attendant meaning, while not being able to perform this double task, the image withdraws both itself and its presumed object from hermeneutic closure. It resembles, to employ Blanchot's figure of thought, without resembling, embodying a picture that cannot picture and that refuses to be pictured. If the image "becomes the object's aftermath, that which comes later, which is left over and allows us still to have the object at our command when there is nothing left of it," the aftermath must always be traversed by a simultaneous withdrawal and refusal in which the image insists on its own non-self-identity and on its prismatic refraction and programmatic dispersal of any concept of unified sense. What remains of our encounter with the withdrawal and dispersal that are lodged at the heart of the image is what Benjamin refers to as the moment of the being-no-longer and what Blanchot, as if echoing Benjamin, names the image's "sordid basis upon which it continues to affirm things in their disappearance."[23] It is in this sense that the withdrawal of the image, if it is to be taken seriously as the experience of a charged and illuminating afterness, is always also a moment of affirmation—the affirmation of the image's enigmatic presence-as-absence.

The unpresentability that resides in the image as withdrawal, even in its affirmation, cannot but inflect the ways in which we think about thought itself. Therefore Deleuze states that what he calls "the powers of difference and repetition" can begin to be thought "only by putting into question the traditional image of thought."[24] "By this," he means "not only that we think according to a given method, but also that there is a more or less implicit, tacit, or presupposed image of thought which determines our goals when we try to think."[25] For Deleuze, as long as a radical critique of the "classic image of thought" has not been carried out, it remains "difficult to conceive of thought as encompassing those problems which point beyond the propositional mode; or as involving encounters which escape all recognition; or as confronting its true enemies, which are quite different from thought; or as attaining that which tears thought from the natural torpor."[26] What is called for, in this Deleuzean perspective, is a "new image of thought—or rather, a liberation of thought from those images which imprison it."[27] Deleuze ultimately distinguishes between two images of thought, the dogmatic one and the one that is still to come. Dogmatic images of thought, he argues, "crush thought under an image which is that of the Same and the Similar in representation, but profoundly betrays what it means to think and alienates the two powers of difference and repetition, of philosophical commencement and recommencement. The thought which is born of thought, the act of thinking which is neither given by innateness nor presupposed by reminiscence but engendered in its genitality, is a thought without image."[28]

The image of thought that requires thought to be identical to itself, to come into its own by corresponding to models of similarity and mimetic perpetuation, is the thought that cannot properly begin, but only repeat, even when it is repeating with a difference, for there can be no other repetition. To commence properly, according to this model, would require a rethinking of the relation between difference and repetition along lines that will not always be capable of keeping the distinction pure and free of internal tension. The thought that generates itself, the one that is not given to itself by an image imported from elsewhere, would require a thinking of the relation between, on the one hand, the conceptualization of the model of difference and repetition as pure difference and, on the other, the conceptualization of the model of difference and repetition as internally non-self-identical, which is also to say potentially involved in its own collapse. If thinking in this Deleuzean vein can rise to these challenges, it does so without an image, for no image, understood as the presentation of a form, even in the formless or in the depiction of the impossibility of the presentation of form, could return thought to the internal self-division and restless self-suspension that makes the kind of thought that is born *of* thought what it is. It is in this sense that Deleuze's project can be understood to suggest that the thought that comes into its own from and as thought is "a thought without an image," a thought that is therefore future-directed in aleatory and unprogrammable ways. As in Benjamin's brooding attachment to the image that is about to disappear; as in Heidegger's intuition that essence, and by extension the essence of thinking, if it is thinkable at all, is imageless (*bildlos*); and as in Blanchot's movement of the image at the limits of what makes it both possible and impossible, in Deleuze's image of the imageless thought, thinking is set on its way and charts its unpredictable course, when its image is absent or, more precisely, in retreat.

This conceptual emphasis on the possibilities of the image in retreat cannot simply be reduced to the onto-theological tradition of the prohibition against images (*Bilderverbot*) that has structured certain Western trajectories of thought, especially in the Judeo-Christian concept of monotheistic religion, which attempted to preserve the dignity of a single God as the one transcendental signified in opposition to the polytheistic worshipping of images and which Freud famously describes as a primordial, if repressive, victory of intellectuality (*Geistigkeit*) over sensuousness and which Max Weber analyzes as intimately tied to a certain genealogical model of a progressive rationalization of mind and consciousness.[29] The image in withdrawal does not operate according to the conventional logic of a *Bilderverbot*. The onto-theological prohibition against images is structured around the idea that an image is an image *of* something, that it works to re-present something, even a deity that is not strictly speaking representable as a form, which by definition must be limited. But the image in withdrawal, as it has been developed here, cannot strictly speaking simply be an image *of* something. It would still be an image, but without the of, if the genitive preposition is meant to signify possession in the sense of mimetic belonging or a parallel creation. Rather, the image in withdrawal partakes of a perpetual leave-taking, indeed stages the very scene of leave-taking precisely there where it is no longer an image of something. This does not mean that it is simply an abstract image, as in an abstract painting, which is, after all, always to some extent still an image *of* abstraction. It is more radical than that. "How much more easily the leave-taker is loved [*wie der Abschiednehmende leichter geliebt wird*]," Benjamin says, how "the flame for the one who is distancing himself burns more purely [*die Flamme des Sichentfernenden reiner brennt*]."[30] The image in withdrawal, the image as leave-taker (*das Abschiednehmende*) would become what it is only to the extent that it steps into something other than that which is merely the case, waiting to be reproduced, in however mediated a fashion. As an originary image, the image in withdrawal claims our attention there where it refuses to leave its own appearance, and our experience of this appearance, untouched.

8 *Afterness and Experience (I)*
Can Hope Be Disappointed?

In a recent conversation about the problem of hope, the American philosopher Alphonso Lingis suggests that "hope is hope against the evidence. Hope arises in a break with the past. There is a kind of cut and the past is let go of."[1] To the extent that hope always runs counter to evidence, something merely other than what would be expected based on past experience and probability, one may speak of "a discontinuity in time," so that "there is a break, and something starts out of nowhere."[2] The examples given include the hope that the desired other will fall in love with me (though there is no "adequate evidence for that") and the hope of overcoming a "disastrous illness." For Lingis, therefore, "hope is a kind of birth . . . it does not come out of what went before, it comes out *in spite of* what went before," so that "every time hope begins again, however late in life, it is a very childlike moment; it is like being born."[3] Stressing the departure from *what is* and from *what was* that every moment of hope performs, this model envisions hope as an interruption of time in which time can start anew, is born or invented, differently, one more time, perhaps not unlike the way in which revolutionaries shot at public clocks in Paris during the French Revolution to indicate that in this new moment of historical and personal hope, conventional time had to be suspended and a new time, even a new calendar, instituted.

Yet, one might add that hope, even when it breaks with the past in the name of a new time to come, *also* remains intimately tied to those patterns of experience that it wishes to overcome and against which it hopes to institute itself. This is to say that hope, even when it is experienced as a birth, is always the experience of an *anticipated afterness*. Not content with affirming what is, hope, in its contrary-to-factness, points to what cannot be reduced to presence, whether this presence is thought in empirical or in theoretical terms, and thus works to come after that which was—that is, even though it comes after, it comes after *something*, which is to say that its afterness still is measured in relation to that with which it has parted. Even the remarkable phrase from Nietzsche's *The Will to Power* that Lingis quotes ("in impossible times when one does not know how old one is or how young one is yet to be") to illustrate the idea that "hope is to hope that things can be born in your life" also carries with it the idea of an afterness that is both a beginning and a perpetuation.[4] If Nietzsche emphasizes the seemingly paradoxical possibility that one's youth may still be to come, even late in life, he holds open the possibility of a transformation into something new and young while at the same time considering the ways in which such a belated youth must always be inscribed in the afterness of a life *already lived*, a lived life that in fact makes the possible experience of one's possibly belated youth thinkable in the first place. The hope that unfolds here is one of a doubly discontinuous time; it breaks with the past and must return to that past over and over again in order to come to terms with its departure (actual or envisioned) from it. The afterness of hope is neither a programmatic futurity nor exclusively the redemptive localization of a "hope in the past," a *Hoffnung im Vergangenen*, to evoke a suggestive phrase that literary critic Peter Szondi once employed with regard to Benjamin.[5] Rather, hope is the name for an enigmatic disjunction in time and experience that will not let itself be understood in isolation from an afterness that always is coming and going, at once departing from and perpetuating.

There is, then, a certain madness to hope: even though that which is cannot vouch for what will be (otherwise hope would not be hope but rather calculation, confident expectation, or even certainty), there is a trajectory within all hope, whether well founded or misguided, reasonable or overly optimistic, that there will have been an after in relation to the state of affairs that now obtains. One may, for instance, hope for political regime change prior to an election or a revolution; one may hope for future forgiveness for a transgression against a friend; one may also hope that a prayer will be answered, a blessing spoken or received. In every instance, there is an implied afterness lodged at the core of hope—an abiding commitment, lucid or mad, to the idea that the way things are will be superseded by a time and a situation after that which is, indeed, that there will be an after at all. Seen from this perspective, hope, as something that endures, "is not a projection into the future," as Andrew Benjamin reminds us: "Such a projection would abandon the present, refusing to grant it any quality except the demand that it be effaced."[6] While hope is unthinkable without an after that will not remain self-identical with what is, it also breaks with forms of projection that are built on expectation, repetition, programming, and sameness.

As a form of afterness, hope is also the hope for hope itself, the hope that in the afterness of that which is, hope still can be hoped for. Hope survives as that which cannot fully be assimilated to the status quo and to the administered world. What would it mean to think afterness along the lines of the negative dialectic of hope and its opposite, discouragement, which always also must be a possibility for hope to exist? After all, we have no hope without the possibility of discouragement, no articulation of hopefulness that has not already faced its possible erasure in discouragement, a discouragement that becomes the condition of possibility for hope.

Hope and Discouragement

As the paradigmatic twentieth-century "committed" scholar, Herbert Marcuse hardly wrote a line that did not, in one way or another, engage theoretical topics such as eros and one-dimensionality while at the same time intervening in the political situation of the day in the United States and in his native Germany. For Marcuse, scholarship was characterized by the dialectical struggle between hope and discouragement, a tension that he envisioned would propel thought into action. Marcuse's friend and colleague, the writer Reinhard Lettau, records an encounter shortly before Marcuse's death in 1979. Marcuse's favorite living author, next to Peter Weiss, was Beckett, who had published a poem on the recent occasion of Marcuse's eightieth birthday. Lettau writes: "Never, as long as I knew him, had he been so unable to conceal how touched he was as during our last meal in La Jolla. He suddenly stopped eating and told me that Beckett had once been asked by a critic what the structure of his writing was. 'I can explain to you the structure of my writing,' he answered. 'I once was hospitalized and in the room next door to a dying woman who screamed all night long. This screaming is the structure of my writing.'"[7] The screaming that Beckett claims as the structure of his writing and that Marcuse seems to have adopted as the motto for his own work as a scholar and public intellectual reverberates both in the imperative that writing intervene in unnecessary human suffering and in the acknowledgment of writing's impotence to transform the world in which this suffering occurs. At the beginning of the twenty-first century, Beckett's scream is heard, even if only faintly, in those academic quarters in which ethico-political questions are still considered important.

The sense of discouragement currently felt by many scholars in the humanities who concern themselves with ethico-political questions and with larger issues relating to the university as an institution of academic freedom and intellectual independence has been articulated eloquently in a series of recent studies. For instance, the literary scholar Jochen Hörisch examines how the once-leading German university system largely has been converted into an unloved knowledge factory bearing little resemblance to the noble institution once so powerfully envisioned by Wilhelm von Humboldt, and Marc Bousquet offers a chilling, fact-based critique of the merciless corporatization, de-intellectualization, and erosion of the modern American university in recent years.[8] The present feeling of despair stands in marked contrast to the optimism that characterized the heady discussions in the 1780s regarding the nature and promise of the Enlightenment. The famous essay question "What Is Enlightenment?," posed in 1784 by Johann Friedrich Zöllner in his journal *Berlinische Monatsschrift*, elicited largely hopeful responses from such thinkers as Kant ("An Answer to the Question: What Is Enlightenment?") and Mendelssohn ("On the Question: What Does to Enlighten Mean?"). A year earlier, the well-respected Berlin physician J. K. W. Moehsen had delivered his own meditation on the question "What Is to Be Done Toward the Enlightenment of the Citizenry?" to a clandestine group of "Friends of the Enlightenment" called the Berlin Wednesday Society, and in April 1789 the writer and political essayist Christoph Martin Wieland furnished his own commentary, "A Couple of Gold Nuggets, from the . . . Wastepaper, or Six Answers to Six Questions," in the influential journal that he edited, *Der Teutsche Merkur*.[9] For all their heterogeneous understandings of what "to enlighten" meant, these thinkers were united in the hope and belief that the process of enlightening, when properly carried out, would lead to human freedom, to a dignity and autonomy that would break with superannuated superstitions such as religious doctrine, irrationality, myth, and dependency. What Kant, Mendelssohn, Moehsen, Wieland, and others imagined was enlightenment as the "science of freedom."[10]

That Kant's contribution to this debate became by far the most widely read in the academy hardly is surprising, given the special status that he accords to the scholar in the project of enlightenment. After all, if *"Enlightenment is mankind's exit from its self-incurred immaturity,"* or *Unmündigkeit* (in German, a "mouthlessness" that also resonates with *Mündigkeit* [to be of legal age], *Vormund* [legal guardian], and *bevormunden* [to impose one's will on another]), then this departure is, in no small part, facilitated by the scholar's public use of reason, as opposed to the merely private use of reason employed by the layman or the more limited use of reason incorporated by clergy members and civil servants who answer to the demands of the office with which they are entrusted rather than to the idea of freedom itself.[11] For Kant, the scholar "has the complete freedom, indeed it is his calling, to communicate to the public all his carefully tested and well-intentioned thoughts on the imperfections" as well as "his proposals for a better arrangement." If the human being, then, was meant to function as more than the mere material substance of *L'Homme machine* as imagined by Julien Offray La Mettrie in 1747, then this Kantian *Freiheit des Geistes*, or "freedom of mind and spirit," hardly could be achieved without a "scholar" (*Gelehrter*) to make use of his reason "before the entire public of the *reading world.*"[12]

The current state of discouragement among scholars in the humanities cannot be solely attributed to the well-known concerns that Horkheimer and Adorno raised with regard to the threat of an undialectical understanding of enlightenment—in which enlightenment reverts to myth, and the freedom that enlightenment claims to sponsor becomes a new form of enslavement—or to the felt knowledge that, as Horkheimer outlines in an essay, the crucial ethico-political differences between *traditional* and *critical* theory have been repressed by an administered world.[13] The experience of discouragement also arises out of a more immediately felt tension between, on the one hand, the optimism and ethico-political hope that the Kantian image of the scholar and his work conjure and, on the other, the sense of frustration and despair that attends our seeming inability to intervene through scholarly work in the injustices perpetrated in the world.[14] Examples include, but by no means are limited to, the exploitation of the poor, war, ethnic cleansing, ecocide, and the hostile imposition of sovereignty that underlies global empire building.

On a more experience-near level, these injustices also include the incremental de-intellectualization and corporatization of the university, one of the last refuges of a free thinking that is not a priori subjected to the profit-driven motives of a world whose technocratic hegemony coercively manufactures consent. Savage budget reductions in the humanities have had devastating consequences. The imposition of corporatist principles of instrumental exchange-value threaten to turn Humboldt's ideal of a modern, independently minded research university—one that establishes its own laws and sets its own course in the unencumbered pursuit of intellectual concerns—into a subservient bureaucratic entity. This university-cum-corporation has fully internalized the demand to "function" in a relentlessly administered world and to surrender, especially within the humanities, the *Geist* of Wilhelm Dilthey's *Geisteswissenschaften* to a dulling of the intellect and a reification of human relations. According to this dystopian model of the university, the role of scholars in the humanities is to provide would-be players in the global economy with a cultural suntan and the ability to write at least semigrammatical reports to the boards of their future companies. In this view, researchers and teachers in the humanities are regarded as *graeculi*, or "little Greeks," the teachers who could still speak Greek and teach Greek language and culture to the children of an elite Roman class, in a time when such knowledge had all but vanished from Roman culture but was still fetishized as an exotic and almost phantasmagorical ability possessed by a dead "other." Given the perceived marginality of the humanities today, one might ask whether there can be any hope for future intellectual work to intervene in unnecessary human suffering. Ethically responsible theoretical interventions of this kind most recently have included Samuel Weber's proposed alternatives to a "targeting" strategy that generates a "militarization of thinking" in response to confrontation with loss and finitude, as well as Judith Butler's attempt to reenvision "precarious life" in such a way as to offer an alternative to violence as the sole outcome of the process of mourning. The question remains open whether such important initiatives will be met with discouragement or hope.[15]

One particularly interesting difficulty in Kant's conceptualization of enlightened thinking offers illumination here. If *"Enlightenment is mankind's exit from its self-incurred immaturity,"* then this immaturity can be understood as "the inability to make use of one's own understanding [or reason, ability to think (*Verstand*)] without the guidance of another." As Kant explains, this inability is self-incurred "if its cause lies not in the lack of understanding but rather in the lack of resolution and the courage to use it without the guidance of another. *Sapere aude*! Have the courage to use your *own Verstand*! is thus the motto of enlightenment."[16] While this well-known passage often has been taken to affirm the status of a self-sufficient and coherent subject that heroically casts aside the shackles of heteronomy, or other-determination, in order to affirm its autonomy, or self-law-giving status, several difficulties arise. First, there seems to be a performative contradiction at work in Kant's exhortation. To the extent that the purpose of his request is to promote the subject's autonomy and self-determination, then in following Kant's exhortation the subject must break with the exhortation's specific demand. After all, by following Kant's request to use one's own *Verstand* and thus to set one's own laws, one does the exact opposite—that is, takes one's law from elsewhere rather than from oneself and as a function of one's own exercise of reason. The subject can follow Kant's demand only by not following it, and by not following, it follows it. This impasse situates the subject and its *Verstand* in an aporia.

Second, and related to the first difficulty, a further reading of this passage may reasonably focus on the word that Kant italicizes, "*own*," in "your *own Verstand.*" What, precisely, is this "own"? Much hinges on this question. On the one hand, the subject's "own" *Verstand* is seen to be an expression of sovereignty and autonomy—I am employing the faculties of understanding that structure *my Verstand* rather than those that structure *yours*. On the other hand, my "own" *Verstand* cannot be simply my own; it also must be yours insofar as it is based on logic to which we both have access. In other words, while any particular turn of thought may be a function of my *Verstand*, to the extent that it is rational, repeatable, challengeable, verifiable, or refutable, it also must be a manifestation of a general *Verstand* or universal reason that is common to all who participate in rational, logical, and enlightened debate. Thus for the subject to be or become itself, it also must be something else; it becomes itself only when it departs from itself, moves elsewhere. The thinking subject thus is both autonomous and heteronomous, since the use of its "own" *Verstand*, to the extent that such thought is consistent with enlightened thinking, always constitutes the singular manifestation of a universal law that, by definition, is not founded by the subject.

It could be argued that a reading of Kant's "own" in which the subject is seen as coming into its own only by departing from itself, by subjecting itself to a nonsubjective structure of reason and understanding, implicitly has been thematized in various ways ever since Kant formulated these lines in

1784. One thinks first of all of the anonymous manifesto "Earliest Program for a System of German Idealism" (1796)—assumed to have been jointly authored by the friends and one-time Tübingen roommates Hölderlin, Schelling, and Hegel—and, a few years later, the Jena Romantics and their insistence on a relational, linguistically mediated subject, as in Novalis's "Soliloquy" (1798) and in Schlegel's "On Incomprehensibility" (1800) and the *Athenäum* fragments. The Jena Romantics' sense of a split in what appears to be the subject's "ownmost" property of thinking is, in the late nineteenth century, extended and radicalized in the genealogical project of Nietzsche and, in the early twentieth century, by Freud, whose project was to explicate the ways in which the self is not at home with itself, the ways in which it answers to the laws of a psychic structure that remain largely opaque and inaccessible to it. We could say that, in various forms and heterogeneous modulations, much of twentieth-century literary, philosophical, and scholarly writing attempts to rethink the ethico-political and historical challenges posed by the split in the Kantian "own" of *Verstand*. While such attempts are legion, I wish to recall here three of the most influential modes of response to this split: the stance of critique (as, for instance, in Adorno and Foucault), a reconsideration of Being (as in Heidegger), and a kind of other-directed hope (as in Kafka).

What unites the projects of Adorno and Foucault across their manifold differences is a perpetual return to the canonical formulations of *Kritik* in Kant (especially, of course, in his three major *Critiques*) in addressing this split. This strategy also returns them to Schlegel, who traces the notion of critique back to Greek thought in order to forge a relation between critique and modernity in his "Concerning the Essence of Critique" (1804). "We should," Schlegel argues, "think of critique as a middle term between history and philosophy, one that shall join both, and in which both are to be united to form a new, third term. Without philosophical spirit, such a critique cannot thrive—everyone agrees on this—nor without historical knowledge." For Schlegel, this "thorough understanding . . . is the real business and the inner essence of critique. We may bring together the most solid results of a historical mass under a concept, or else we may specify a concept not merely in order to allow distinctions, but rather to construct the concept in its becoming, from its earliest origins to its final completion, giving thus, together with the concept, its own inner history. Both of these are characterizations, the highest task of critique and the most intimate union of history and philosophy."[17] It is this interpenetration of philosophy and history as the moment of an ethico-political critique that Adorno and Foucault share. Adorno, in his essay "Critique," defends the valorization of negativity that is implicit in the act of critique. Referring to Kant's three *Critiques* and his essay "What Is Enlightenment?," Adorno insists that "the false, once determinately known and precisely expressed, is already an index of what is right and better."[18] This view of critique as absolute negation, as intransigent negativity that will not betray what is to come by triumphantly endorsing what is, remains a central concern from Adorno's early works through his late magnum opus *Negative Dialectics*.

Like Adorno, Foucault responds to Kant's essay "What Is Enlightenment?" and its reception within the Frankfurt School by echoing Schlegel's reading of critique when, in his 1978 lecture "What Is Critique?," he emphasizes that a part of his genealogical practice deserves to be called "historicophilosophical, which is nothing like the philosophy of history and the history of philosophy"; rather, the "domain of experience to which this philosophical labor refers does not absolutely exclude any other."[19] In contrast to the Frankfurt School, however, Foucault wishes to stress the relationship of enlightened critique to questions of governmentality, power relations, and the effects of discursively mediated regimes of coercion, including those that govern how mental illness, punishment, sexuality, and delinquency are thought and talked about. It is through these questions of critique that, for Adorno and Foucault, the split in the "own" can be made epistemologically and ethico-politically productive.

For Heidegger's fundamental ontology, the self that is not at home with itself is to be thought in terms of its *Seinsvergessenheit*, its "having-forgotten-Being." For him, the metaphysics of the subject has worked to obscure the essential condition of the self in its relation to Being, time, and the idea of finitude itself. It is in the poetry of Rilke, George, Trakl, and, above all, Hölderlin that we may encounter ourselves in our relation to Being. For instance, in the preliminary remarks to the July 1959 Stuttgart version of his lecture "Hölderlin's 'Heaven and Earth,'" Heidegger writes:

> In the meantime, the question has been raised as to whether Hölderlin belongs to the philologists or to the philosophers. He belongs neither to one nor to the other, nor even to both. This either-or, however it may be resolved, missed the crucial point. In what way? Inasmuch as the question which needs to be clarified is not to whom among us Hölderlin belongs; rather, the sole question is whether we in the present age are capable of belonging to Hölderlin's poem.

> Our reflection is concerned solely with Hölderlin's poem. It is an attempt to transform our accustomed way of representing things into an unaccustomed, because simple, thinking experience. (The transformation into the thinking experience of the center of the infinite relation—out of the collected framework [*Ge-stell*] as the self-dissimulating event [*Ereignis*] of the fourfold.)
>
> There is no *one* true way into the greatness of Hölderlin's poem. Each of the various ways is, as a mortal one—an errant way.
>
> If what Paul Valéry says of the poem is true: "The poem—this prolonged lingering between sound and sense," then the listening to the poem, and even the thinking which prepares such listening, lingers even longer than the poem itself. After all, such lingering has its own lofty resoluteness; it is no mere vacillation.[20]

For Heidegger, then, it is not a question of ownership of Hölderlin. Rather, Hölderlin's poetry opens up for its readers the question of their Being and belonging, to the extent that the encounter with his poetry, suspended between literature and philosophy, reopens the question of whether and how we belong to language, not whether and how language belongs to us. For it is in language, Heidegger believes, that the path of an impossible return of the self to itself in relation to Being is traced. We might say that, along the paths of this impossible return, the self implicitly encounters a poeticized version of the Kantian split's "own" that suspends it between singularity and universality in language itself.

While Heidegger's path relates the self to itself—that is, relates the self that lives under the condition of having-forgotten-Being to the self that encounters this having-forgotten in its engagement with language itself—Kafka's writing offers no such encounters or turns. The hope that any such encounter of the self with itself in language may harbor strictly speaking cannot benefit the reading and writing self. There can be no return to an unfragmented self in, say, "The Judgment" any more than there can be a subjectively livable outside to the dehumanizing condition of having been transformed into a vermin in "The Metamorphosis." Kafka's friend Max Brod recalls a conversation with Kafka about whether hope exists. Kafka responded: "Oh, plenty of hope, an infinite amount of hope even—but not for us."[21] Kafka's writing, then, refuses to sponsor an encounter between an authentic self and an inauthentic self in language, an encounter that could be understood as offering hope to that self inasmuch as its newly found wisdom about its condition could be regarded as the condition of possibility for change. No, to the extent that there is hope in Kafka, it is always *other-directed*, a matter addressed to and for the other who is still to come. Certain elements of Kafka's other-directed hope resurface in Levinas's ethical philosophy of the *tout-autre*, the "wholly other" who remains eternally unintelligible to me but who nevertheless makes infinite—and infinitely ethical—demands on me, that is, calls me into responsibility by always eliciting a response that I must deliver without quite knowing how.

The Radical Disappointability of Hope

Beyond these three responses to the ethico-political question of the split in the Kantian "own"—critique, relatedness to Being, and the other-directedness of hope—what interests me most apropos of discouragement and hope is a fourth analysis of responding in Bloch: the question of hope itself and its disappointability. Having written the twentieth century's major philosophical treatment of hope, the three-volume *Principle of Hope* (1949) in American exile, Bloch returned to Europe in 1948 to assume a professorship at Karl-Marx-Universität Leipzig in the German Democratic Republic. Because of his disenchantment with the authoritarian GDR regime, which attempted to place various humiliating constraints on his unorthodox way of thinking, he decided, during a visit to West Germany in 1961, to continue his ethico-political philosophical project in the West just months before the Berlin Wall was erected. In West Germany, he quickly was granted a professorship at the University of Tübingen.

Returning to the leitmotif—the question of hope—that traverses his oeuvre from the influential *Sprit of Utopia* (1918) onward, his 1961 inaugural lecture at the University of Tübingen carried the title "Can Hope Be Disappointed?"[22] Formulating a "question of particular relevance," Bloch asks, "can hope, or more precisely, can every kind and every degree of hope be disappointed?" Because people too often have been seduced "by the pied piper" when they "run blindly after conformist and escapist hopes," the unequivocal answer must be yes (339). Myriad false hopes such as the political delusions perpetrated by the so-called Third Reich, a period that Bloch refers to as "the most terrible episode in the history of squandered faith" and a "betrayal by criminals of Shakespearean size, accompanied by the odor of urine from petit-bourgeois chamber pots," must be resisted. The same holds true for mere wishful thinking of the kind that is "the vilest caricature of Adventism, of the false Messiah," that once started a "utopian psychosis" in Chicago: "God arrives next Tuesday at 11:25 A.M. at the Illinois Central, hurry to welcome him!" (340). (Bloch, were he alive today, no doubt would be interested in knowing that the pertinence of his example persists to the present, down to its geographical specificity: in April 2005, crowds of people had been gathered for days under a Chicago freeway underpass because they believed that a stain on the wall represented the Virgin Mary. According to the Illinois Department of Transportation, the stain most likely resulted from a salt run-off. The underpass festivities continued until a spray painter eventually defaced the stain, a misdemeanor for which the city has pressed charges.)

Bloch therefore arrives at the following conclusion: hope must be disappointable *"or else it would not be hope."* Hope is inseparable from a "specific disappointability [*Enttäuschbarkeit*] of informed, and therefore self-informed *docto spes* (educated hope)" (340). He continues:

> Pertaining not only to the need for mediation with respect to the course of things, but also—after this indispensable precondition—most importantly to the question of hope itself, as something that does not, in spite of all, make peace with the existing world. Therefore hope must be unconditionally disappointable, *first*, because it is open in a forward direction, in a future-oriented direction; it does not address itself to what already exists. For this reason, hope—while actually in a state of suspension—is committed to change rather than repetition, and what is more, incorporates the element of chance, without which there can be nothing new. Through this portion of chance, however sufficiently limited it may be, openness is at the same time also *kept open*. At least to the extent that hope, whose field of action this is, pays in the coin of hazard so as not to be indebted to the past. *Second* . . . hope must be disappointable because, even when concretely mediated, it can never be mediated by solid facts. For these are always, in the face of what informs hope, merely subjectively reified moments or objectively reified stoppages within a historical course of events. . . . In other words, referring directly to disappointability: hope holds *eo ipso* the condition of defeat precariously within itself: it is not confidence. It stands too close to the indeterminacy of the historical process, of the world-process

that, indeed, has not yet been defeated, but likewise has not yet won. (340–341)

Understood in this way, hope can be what it is only because it is perpetually exposed to the radical danger of disappointment. Without the real possibility of disappointment, there could be no hope—only the certainty that this or that phenomenon will be achieved and implemented. Hope is the name of the disappointable as such. Hope cannot be thought undialectically, without an eye to that which, within it, already threatens to undo it, even in the moment of its articulation. Hope is processual, dependent for its existence on the danger of its own undoing even while striving to overcome that danger. The dream of hope, for Bloch, is lodged in the ways in which the world is at odds with itself and deserves to be rethought and reorganized—not with the purpose of erasing its non-self-identity in the name of some rectificatory program of self-identity, but to radicalize that non-self-identity to such a degree that the potentially liberating contours of its opposite become visible.

For Bloch, the concept that "hope must be unconditionally disappointable" means that it is "open in a forward direction, in a future-oriented direction; it does not address itself to that which already exists." In this regard, the disappointability of hope ties hope to a commitment to change and transformation "rather than repetition and, what is more, incorporates the element of chance, without which there can be nothing new." According to this logic, "openness is at the same time also *kept open*." Bloch here implies that there is a kind of openness that is not fully open—that is, foreclosed in advance by predictability, programmability, or even confidence itself. To the extent that hope is not confident—that is, keeps the openness of openness open as the concept of openness itself—it belongs to the realm of the "not yet," a realm in which "not only hope's affect (with its pendant, fear) but, even more so, hope's methodology (with its pendant, memory) dwells" (341).

What is further decisive for Bloch is that within this disappointable hope "nothing has been settled yet as irrevocable fact, completed in its becoming" (341). It is here, in the refusal of hope to be dictated by a set of putative facts—facts that have not yet become what they are—that its unpredictable otherness, its future-directedness, makes itself felt. This is so, Bloch explains,

> because concrete hope does not surrender when setbacks occur; with a renegade spirit, it even gambles on whatever has been negated up to now (thereby becoming abstract once again). True disappointment, in a way

that is equally immanent, becomes wiser through injury. Not, however, through an encounter with crude facts, for these always are taken into account by well-founded hope: so much the worse for the obstructing facts. Well-founded hope, on the contrary, becomes wiser through faithful attention to the *tendency* in which the so-called facts are not standing still, but are circulating and developing. (342–343)

The relation between the factual and hope is constantly in flux because it is in hope that what could in the future be considered a fact has not yet shucked the traces of its own contingency, the various labors and discourses of interpretation and reinterpretation that will have made it what it is. Hope, then, will have been the name for the centrifugal movement of forces that will not let a "fact" simply come into its own as a form of self-identity.

The hope that is disappointable is the hope that cannot be fully annihilated. By the same token, hope as confidence or calculating certainty is the hope that can. As Bloch argues:

For if hope could be annihilated, that is, if it could literally be *made nihilistic*, it would never have proved so intractable to those despots who represent its opposite. A Ninth Symphony cannot be revoked, and the truth of its hope can never be undone: it points out, and holds open, the pathways that cannot be discredited. The same goes for genius, and for what humanity shares in genius; if it could be suppressed, Jean Paul said, it never would have existed. The history of our culture is, after all, filled with figures other than Nero and Moloch—indeed, even the death of Christ was only his beginning. (344)

The kind of hope that Bloch imagines, the kind that is radically disappointable, is a form of "transgressing" (*überschreiten*) of that which merely is or claims to be. Taking up the trope of transgression that permeates so much of his oeuvre, Bloch enlists Heraclitus, who says, "'Whoever does not hope for the unexpected will not find it.' This should be enough to invoke the call to action, according to which human existence—in the transcendental sense upon which this existence is founded—means *that which transgresses or goes beyond*" (345). We could say, then, that disappointable hope, for Bloch, is the condition of possibility for the act of transgression, not only the engagement with the border between two realms but also, in the very gesture of departing without fully knowing where one will arrive, the performance of a thinking that is always already under way and that will not take its programmed delimitation and transparent self-identity for granted.

I wish to suggest, then, that the various forms of discouragement that haunt the humanistic disciplines today deserve to be rethought in terms of the forms of hope that they harbor as their ownmost inner other. The hope with which this discouragement could be confronted, however, neither would exhaust itself in a renewed appeal to the optimism of certain enlightenment discourses nor merely would seek refuge in the view that the hope that remains is to be understood as a function of an unshakable belief in perfectibility and progress, a view, in short, that regards modernity merely as an unfinished—but in principle finishable and perfectible—project. On the contrary, the discouragement that many writers and thinkers feel today when faced with the seeming inability of their intellectual and artistic projects to effect meaningful change in the public sphere begs to be rethought from the perspective of a radical hope—that is, from the perspective of that permanent threat and perpetual promise that hover undecidably within the figure of disappointability itself. The negative knowledge that is unpredictably interjected by an undecidable disappointability into any discourse of closure and abjection prevents even the deep mourning that is born of political and personal discouragement from simply remaining itself. It has an afterlife, and it affirms the idea of a radical afterness.

For those among us who, living in the afterness of the struggle between hope and discouragement, are content neither to be confined to the role of highly educated bureaucrats nor to play the part of institutional *Wissensverwalter*, administrators of knowledge who file their reports away in creaky cabinets after each dutiful performance as an information-delivery device, this eminently disappointable hope is, for once, good news indeed. It's a *scream*.

9 Afterness and Experience (II)
Crude Thinking Rethought

As we have seen in our articulation of the relation between afterness and the experience of hope, afterness can never be an unpolitical category. Indeed, as we are now in a position to argue, there can be no concept of afterness that is not explicitly or implicitly propelled to confront its ethico-political stakes. For something to have followed something else, to have superseded it through critique, rejection, or historical succession, also involves a confrontation with the specific demands of thinking that this afterness calls into presence. To experience afterness is to open up a certain situatedness in the wake of what has come to pass, while remaining without a predetermined concept of a futurity to come.[1] The attempt to articulate the situatedness of afterness, which can never not be in a situation—extricated from the contingencies of this or that *particular form* of the after—necessitates an orientation of the after in relation to ethical and political commitments. Indeed, these issues come to the fore most urgently when the afterness in question entails a felt or an actual departure from established political regimes or norms, a departure from this or that "master narrative," as Lyotard would say, or from an order of thinking that no longer can be assumed to be self-evident. If for Carl Schmitt the concept of the political is inseparable from the distinction between friend and enemy, the question arises, in our own context, to what extent the concept of the political and the ethical demands inscribed within it are intertwined with the experiential and cognitive structure of a before and an after, a structure that engenders the very thinking of afterness. Viewed from an ethico-political perspective, what kind of a thinking would afterness require? Is there a gesture, a mode, a *style* of thinking that would attempt to do justice both to the actuality of ethico-political concerns and to the precarious demands of afterness with which they are saturated? Do some styles of thinking stand in closer proximity to afterness than others? Such questions would have to be addressed *aus der Erfahrung des Denkens*, "from out of the experience of thinking," to borrow a phrase from Heidegger.[2]

During the time of afterness, when so much has come and gone, has been assumed and left behind, at a time when so little still seems capable of really surprising us, it is perhaps not superfluous to recall that at the origin of all philosophy, all love of wisdom, lies the moment of *thaumazein*, the feeling of astonishment and wonder that gives rise to questioning and reflection. When Plato, in the rhetorical afterness that is his own preferred style, has someone who he says came before him, Socrates, say to young Theaetetus in their dialogue on the nature of wisdom and knowledge that the latter's "sense of wonder is the mark of the philosopher" and that "philosophy has indeed no other origin," he locates the primal scene of Western thought in the moment of *thaumazein*.[3] All thinking that emerges in the wake of Greek philosophy, in the afterness of thinking that the Greek invention of philosophy always will have established, must remain faithful to the experience of that event of amazement and awe, both to become what it is and to preserve, in various forms, its classical inheritance. In fact, one way of tracing the history of Western thought, and the various modes of afterness it has occasioned, would be to record the variegated articulations of, and responses to, this singular event. Because in its radical sense the event of *thaumazein* never can be predicted—what would a surprise be if I had expected it? what would amazement be if it had announced itself long before?—my particular relation to this experience can be neither preprogrammed nor anticipated. Rather, my response to the event, and even the very logic of responding, must be reinvented with each new moment of *thaumazein*, and, in a sense, philosophy, even though it always unfolds in the afterness of its Greek invention, itself must begin anew, and somewhat differently, each time. Yet, my experience of astonishment demands not only an articulation of my relation to the event that provoked it and in whose afterness I now stand, but also a consideration of the very logic and language of my response—its structure and stance as a matter of the before and the after. For instance, will I allow the event to activate in me a desire to change the world, or will I see it merely as an affirmation of what is and already ought to be? And will I allow my response to, and articulation of, the event of *thaumazein* be careful and subtle, or will it be hasty and crude?

The philosophical and political consequences at stake in my response to the afterness of the event of *thaumazein* are high. While such an event would seem to demand of those who follow a responsible departure from crude thinking, perhaps we should not yet put too fine a point on it, since there is nothing self-evident or natural about the self-imposed requirement that our thinking not be crude. To state it somewhat bluntly: the gold standard for measuring what remains of the "theoretical humanities" in an age of global corporatization is the magnitude of the unregulated ethico-political promise and transformative potential that may still reside in speculative thinking, whether or not it is realized in the variegated forms of a familiar praxis. In modern theoretical thought, at least, this potential and promise travel, in heterogeneous formulations, from Marx's eleventh thesis on Feuerbach through Gramsci's prison-house reflections on the manufacture of consent in state hegemonies and the efforts of Ernesto Laclau and Chantal Mouffe to theorize a postessentialist political sphere, to Edward Said's quasi-testimonial admonition that scholars in the humanities "not only hope, but also do."[4] The appeal of this gold standard, the distinctly political legacy of young Theaetetus's Greek inheritance, today remains palpable in a variety of discourses.

But this political standard for speculative scholarship, and thus for all responsible responses to the afterness of *thaumazein*, often has been tied to a model of thinking that subjects theoretical work to a kind of praxis-based precensorship, according to which a project is considered suspect and worthy of abandonment if the work to be carried out appears unusable as an instrument of practical intervention. As such, the concepts and figures of thought that may arise from speculative work are subjected to evaluation in advance of themselves and in advance of the futurity that they may encode but that cannot yet have been actualized as a concrete form of critique or as a manifest truth content. All of this occurs in spite of the fact that precisely those works not originally intended as revolutionary can have the most far-reaching political and epistemological consequences. Indeed, such works have, throughout intellectual history, transformed not only the thinking of this or that field but also the very way in which we think.[5] Writing produced in the theoretical humanities, like all writing, relies by definition on an imagined reader who does not yet exist, an unknown reader who may or may not one day discover the text like a message in a bottle that, as its own singular form of afterness, has washed ashore in another time and place. A stranded text such as this, its author's signature faded, is capable of signifying, if it does anything at all, apart from any consideration of its creator—that is, in the absence of any authorial control being exercised over its ethical imperatives and political marching plan. A text sent on its way in this fashion encodes the radical or wild element of afterness that is in no need of an author or an intention.

Such autonomy from authorial control means that a reader may at any time fall prey to the dictates of a certain repetition compulsion when attempting to understand the promise and potential of a text. This threat is vividly illustrated by an image presented to me as a beginning university student enrolled in a seminar with Reinhard Lettau, the late German writer and member of the fabled Group 47. Lettau explained that readers who wish to see their preexisting ideas and philosophical assumptions reproduced in every new text that they encounter behave like a man who, standing before a window that is opaque with condensation, makes a bet with himself that, if he were to wipe his hand across the pane, a swath would appear just wide enough for him to see the world outside. Then, having performed the gesture, he happily congratulates himself on having won the bet. In other words, the compulsion to perform this seductively repetitive gesture would seem to foreclose the unpredictable event of *thaumazein*.

That there is pleasure to be experienced in the enactment of this compelling gesture, in which an after may emerge as a more or less predictable before, is undeniable. Barbara Johnson's circumspect observations regarding the repetitive element in scholarly work is apropos in this regard. In an interview, she suggests:

> I think that it's like saying that from the outside someone's behavior looks like repetition, but from the inside it feels like life, or it feels like pleasure. Someone who repeatedly drinks too much or marries and divorces or buys a car and sells it for less than he paid for it. Whatever it is where you would say, This person seems to be living an absurd

and repetitive life, always falling into the same mistake. But from the inside, the way the choices keep presenting themselves are what makes the person feel that they are alive. And so, any kind of criticism that you're not involved in looks more repetitive from the outside than it feels from the inside. Not that you can't say there are some similarities and predictabilities. Take a hundred essays [of deconstructive criticism] and you would certainly find similarities, but I think that people say the same thing about Marxist criticism or about feminist criticism or about New Criticism or about religious criticism or whatever, that, in fact, the repetition comes in the way an argument concludes. Therefore, that is not of interest. What is of interest is the possibility of there being an encounter somewhere along the way of the analysis with the unexpected or the overturning of presuppositions of the argument itself. It may look as if these are not overturning the expected, but I think the whole pleasure of analysis is when you say, Wow, the text has made me see something that I really didn't see the first time. . . . Pushing the text until it tells you something you didn't already know is probably what all good criticism does.[6]

What appears like the repetitive bet I make with myself in front of a steamed-over window, the bet I cannot lose, thus also can be thought as a reading against the grain. At the same time that such a reading remains faithful to the basic assumptions and theoretical intuitions that sponsor it, it never simply repeats the very same gesture, working instead to uncover an unexpected—and therefore unknown—element that will not allow it simply to remain itself. The reading vacillates between repetition and alteration, between the repetition that also is alteration and the alteration that also is repetition. The compulsive repetition of the unlosable bet therefore can also generate a transformative kind of pleasure in which the internal alterities of a text both expose and safeguard their secret.

But no matter what form of pleasure one's speculative activity sponsors, the relation between mobilized concepts and what they may be meant to address is by no means self-evident. After all, the measuring stick for gauging the validity and usefulness of dialectical concepts and deconstructive movements of thought hardly can be how well they describe an empirical reality believed to exist independent of them. In a certain sense, they would have to be without measure: without common measure with empirical reality and even without measure as such. For, if one wanted to make this common measure and its descriptive element the sole criterion, one would have restricted any such concepts or movements of thought from the start to the enactment of a certain repetition that reproduces, if not so-called reality itself, then certainly the entrenched logic and hidden assumptions that structure the perception of this reality even when the latter powerfully suggests the opposite. If they allowed themselves to be measured by allegedly unshakable givens that are "in themselves" not open to a perpetual questioning of the very concept of having a common measure and thus to a potential unraveling, both dialectical concepts and deconstructive movements of thought would tacitly work to perpetuate precisely what they may have set out to question, inasmuch as the terms of their interventions, inscribed in afterness, would always already be dictated by, and contingent on, that with which they may have intended to break. A critical break with something then also would amount to a perpetuation of the same thing, to an undoing that is also an affirmation. Clearly, then, the relation between, on the one hand, dialectical concepts and deconstructive movements of thought and, on the other, the referential world to which they may point can itself not simply be taken for granted as something either to be celebrated or to be disowned but itself must figure as an abiding touchstone that also is to be thought and addressed even when the primary object of a thought or critique seems to be something else. But what if we wished to remain faithful to this double relation without relinquishing a *possible* relationship between one's conceptual work and a certain transformative potential that, however weakly and obscurely, the work may still harbor? The task—an infinite task, to be sure—would be to engage in an articulation of dialectical concepts and deconstructive movements of thought that would remain faithful to their radical singularity, autonomy, and otherness and *at the same time* break with that fidelity to allow us to relate to the possible and nonnaïve transformative reverberations of the material inscriptions that these thoughts and movements leave in the world.

To be sure, speculative thought, even when it addresses politically charged issues, can hardly be the space from which concrete and specific tasks are directly issued or deduced. It unfolds on the level of the concept. Another kind of thinking of politics and the political may well result in specific imperatives to effect change in the world. It unfolds on the level of praxis. But how do these two spheres *relate* to each other—even when they occur in one and the same intellectual project, perhaps even crisscrossing and touching each other there? Especially when thinking takes place in times of terrorism, reinvigorated fundamentalisms of various stripes, perpetual implementations of globalization at the expense of the true universalization of human rights and dignities, tele-technologically mediated imperialisms, and continued state-sponsored homicides and ecocides legitimated by violently renewed assertions of national sovereignties and their attendant politico-economic interests, does it not behoove us to allow our thinking to be inflected by a consideration of this relation between the two spheres? Should this thinking not be one that identifies the infinite task of thinking philosophically precisely along the lines of the radical alterities within conceptual thought that allow Deleuze and Guattari to think thinking so memorably as a form of perpetual deterritorialization?[7] Should this thinking of the relation between different kinds of thinking to each other and to praxis not also help us to meditate on the question as to how far it is possible for specialist intellectuals (critical and cultural theorists) to raise such questions in the public domain and actually get themselves heard?[8]

It certainly should. But can we ever be sure that such thinking—or any kind of thinking—is in fact under way? We recall that in his 1952 lecture "Was heißt Denken?" (What Is Called Thinking?), Heidegger worries that we are still, after everything, not thinking, have not yet learned really to think, even as the condition of the world is becoming ever more serious and therefore worthy of thought (*"fortgesetzt bedenklicher wird"*). The world's becoming ever more an object of concern and therefore of questioning seems to dictate that we act swiftly rather than only "speaking at congresses and conferences and [limiting] ourselves to merely imagining what should be and how it would have to be accomplished." However, what appears to be a lack of action rather than of thought also sponsors the possibility, at least for Heidegger, that "perhaps the conventional human being has, over the centuries, already acted too much and thought too little [*bereits zu viel gehandelt und zu wenig gedacht hat*]."[9] From this perspective, the object of a future thinking would not simply be what it thinks about but also its own state of being and its own conditions of possibility. Learning to think—and for Heidegger, this learning to think, which can be neither taken for granted nor simply completed, would be a learning to think philosophically, not merely acquiring an interest in philosophy or pursuing, say, a science, since science for Heidegger does not really think—this learning would be the learning of how to think thinking itself. In principle, there is nothing to prevent this doubly coded thinking—the thinking that thinks about something and the thinking that takes itself as its own object—from interacting in important and concrete ways with the world in which it takes place.

For all the differences between thinking thinking in terms of a fundamental ontology and thinking thinking as effects of a negative dialectic, the projects of Heidegger and of Adorno relate in the ways in which for each the potentially transformative potential of thinking thinking cannot simply be arrested by the iron collar of political conviction and the dictates of too narrowly conceived models of intervention. When during the political revolutions of the 1960s, Adorno, along with other older members of what by then was beginning to be named the Frankfurt School, was attacked for not being sufficiently committed to political struggle and, by extension, for having given in to resignation, he responded with the following lines:

> By contrast the uncompromisingly critical thinker, who neither writes over his consciousness nor lets himself be terrorized into action, is in truth the one who does not give up. Thinking is not the intellectual reproduction of what already is anyway. As long as it does not break off, thinking holds on to possibility. Its insatiability, its aversion to being easily appeased, refuses itself to the foolish wisdom of resignation. The utopian moment in thinking is all the stronger the less it—this too a form of relapse—objectifies itself into a utopia and thus sabotages its realization. Open thinking points beyond itself [*Offenes Denken weist über sich hinaus*]. For its part a behavior, a form of praxis, it is more akin to a transformative praxis than a behavior that, for the sake of praxis, does what it is told. Prior to all particular content, thinking actually is the power of resistance. . . . To be sure, such an emphatic concept of thinking is not securely anchored, neither by existing conditions nor by any goals to be reached, nor by any battalions. What has once been thought can be suppressed, forgotten, or blown away by the wind. But it cannot be denied that something of it survives. For thinking has the moment of the universal. Whatever once was rigorously thought must be thought elsewhere, by others [*Was triftig gedacht wurde, muß woanders, von anderen gedacht werden*]: this confidence accompanies even the most solitary and powerless thought. . . . The happiness that arises in the eye of the one who thinks is the happiness of humanity. The universal tendency of oppression is directed against thought as such. Thought is happiness, even where it defines unhappiness: by

articulating it. With this alone happiness reaches into universal unhappiness. Whoever will not let it wither away has not resigned.[10]

Because true thinking, even when it is situated in afterness, always points beyond itself, is always also something other than merely itself, even when it attempts to remain with itself, it remains open: open to being pointed elsewhere and open to being thought in another place and by an other. While every moment of thinking is singular—one thinks about something, even if the object of this "aboutness" of thinking is thinking as such—every moment of thinking, *as* thinking, is also universal, that is to say, singular in its universality and universal in its singularity. It affirms the universal in its singularity, and it affirms the singular in its universality, to the extent that these two modes stand in a supplementary or radically dialectical relation to each other. But because thinking is both singular in its aboutness and universal in the ways in which each singular act of thinking opens onto questions of the universal, each act of thinking makes itself available, potentially, to the other who is called on to continue to think one's particular thought and even to think one's thinking. What places acts of thinking into relation with each other is therefore the gift of excess, the gift to and from the other that hardly can be calculated in advance by this or that program or fixed ideology. It is for this reason, too, that if the thinking of thinking took place only in the name of a determined and stable model of praxis, the utopian or transformative hope that may attach to it would be cancelled. The thinking of thinking that allows itself to be determined by certain goals also betrays the thinking of thinking, and thereby thought itself. It becomes a form of instrumental reason that relies on a means–end relationship that has always already been determined and thus sealed off from true thinking and the potentially transformative effects of the thinking of thinking. Only the thinking that is non-self-identical, the thinking that thinks thinking as that which points beyond itself, would then remain faithful to the idea of transformation, the view that the last word has not been spoken and that the world could be—and indeed deserves to be—*entirely* different. The thinking of thinking, then, would indeed be a thinking without common measure. This thinking of thinking affirms the absence of a common measure that would allow us in advance to judge this or that singular act of thinking and therefore strives to preserve its weak but present hopefulness, an ephemeral prayer that could be disappointed at any moment. This thinking of thinking would not fail to remain faithful, in as yet unforeseeable ways, to everything that follows from Hölderlin's poetic question, uttered some two hundred years ago: "Is there a measure on earth? There is none [*Giebt es auf Erden ein Maaß? Es giebt keines*]."[11]

One of the many spaces in which both Adorno's concept of a thinking that points beyond itself and Heidegger's double emphasis on the thinking of something and the thinking of thinking may speak to each other—precisely by leaving behind material (and therefore potentially transformative) inscriptions—is the sphere of the aesthetic and the artworks that inhabit it. One of the most consistently effective, and in this very effectiveness perhaps even posthuman and machine-like, thinkers of the dialectic encrypts the transformative potential that may still be found in speculative thinking and in artworks when he has one of his literary characters famously say: "To be sure, it is crudely thought, but this thinking is close to reality. The main thing is to learn how to think in a crude manner. Crude thinking, that is the thinking of the great [*Es ist freilich plump gedacht, aber der Wirklichkeit ist dieses Denken sehr nahe. Die Hauptsache ist, plump denken lernen. Plumpes Denken, das ist das Denken der Großen*]."[12] Brecht's three short sentences, which read like an apodictic gloss on all his sentences, give us a lot to think, crudely or otherwise.

From the perspective of the afterness of a traditional Marxism, *plumpes Denken* of the kind that Brecht advocates is to be understood as a gesture of demystification and epistemo-political enlightenment. For instance, as early as his essay "Criticism and History" (1976), Fredric Jameson takes up what he calls a "defense of *plumpes Denken*—crude thinking," when he reminds us that, "as all real Marxists know, there is something intolerable about the use of the accusation of 'vulgar Marxism' to frighten us away from the real issues and to encourage a kind of intellectual discourse more . . . acceptable in the university." For him, it is crucial to recall that "we are always *in situation* with respect to class and ideology and cultural history . . . and that truth can never exist as a static system, but always has to be part of a more general process of *demystification*." This, Jameson continues, "is the justification and the essence of the dialectical method; and the proof is that even *plumpes Denken* takes its value from the intellectual position that it corrects—the overcomplicated Hegelianism or philosophic Marxism for which it substitutes some hard truths and plain language." Therefore, he concludes, "*plumpes Denken* is not a position in its own right either, but the demystification of some prior position from which it derives its . . . momentum and of which it comes as a genuinely Hegelian *Aufhebung*."[13] According to this model, then, *plumpes Denken* emerges as the term of a substitution rather than as a presentation or mediation: it can be entrusted with delivering, albeit in somewhat crude and reduced form, the truth content of a complex concept or movement of thought—considered to be detachable in principle from the specific and singular form of its presentation in the texts of, say, Hegel and Marx—while itself remaining relatively unaffected by this procedure. *Plumpes Denken*, as demystification, would be a straight thinking, one that gives us, as they say, the straight dope, the way things are when they have been stripped of any obscurantist complications. According to this view, *plumpes Denken* acts as a kind of police for clarity and transparency, reaching for the crudeness in its holster whenever it encounters subtleties that threaten to violate a demystificatory model of clarity, communication, and transparency. But *plumpes Denken* in this view cannot itself be thought in terms of its own internal self-differentiations—that is, in terms of the ways in which it necessarily also is traversed and conditioned by its alleged other, subtle or refined thinking. What if *plumpes Denken* were not always and crudely self-identical, as in Jameson's account, but could be opened up to the ways in which it is also at odds with itself, at once crude and subtle? And what if this being-at-odds-with-itself were not merely an embarrassing obstacle to be overcome in the recuperation and affirmation of an occluded gold standard of demystification but politically charged *in a different way*?[14]

Any such consideration should first turn to the linguistic specificity of the term *plumpes Denken* itself. To begin with, *plumpes Denken*, although readily understandable in present-day German, cannot easily be translated into contemporary idiomatic English. The German adjective *plump* has, since the end of the fifteenth century, referred to something thick, clumsy, and slow-witted, but also, in Middle Low German, to something massive and dull. Since the nineteenth century, it has acquired the more figurative meaning of "coarse" and of something importunate (as in the inappropriately coarse and overly familiar address of a presumptuous stranger who in German acts *plump vertraulich*). Having evolved onomatopoeically from the sound *plumps*, which can be heard when a massive object hits the ground, the word in modern German also can denote the sound that a person or an object makes when falling clumsily into the water (*ins Wasser plumpsen*) or onto the ground (*einen Plumps auf den Boden machen*). *Plump*, along with its Low German counterpart *plomp*, signifies what is noticeably loud and crass, unformed and unrefined, rather than what is subtle, tender, intricate, and fine—in both a physical and an intellectual sense.[15] To translate *plump* with its contemporary English cognate would perhaps be to overemphasize the aspect of thickness or podgy massiveness that the adjective implies today, if one does not also hear the massive thud that reverberates in the adjective's etymology. To translate it as "awkward" or "clumsy" would be to foreground the particular qualities of its movements, while both "crude" or "blatantly obvious" are somewhat more negatively coded in English. "Crass" or "embarrassingly overfamiliar" do not fully capture the ponderousness that *plump* also implies, while "blatant" fails to render the fallenness of *plump*, the sudden plummeting and plunging, the splashing thud or bump with which a body hits the water or the ground. These difficulties in translating *plump* are far from secondary philological considerations; they speak to the heterogeneous meanings that traverse the concept itself.

On the one hand, it is as though any translation of *plump* into contemporary English would violate the blunt coarseness of its concept because it would have to activate a subtle etymological genealogy that links the two languages in history. Such a translation of *plump* as "plump" in the older English senses would be historically erudite, conceptually subtle, and therefore at odds with what is truly *plump*. On the other hand, it is as though any translation of *plumpes Denken* could itself only be *plump*. In its very resistance to idiomatic translation, *plumpes Denken* denies itself, on the constative level, to the subtleties of a good or successful translation, while simultaneously offering itself, on the performative level, as an instantiation of the crude *plump*-ness that it names. While, on the one hand, there can be no good translation of *plumpes Denken*, on the other, there can be *only* good translations of the phrase. After all, every translation of *plumpes Denken*, no matter how bad, could also be considered a good translation to the extent that it exemplifies and stages precisely that of which the object of its translation speaks and which that object will not relinquish in any denotative and constative transfer.

If Brecht's first sentence makes a concession ("*freilich*" [to be sure]) with regard to the lack of subtlety in *plumpes Denken*, then the lack that this concession acknowledges is redeemed by the assertion that this very lack is justified because of its close relation ("*sehr nahe*") to reality. A *qualitative* assessment is thus translated into a *relational* assessment, with the latter putatively compensating for the shortcomings of the former. Could it be, then, that *plumpes Denken* only ever justifies itself *in and as translation*, even when it is not being translated into another language—that is, even when its translation occurs in the language it claims as its own?

Is not the narrative perspective from which the assertion on behalf of *plumpes Denken* is made already an expression of what it advocates? Could a thinking characterized by subtlety and refinement endorse *plumpes Denken* in this way, or would the thinking that speaks out on behalf of *plumpes Denken*—that is, the thinking that has spent considerable energy pondering various advantages and disadvantages of different modes of thinking and arrived at the conclusion that *plumpes Denken* is to be favored—not itself already be an expression of *plumpes Denken*? In that case, *plumpes Denken* could only ever endorse itself, calling for ever more instantiations, articulations, and even diagnoses of itself—to the point of the tautological threat, which itself would eventually become indistinguishable from *plumpes Denken*.

Yet *plumpes Denken*, we are told, is not merely one garden-variety form of thinking among others. Rather, it is "the thinking of the great" ("*das Denken der Großen*"). The logic that is implicitly at work here—that subtle or refined thinking is the thinking of the less-than-great or even mediocre and that only the great may think in a *plump* manner and that, perhaps, only truly *plump* thinking is worthy of occupying the great thinkers—is not entirely unrelated to the view that Heidegger articulates in his lectures on Hölderlin: that only second-rate poets are, or are concerned with being, "original."[16] Only the greats, like Hölderlin himself, are capacious enough not to be original but to be receptive to the influence of the voices of former greats. Minor poets are utterly original and therefore dull; only great ones like Hölderlin are capable of receiving the voice of a Sophocles and of allowing other, previous voices to resonate in them prosopopoeiacally. They live and think their afterness fully. Just as, according to this logic, to be great is to be unoriginal and capable of being influenced and spoken through by the great dead or absent ones, so to be a truly great thinker is to be *plump* rather than subtle or refined. Subtlety of thought would be reserved for the speculative bench of reserve players and lesser talents.

The paradox of *plumpes Denken* is that when one attempts to theorize it, it is no longer simply *plump*. It cannot withstand that kind of afterness. One must perform it without reflecting on it too much, without thinking about it too much. It is thus a kind of thinking without thinking, a thinking that also refuses thinking, a thinking that is both an affirmation and a foreclosure of thinking. If we are given the task of learning to think in a *plump* manner— the "main thing is to learn how to think in a crude [or *plump*] manner [*Die Hauptsache ist, plump denken lernen*]"—then the learning we are to accomplish is both a conscious, thinking form of learning and a nonthinking, not fully conscious form of learning, since too much thinking or theorizing about thinking would stand in contradiction to the very thinking that is to be learned. It may hence be no accident that the main thing, "*die Hauptsache*," is not thinking in a *plump* manner but *learning* to think in a *plump* manner, as if, once the learning of *plump* thinking were actually accomplished, the thinking no longer would be exclusively and purely *plump*. In that case, having learned *plumpes Denken* once and for all, one also would lose the learning of it immediately and, by extension, *plumpes Denken* itself.[17]

Yet, one may legitimately wonder, from a different perspective, whether the learning of *plumpes Denken* must indeed also be *plump*—that is, reproduce the qualities of what it is meant to enable one to learn—or if *plumpes Denken* also can be learned by means of considerable subtlety of thought. In the latter case, the desired outcome of subtle thinking would be, in its completion, *plumpes Denken*; and, by extension, there could only be *plumpes Denken* where there once was rather subtle thinking, that is, the kind of thinking that first enabled one to learn what it means to think in a truly *plump* manner, as only "the greats" can.

In a 1935 essay, Benjamin, Brecht's friend and houseguest in Danish exile, remarks on how the passage on *plumpes Denken*, in its italicization, interrupts his friend's novel to draw attention to its own status as presentation, similar to the way an illustration functions. As an interruption, the passage transforms both what it interrupts and any thinking that would unfold "after" this interruption. Of *plumpes Denken*, Benjamin then writes:

> There are those who imagine a dialectician as a lover of subtleties. So it is uncommonly useful when Brecht puts his finger on the "crude thinking" [*plumpes Denken*] that dialectics produces as its antithesis, engulfs within itself, and needs. Crude thoughts belong especially to the household of dialectical thinking because they present nothing else but the directing of theory toward practice [*die Anweisung der Theorie auf die Praxis*]. Toward practice, not for it [*Auf die Praxis, nicht an sie*]: taking action can, of course, turn out as subtly as thinking. But a thought must be crude to receive its due in action.
>
> The forms of crude thinking change slowly, for they were created by the masses. We can learn even from extinct forms. One of these we encounter in the proverb, and the proverb is a school of crude thinking [*eine Schule des plumpen Denkens*].[18]

Benjamin's dialectical reading of *plumpes Denken* stages itself as a dialectic as well. It cannot be decided, based on his grammar, whether *plumpes Denken* produces a dialectic as its other, the other that it requires and houses within itself, or whether, conversely, the dialectic produces and houses *plumpes Denken* as its necessary other. The relationship of dialectical thinking to *plumpes Denken* is thus itself dialectical, and the two cannot proceed in simple isolation from each other. *Plumpes Denken* belongs to dialectical thinking, in Benjamin's reading, because it points theory to praxis (*"Anweisung der Theorie auf die Praxis"*), rather than having theory give commands to praxis (*"Anweisung der Theorie an die Praxis"*). *Auf die Praxis* versus *an die Praxis*: Benjamin's serious play with his prepositions marks the difference between the concept of a sovereign and autonomous theory that resolutely provides praxis with specific modes of intervention and a different concept, that of theory which, dethroned from its position of absolute mastery, must itself be reminded that it is connected to, and does not stand in mere opposition to, praxis. It is only here, in the dialectical play of these two concepts of theory, that action can emerge, potentially, as something as subtle as thinking itself. While there is nothing to justify the view that acting must be less subtle than thinking, thinking, even of the subtle variety, can come into its own as a form of praxis only when it stages itself in accordance with the precepts of *plumpes Denken*. If the proverb is a school of *plumpes Denken*, then the graduates of this proverbial school have learned that they never can be sure that any given act of thinking belongs squarely either to what is *plump* or to what is subtle and dialectically refined. Insisting on the detected difference too triumphantly only would be another form of *plumpes Denken*.

Having graduated, perhaps with the help of some extra-credit conceptual work, from this proverbial school of *plumpes Denken*, it is necessary for us to consider the possibility that *plumpes Denken* does not leave even a reflecting about it unaffected. What will it have meant to have thought in a *plump* manner, both for *plumpes Denken* and for the thinking that thinks about it?

Because *plumpes Denken* cannot be explained without activating the possibility of its being transformed into its opposite without its explanations explaining why it cannot be explained and why the explanations of its inexplicability not only depart from the giving of this or that explanation but also depart from the blind assumption that an explanation simply is opposed to a nonexplanation in the face of the inexplicable. Following the logic of Giorgio Agamben's reading of Kafka, we could even say that "explanations are . . . only a moment in the tradition of the inexplicable: they are the moment . . . which keeps watch over it by leaving it unexplained. Emptied of their content, explanations thus fulfill their task. But at the point where explanations, by showing their emptiness, leave it be, the inexplicable itself is in jeopardy.

Only the explanations were, in truth, inexplicable," so that what "was to be explained is perfectly contained in what no longer explains anything."[19] What no longer explains anything, such as the explanation that would venture to give a conceptual account of *plumpes Denken*, would then be no longer simply the absence of a desired explanation but at the same time the continued presence of what is to be explained, harbored in the articulations and disarticulations of those explanations that are strictly inoperative. *Plumpes Denken* perpetually opens and seals off the explanations that make it what it is, living on within the citable gesture of what perpetually is adduced—but never fails to fail—to explain it.

Seen in this light, the incessant movement of revealing and retreating that is *plumpes Denken* sponsors an infinite conversation, a limitless afterness, in which thinking itself becomes the theme of aesthetic production. In his meditation on the relationship among thinking, time, modernity, and the work of art, Lyotard argues: "Being prepared to receive what thought is not prepared to think is what deserves the name of thinking."[20] The thinking of *plumpes Denken* that becomes thinkable in the aporetic terms outlined here offers us, if it is capable of doing anything at all, a receptiveness that paves the way for a preparedness for what thought is not normally prepared to think. Being prepared to receive—which is not the same as merely receiving or knowing that receiving will indeed occur—that which eludes thought because thought is not prepared for it returns thinking to itself, to the core at which thinking is at odds with itself. The realm of the aesthetic, including the novel in which Brecht sets *plumpes Denken* into motion, may be thought as the space in which such thinking performs itself—not a space in which an autonomous subject sovereignly thinks thinking in this sense, but a space in which thinking itself comes to pass, not unlike the thinking that takes place in Heidegger's haunting confession: "*Es denkt in mir. Ich kann mich nicht dagegen wehren*" ("It thinks within me," or "There is thinking going on within me. I cannot fight it").[21] Both artistic production itself and all critical commentary on that production work to open up a space in which the aporetic forms of *plumpes Denken* are exposed as thinking is permitted to perform itself.

What *plumpes Denken* ultimately would require of us in the uncontainable Greek event of *thaumazein* and its afterness would also be to remain faithful to its opposite, subtlety and refined thinking, without simply betraying crude thinking. Because any explanation of *plumpes Denken* already partially will have betrayed it, we may think of *plumpes Denken* as that which we do without quite knowing how to do it and while, at the same time, also doing the opposite. If they could be fathomed at all, philosophical positions and even artworks based on such a model of crude thinking would have the qualities that Adorno once declared to be music's concrete possibility; like Kant's perpetual peace, it *theoretically* could be realized but it also is an Idea. For Adorno, the "form of all artistic utopias today is: doing or making things of which we know nothing of what they are [*Die Gestalt aller künstlerischen Utopie heute ist: Dinge machen, von denen wir nicht wissen, was sie sind*]."[22] To do and make things that we do not know requires that we remain open to their afterness as well as to the unpredictable significations of their futurity. Coming after without having overcome, knowing it and not knowing it at the same time, we both honor and betray the infinite responsibility of having to explain ourselves and our thinking without quite knowing how, of having to give an account of what it is we are doing or creating even when that something resists our efforts at explanation. It is in the context of the urgent struggle to come to terms with this resistance that certain forms of *plumpes Denken*, as an afterness yet to come, perhaps still require to be thought, spoken of, and practiced. Hopefully without measure, but not without measureless hope.

10 *Afterness and Experience (III)*
Mourning, Memory, and the Fictions of Anteriority

> Of the two springs called Mnemosyne and Lethe, which is the right one for Narcissus? The other.
> —Jacques Derrida, *Memoires for Paul de Man*

In a remarkable letter to Käthchen Schönkopf, a former love interest, on December 12, 1769, the young Goethe records a description of her as she appeared in his guilt-ridden dream the night before. Having failed to respond to her most recent missive for what suddenly seemed like an eternity, his sleep was fitful: "A dream last night reminded me that I owe you an answer. It is neither as though I had forgotten entirely, nor as though I never think of you; no, my friend, every day tells me something of you and of my debts." Goethe continues:

> But it is strange—and this is an experience with which you may be familiar—time does not erase our memory of absent ones but it does conceal them. Our life's diversions, our making the acquaintance of new things, in short, every change in our condition, do to our heart what dust and smoke do to a painting; they render the subtle traits wholly unrecognizable and the strong ones less visible, all in a manner so unnoticeable that one does not even know how it comes about. A thousand

things remind me of you, I see your image a thousand times, but so weakly and often with so little sentiment as if I were thinking of a stranger.[1]

Even the image of the beautiful head of Fräulein Schönkopf, the woman whom Goethe privately referred to as his "first girl" and with whom he had ended his courtship almost two years earlier, proves no match for the effects of time on memory. While memory requires time to become what it is—no memory without time, no time without memory—time also hinders memory, veiling its specificities, blurring its details, accentuating too selectively and, in so doing, uncannily rendering the familiar strange while, at the same time, causing the estranged gradually to appear more and more familiar. Like the painting whose original vibrancy is covered over time with the sediments of life, the image of the other in memory lives on, submerged beneath ever-thickening layers of temporality and finitude. These memories, however, cannot be delivered from their fate in the way that the colors of Michelangelo's frescoes on the ceiling of the Sistine Chapel have been returned to their alleged sixteenth-century intensity, since memory cannot happen without the obscuring layers of time and dusty markers of mortality. To the extent that memory occurs—at least the kind of memory that is perceived as being "individual" or more experientially inflected than what in late modernity, perhaps too hastily, is called "collective" or "cultural" memory—this memory depends on the very effects of time that also threaten its undoing. *Memory and afterness are constitutive of each other.*

The double movement by which the afterness of memory is constructed and obscured, built and dismantled, offered and withheld is one of the multiple names—but not just any name—that Derrida bestows on the project of deconstruction. Questions of memory, remembrance, recalling, living on, forgetting, retrieving, losing, saving, surviving, and mourning traverse his work, in heterogeneous modulations, from *Of Grammatology* in the late 1960s onward. In a conversation with Anne Berger, Derrida makes explicit the centrality of the trope and experience of memory for his entire project, explaining that

> if there were an experience of loss at the heart of all this, the only loss for which I could never be consoled and that brings together all the others, I would call it loss of memory. The suffering at the origin of writing for me is the suffering from the loss of memory, not only forgetting

or amnesia, but the effacement of traces. I would not need to write otherwise; my writing is not in the first place a philosophical writing or that of an artist, even if, in certain cases, it might look like that or take over from these other kinds of writing. My first desire is not to produce a philosophical work or a work of art: it is to preserve memory.

Therefore, he confesses, "I struggle against this loss, this loss of memory."[2] Neither philosophy nor poetry, neither logic by itself nor rhetoric in isolation, Derrida's undertaking is touched by the stringent and ethical demands of each. He sees his writing both as an enactment of and a self-conscious resistance to the eradication of the trace, the very precondition of legibility and, by extension, the concept of meaning itself. Like a reader of Goethe's vanishing mnemonic image, Derrida conceptualizes his work, in all its multiplicities and refractions, as the attempt to preserve a memory and memory itself, even if that memory is but the faint outline of an absence, mere remnants of the ashen traces of a genocidal burning that he evokes, in all their melancholia but also in their potentially affirmative future-directedness, in his book *Cinders*. The trace of Derrida's itinerary always moves, as David Farrell Krell reminds us, from the buoyant phenomenological credo, *zu den Sachen selbst* (to the things themselves) toward the ashen remains of its anagrammatic version, *zu den Aschen selbst*.[3] The minute anagrammatic transposition of the letters "s" and "a" announces deconstruction's epic theater. We even could say that the trace, ashen or otherwise, that for Derrida connects the material practice of his work with its ethico-political impetus is visible in the movement from the Greek sense of *philosophia*, the "love of wisdom," to a certain *mnemophilia*, the "love of memory." The practice of mnemophilia involves a striving to come to terms with the threat of a potentially inconsolable loss, a relation to the object of memory without which writing's ethical, historical, political, and personal commitments would be erased.

But can a kind of thinking be imagined that strives to retain its speculative rigor while answering first to the stringent demands of its mnemonic commitment rather than to the classical labor of the concept? As Nietzsche warns us in *Human, All Too Human*, "many do not become thinkers merely because their memory is too good."[4] He may have had in mind, among other things, paragraph 464 of the *Encyclopedia*, where Hegel remarks that it is no accident that youths possess a better memory than older people, because youth "does not yet behave in a thinking manner [*sich noch nicht nachdenklich verhält*]."[5] In this view, thinking and remembering are at odds with each other such that an overly acute memory impedes the kind of rigorous and self-reflexive thought that would clear the mind of mnemonic debris. Nietzsche seems to suggest, *pace* Hegel, that memory—the very thing Derrida wishes to preserve—stands in the way of true thinking. Understood in the Heideggerean sense, even before Heidegger, Nietzsche advocates a kind of innovative movement of thought that is not at all confined to the limits of conventional, and institutionalized, philosophizing, but that instead accepts the challenge of inventing its own methods each time it encounters a new object or question—that is to say, each time it allows itself to redefine what truly rigorous thinking is and calls for. His target, though, is the concept of memory that informs a nineteenth-century Germanic historicism, whose unacknowledged aim frequently was the nationalistic endorsement of a history of linearity and continuity in the service of a largely affirmative, unquestioning engine of totalizing consciousness. This kind of memory prevents the actualization of a new thinking. Believing itself to know too much already, it is weighed down by the sheer facticity of its empirical attachments. Such memory cannot think the to-come of thinking because it is shackled by a predictable future in much the same way that Bill Murray's character in the film *Groundhog Day* is condemned to wake up, day after day, to the historical sameness of the identical day, without being able to change it.

Derrida's notion of memory, by contrast, does not simply reproduce what is assumed, or once was assumed, simply to be present, ready to be passed on to a new generation of heirs and epigones. Rather, encouraging himself and us to learn to accept an inheritance—as, for instance, the inheritance of Marx's oppositional spirit in *Specters of Marx*—Derrida's writing works to define and perpetually to redefine the meaning of inheriting without following, the meaning of accepting without repeating, the meaning of following even by betraying, and the meaning of setting to work an idea even while taking it in a different direction.[6] His work asks again and again how we can show ourselves responsible to a memory whose laws we have not fully understood, whose history escapes us, and yet whose ethico-political requirements already have reached us, as though always already emanating from the transcendence of the wholly other that his interlocutor Levinas so often evoked.

No overall summary of Derrida's "concept" of memory could responsibly reduce the multiple singularities of its iterations from *Of Grammatology* onward to a well-defined, single meaning. As Gasché reminds us, Derrida's "singular reworking of traditional forms of thinking . . . always escapes for essential reasons any essentialist determination." Instead, readers are enjoined to "seek in his writings precisely those structures that singularize, extend, and overflow any totalization," thereby rendering these texts as stages on which "an ever incalculable and unpredictable response" may be performed.[7] It is no different with the vexed and elusive question of memory. With these caveats in mind, which also always are promises, we may turn to two specific texts in which Derrida further elaborates the multiple relationships of memory to his project of thinking and writing: the series of lectures entitled *Memoires for Paul de Man* (1984) and the collection *The Work of Mourning* (2001), which gathers essays, addresses, and meditations written shortly after the death of a friend or colleague over a period of some twenty years. A perpetual and obsessive engagement with the uncontainable logic of memory itself is performed in language each time memory is evoked as though we already knew what the word meant:

> What is memory? If the essence of memory maneuvers between Being and the law, what sense does it make to wonder about the being and the law of memory? These are questions that cannot be posed outside language, questions that cannot be formulated without entrusting them to transference and translation, above the abyss. For they require, from one language to another, impossible passageways: the fragile resistance of a span. What is the meaning of the word "mémoire(s)" in French, in its masculine and feminine forms (*un mémoire, une mémoire*); and in its singular and plural forms (*un mémoire, une memoire, des mémoires*). If there is no meaning outside memory, there will always be something paradoxical about interrogating "*mémoire*" as a unit of meaning, as that which links memory to narrative or to all the uses of the word "histoire" (story, history, *Historie, Geschichte*, etc.).[8]

The figurative and allegorical investments of memory in its various articulations preclude any totalization; memory always will have been that whose pastness, present claims, and future-oriented commitments pull it elsewhere, to a different time and space, a different language, a different nation, a different politics.

Meditating, inconsolably, on the passing of his friend Paul de Man, Derrida in *Memoires* places memory and mourning into philosophical and experiential relation. While there can be "no singular memory,"[9] no mnemonic act or object that would once and for all shuck the traces of its multiple contingencies, the uncontainable memories that bear upon us, traverse and haunt us, are nevertheless connected by a double affirmation: the "yes, yes." The double affirmation works to authorize itself in that the second affirmation, the second "yes," always seconds the first yes, sanctioning it, giving it legitimacy. The validity of the first "yes," its structure as a promise, can be confirmed and countersigned only by another "yes" that remains to come; that is, it must defer its validation to a future act that remains bound in the promise of its very first utterance. The second affirmation of the "yes, yes" acts to "preserve memory; it must commit itself to keeping its own memory; it must promise itself to itself; it must bind itself to memory for memory, if anything is ever to come from the future."[10] What Derrida names the "alliance between memory and the seal of the 'yes, yes'" can be said to reside, in different formulations and manifestations, "at the heart of deconstruction."[11] The inscription of the initial "yes," whether in written or spoken form, or in texts and situations of any kind, must carry within itself the ashen trace of its erasability—not that it will be erased of necessity, nor that it will survive intact, but rather that its very performance is contingent on its possible disappearance. When he says that we "cannot write what we do not wish to erase, we can only promise it in terms of what can always be erased," and that "otherwise, there would be neither memory nor promise," Derrida shows us that the very person or thing that is to be remembered, by virtue of the awareness of mortality on which existence is predicated, carries its own memory within itself.[12]

One of the central wagers of *Memoires for Paul de Man* is that this alliance between the doubly affirmative memory and the work of deconstructive thought is inextricably bound up with the experience of an impossible mourning. Derrida argues that we can enter a friendship—and, by extension, meditate on it in memory—only to the extent that we acknowledge our own finitude and the finitude of the friend. The two friends encounter each other as mortal beings, as bearers of a signature that one day will have been signed in a prosopopoeiac gesture from beyond the grave. As he writes:

> If there is a finitude of memory, it is because there is something of the other, and of memory as a memory of the other, which comes from the other and comes back to the other. It defies any totalization, and directs us to a scene of allegory, to prosopopeia, that is, to tropologies of mourning: to the memory of mourning and to the mourning for memory. This is why there can be no true mourning, even if truth and lucidity always presuppose it, and in truth, take place only as the truth of mourning.[13]

Like the mourning that memory evokes in us, the memory that mourning leaves behind for us resists the imposition of closure and the stability of a relation defined once and for all. Instead, the mourning of memory and the memory of mourning require of us an impossible affirmation, one that cannot anymore be spelled out in advance than it can proceed according to the curriculum of a described sequence, or be implemented in accordance with an eye toward full transparency. It is the thought of the mortal other that I bear within me, and whose bearing within me exhibits me to myself as an other who is linked to other others in his mortality, whose memory always will have been that of the one who can die and who is capable of being entrusted with an other's memory of his or her mortality.

The poetry of Hölderlin, texts to which both Derrida and de Man, like Hegel and Heidegger before them, often return, is in many ways a sustained engagement with this memory of the other's mortality. In the poem "Die Titanen" (1802–1806), the lyrical voice submits: *"Gut ist es, an andern sich // Zu halten. Denn keiner trägt das Leben allein"* (It is good to rely on others [or to orient oneself toward others]. For no one bears [or carries] life alone).[14] Derrida himself cites the second of these lines in the final sentence of his 2003 memorial lecture for Gadamer on dialogue and poetry at the University of Heidelberg.[15] The responsible memory of the friend, never responsible enough and always too responsible for its own good, propels us to interrogate this Hölderlinian concept of bearing or carrying. What does it mean to bear life not alone but always together, through, and jointly with an other, even an otherness? What is this being-with, the "with-ness" and witness of life, of bearing life that attaches us to the other and his memory? But Hölderlin's lines, *"Denn keiner trägt das Leben allein"* (For no one bears [or carries] life alone), also can be read to mean that no one bears or carries within himself only life (*das* Leben *allein*, in the sense of *nur das Leben*), which is to say, that we always also carry death within us and among us as friends. Our relation to the other, to the memory of the friend, thus always is characterized by a communal bearing or a mutual carrying *and* by the prospects or memory of sadness, finitude, and mourning.

Derrida reflects on these questions both theoretically in his philosophical writings devoted to finitude and mourning and experientially in his more personally inflected texts devoted to recently deceased friends and colleagues in *The Work of Mourning*. These include eulogies and meditations on such dead friends as Barthes, de Man, Foucault, Althusser, Kofman, Deleuze, Levinas, and Lyotard. More recently, these texts were joined by ones on the East German playwright Heiner Müller and on Gadamer.[16] There are also meditations on the losses of family members, such as Derrida's reflections on his experience of the dying and eventual death of his mother in "Circumfession," a text printed in the lower margins of a book about Derrida written by a friend, Geoffrey Bennington—where the reader is confronted with two competing and supplementary texts on each page, the one explicating Derrida, the other written by Derrida himself, embracing, affirming, protesting, clarifying, supplementing, and memorializing the voice of the friend.[17] Leaving the word to someone else—*jemandem das Wort überlassen*, as one says in German—letting the other speak instead of oneself, and yet continuing to think and write with and for that other is the act of memory and mourning par excellence.

If the law of friendship is the law of mourning and memory, there can be no friendship without the permanent possibility and threat of mourning. One cannot die together with the friend—two can die at the same time, but not really, in the deepest sense, together, as in Kafka's melancholic diction, in "The Judgment," where a son and a father are described as eating their meal *gleichzeitig* (simultaneously) rather than *zusammen* (together). Our friendships will always have been conditioned by the future absence of the other, even of the self in the other, and by the fact that one of us inevitably will be left behind to bury, to mourn, to commemorate the other, situated among the friends who have been left behind, the survivors who are now left to walk all alone, in memory of the other. While Derrida works to formulate a series of axioms and laws that respond to the structures of friendship as mourning and finitude, he also reminds us that each death of a friend is singular, each time, as he puts it, the end of the world. Our friends, whether dead or alive, are thus both absolutely singular and unique, and at the same time connected to one another through the possibility and prospect of their and our shared finitude, a finitude that sooner or later will give rise to the tear of memory, of mourning, and of commemoration.

This tear of mourning and of memory flows in a passage from "The Taste of Tears" (1990), a text written on the occasion of the death of Derrida's friend Jean-Marie Benoist, There, we read:

> To have a friend, to look at him, to follow him with your eyes, to admire him in friendship, is to know in a more intense way, already injured, always insistent, and more and more unforgettable, that one of the two

of you will inevitably see the other die. One of us, each says to himself, the day will come when one of the two of us will see himself no longer seeing the other and so will carry the other within him a while longer, his eyes following without seeing, the world suspended by some unique tear, each time unique, through which everything from then on, through which the world itself—and this day will come—will come to be reflected quivering, reflecting disappearance itself: the world, the whole world, the world itself, for death takes from us not only some particular life within the world, some moment that belongs to us, but, each time, without limit, someone through whom the world, and first of all our own world, will have opened up in a both finite and infinite—mortally infinite—way. That is the blurred and transparent testimony borne by this tear, this small, infinitely small, tear, which the mourning of friends passes through and endures even before death, and always singularly so, always irreplaceably.[18]

The questions toward which Derrida asks us to open up revolve around the memory and mourning that the tear, this time not an ashen but a translucent trace, inscribes in our relation to the other and his or her mortality. The tear, veiling the eye and withdrawing vision, is the forbidden taste of passing. What will the relation between the tear and the memory of the friend have signified? The tear of mourning forms even before the empirical death of the friend because, from the beginning, the relation to that friend was touched by finitude and mortality. The memory and mourning of the friend passes through the tear, and the tear, as that which binds all friends in a community without community, is always already both singular and universal. If one must never taste a tear because the act of tasting the tear is an attempt to reappropriate or reannex the other, the tear also is the very figure of that which, within me, always already was other, an otherness that makes me who I am.

The potential reappropriation or reannexation of the other in mourning is inflected by the ways in which the very process of memory is conceptualized. In *Memoires*, Derrida therefore reminds us of de Man's interest in the distinction between two types of memory that worry Hegel in paragraphs 460 to 464 of the *Encyclopedia*. In German, there are two different words for "memory," *die Erinnerung* and *das Gedächtnis*. *Erinnerung*, in that its etymology has evolved from the phrase *er innert*, which literally means "he inners" or "he interiorizes," bespeaks a kind of incorporative or interiorizing memory, a memory that emphasizes an experiential relation of the self as the object of its mnemonic act, an act that works through annexation and psychic appropriation. *Gedächtnis*, by contrast, is a thinking kind of memory, one that emphasizes the etymology of the term that relates it to *denken* (thinking) and *der Gedanke* (thought). (Elsewhere, Heidegger points to the significance of the relation between *denken* and *danken* [thanking] that propel both *der Gedanke* and, by extension, *das Gedächtnis*.) As Hegel writes, "*das Gedächtnis* in this way is the transition into the activity of thought [*Tätigkeit des Gedankens*]."[19] *Die Erinnerung* is the kind of memory that touches me as a form of emotional experience, but it is prereflexive, precritical; *das Gedächtnis* is the memory that sponsors reflection—that is, calls for thinking about both its object and the very logic by which that thinking occurs as a mnemonic act. *Die Erinnerung* always already has posited a self's relation to its memory and to the object of its mnemonic act: it propels the self to incorporate the object of the mnemonic act so that it becomes coextensive with it. *Das Gedächtnis* is always ahead of itself, in search of a new relation, always in need of articulating, through the labor of the concept, just *how* it should relate to the object of its mnemonic act, a relation that, as a form of perpetual reflection, it cannot take for granted once and for all.

Bracketing the question as to whether de Man's reading of this structure as it is set to work in Hegel ultimately gets the distinction right and leaving open the question of whether Derrida correctly understands de Man's reading of Hegel, what should interest us here is what Derrida understands Hegel's and de Man's interest in the distinction between *die Erinnerung* and *das Gedächtnis* implies for the twin projects of memory and deconstruction.[20] Here, Derrida reminds us that, based on de Man's understanding, the "relation between *Gedächtnis* and *Erinnerung*, between memory and interiorizing recollection, is not 'dialectical,' as Hegelian interpretations and Hegel's interpretation would have it, but one of rupture, heterogeneity, disjunction."[21] As Derrida therefore emphasizes, we can read the failure of memory's "apparent negativity, its very finitude, what affects its experience of discontinuity and distance, as a power, as the very opening of difference."[22] This view leads him to the suggestion that if "art is a thing of the past, this comes from its link, through writing, the sign, *tekhnè*, with that thinking memory, that memory without memory, with that power of *Gedächtnis* without *Erinnerung*. This power, we now know, is *pre-occupied* by a past which has never been present and will never allow itself to be reanimated in the interiority of consciousness."[23] We see in Derrida's argument his insistence on the way in which memory is not a form of recuperation or restoration of a past that once was assumed to be present or even of a past, imagined or not, that claims our attention for its own sake. Rather, just as *das Gedächtnis*, never able to benefit from the comforts of interiorization, perpetually must revisit and reformulate its own relationality to the object of its mnemonic thinking and even to thinking itself, memory as a radical form of *Gedächtnis* is directed toward the future. To recognize that its "proper" form always remains still to come also is to acknowledge that memory is not simply a form of afterness but rather an elusive encounter between the "after" of something that never was present and a futurity that has not yet been thought.

The Hegelian distinction between *Gedächtnis* and *Erinnerung* as it figures in de Man provides Derrida with the occasion to interrogate memory's temporality or genealogy as it occupies, of necessity, any discourse on memory. One might inquire into the status of the mnemonic object or idea in relation to a thinking and recollecting self—but who will this self have been if not the Hölderlinean bearer of the other?—that, in spite of its acknowledgment of the concept of a present that is not really present or accessible in any transparent or lucid fashion, nevertheless wonders about the other-directedness of its mnemonic investments. Here, the reality of the mnemonic subject cannot be reduced to the perception of its presence. The recollecting self, the self that exists to the extent that it remembers, always also is invested elsewhere, in a complex network of overlapping and only sporadically conscious commitments. Psychoanalysis, as the study of decentered consciousness, of a lost self-mastery one never possessed, speaks of nothing else. We may recall the rather kitschy film *The Story of Us* (1999), which is redeemed by one brief and brilliant scene. The two protagonists, a constantly warring husband and wife portrayed by Bruce Willis and Michelle Pfeiffer, are shown sitting next to each other in bed, engaged in yet another of their frequent arguments. After we see the couple quarreling in a medium close-up, the camera pans out to show that, next to both Willis and Pfeiffer, their sets of parents are perched in bed with them, arguing along. We realize that these parents are not really sitting in bed with the fighting couple—though, from the empirical standpoint of the rolling camera, they are—but rather that their otherwise unacknowledged influence over their respective offspring, their attitudes, wishes, and complaints, continues to determine the lives of these now-adult children in uncontrollable and ghostly ways. The "reality" and "presence" of the bickering husband and wife is overdetermined by the ghostly order of discourses that are not present as such but nevertheless are real. The intricate and elusive memories of a childhood long in the past tense, mostly unconscious, continue to structure a reality that believes itself to have declared its independence from them.

Yet, while even our mainstream cultural consciousness appears prepared to concede that one's historical and psychological reality cannot be reduced to presence in the sense of a reality structured by visibility and concreteness, we may be more reluctant to follow Derrida's challenge to the metaphysics of presence in the other direction—that is, toward the past. As he writes in his reading of de Man, the "memory we are considering here is not essentially oriented toward the past, toward a past present deemed to have really and previously existed. Memory stays with traces, in order to 'preserve' them, but traces of a past that has never been present, traces which themselves never occupy the form of presence and always remain, as it were, to come." Therefore, Derrida continues, "resurrection, which is always the formal element of 'truth,' a recurrent difference between a present and its presence, does not resuscitate a past which had been present; it engages the future."[24] According to this logic, then, the act and object of memory is not recuperation of something that once was, because this would presuppose that, even though the present is not fully present in the present, it once was present to itself as presence, in the past. This view, a kind of inverted eschatology of the mnemonic, would view the past presentness of the present with a nostalgic longing for the resurrection of a lost presence, a present that once granted access to presence in a way that the current present, to the extent that it no longer is coextensive with the past, has forgotten or unlearned.

What might be named the afterness of memory, then, would have to come to terms with the difficult double movement by which it is both imbricated with the past and simultaneously divorced from it. That is to say, the "after" of the afterness of memory cannot view itself in terms of a relation to a former presence that it now claims to follow. This is why "there is only memory but strictly speaking, the past does not exist," which is to say that it "will never have existed in the present, never been present."[25] The afterness of memory, rigorously conceived, then would have to divorce itself from a certain "fiction of anteriority" with an eye toward accepting its uneasy relation to what is to come, to the futurity of its trajectory.[26]

We may recall here Heidegger's remark, transcribed in his 1936/1937 seminar on Schiller's *Letters on the Aesthetic Education of Mankind* and discussed in chapter 5, that the purpose of the seminar is not "to find the appropriate place of Schiller in intellectual history" or to read his texts with a "general historical intention that aims to know what happened *back then*, but rather to ask for ourselves and that means for the *future* [*sondern wir fragen für uns und d.h. für die* Zukunft]."²⁷ To ask for ourselves—"*wir fragen für uns*"—does not mean shunning historical knowledge or genealogical insight for the sake of an aggressive and ill-informed presentism that knows no historical awareness or has no *Geschichtssinn*, or "historical sensibility," as German eighteenth-century writers like to say. Rather, Heidegger suggests that the act of reading in the present, that is, carefully and with a rigorous eye, is an act for the future—*für uns, d.h. die Zukunft*; to read for oneself, to think, recollect, mourn, understand, write, create, affirm, protect, criticize, or love something or someone now, for us, here, is to affirm a future, insofar as all these acts remain promises that will need to be reaffirmed always one more time, always in memory of what is still to come. Like Heidegger's remark at the beginning of his Schiller seminar—*für uns, d.h. die Zukunft*—Derrida's understanding of the act of memory cannot be thought in isolation from the ways in which it will not turn its back on the future, even when it seems to face the past through a series of fictions of anteriority.

The mnemonic act, thus conceived, resides in an afterness that has as its object the futurity with which it is not yet familiar, a time that remains open and, of necessity, to come. An analysis of the fiction of anteriority as it inflects memory and its various concepts would strive to articulate the ways in which remembrance, recollection, memorializing, and recalling are eminently future-directed—that is, performed not for their own sake, or for the comforting resurrection of an assumed past presence or presenced past, but rather in the name of something else, something that by definition cannot yet have been articulated, cannot yet have assumed the promise and burden of a proper name. The afterness of memory, then, is really the open futurity that our acts of mourning and remembrance so often consider, even with the best of intentions, merely to belong to the presence of the past. Here, in mourning the afterness of the mnemonic "after," the ethical implications of a deconstructive politics of memory may begin to assume form: the future of memory and the memory that there is a future—that is, for us.

11 *Afterness and Empty Space*
No Longer and Not Yet

As the German word *Zeitraum*, which, idiomatically translated, indicates a period of time but literally means "time-space," suggests, time not merely is *related* to space but also can be thought, somewhat curiously, as *having* a space. Having come in the course of this book on a long journey through heterogeneous engagements with and articulations of the after—from the Greek *krinein* via the rhetoric of *Nachfolge* in Kant's third *Critique* and the afterness of translation in Heidegger all the way to Derrida's analysis of mourning and the fictions of anteriority—we might now ask if the after is situated not only temporally but also spatially. Can afterness have a space? If so, how could its space be thought?

In her 1946 review essay, published in the *Nation*, of the English translation of Austrian modernist Hermann Broch's magisterial novel *The Death of Virgil*, Hannah Arendt seeks to articulate, in relation to a literary text, the peculiar logic and unsettling experience of an afterness that feels itself to reside somewhere in between the past and the future, in a peculiar space that nevertheless cannot simply be considered the presence of a now or the prelude to what is to come. She names this scene of abandonment "empty space." Evoking David Hume, Arendt writes:

> Hume once remarked that the whole of human civilization depends upon the fact that "one generation does not go off the stage at once and another succeed, as is the case with silkworms and butterflies." At some turning-point of history, however, at some heights of crisis, a fate similar to that of silkworms and butterflies may befall a generation of men. For the decline of the old, and the birth of the new, is not necessarily an affair of continuity; between the generations, between those who for some reason or other still belong to the old and those who either feel the catastrophe in their bones or have already grown up with it, the chain is broken and an "empty space," a kind of historical no man's land, comes to the surface which can be described only in terms of "no longer and not yet." . . . All the loose talk of intellectuals about the necessary decline of Western civilization or the famous last generation . . . has its basis of truth in this break, and consequently has proved much more attractive than the corresponding triviality of the "liberal" mind that puts before us the alternative of going ahead or going backward, an alternative which appears so devoid of sense precisely because it still presupposes an unbroken chain of continuity.[1]

If Arendt here refers to Hume's striking figure of silkworms and butterflies, a metamorphic image of generationality that also has occupied thinkers as disparate as Karl Mannheim and François Mentré in their engagements with the Scottish philosopher, she does so in order to emphasize the inextricable interlacing of so-called generations and even historical-epistemic successions that cannot be reduced to the determined and clear-cut model of replacement that governs the relation of a being's earlier instantiation, the silkworm, and its subsequent, seemingly independent version, the butterfly. The silkworm and butterfly are incapable of existing at the same time; the latter replaces the former by having emerged from it and by having left behind the forms of its previous modes of being in the world. To argue that the succession of human generations and the concept of continuity within a subject's experience could be thought according to the model of a determined and "clean" break akin to the one that exists between silkworms and butterflies would be highly questionable, because the overdetermined experience of a human psyche hardly would allow for this kind of a categorical break. In fact, it is one of the major tenets of psychoanalysis to insist on the peculiar *simultaneity* of various historical and experiential layers of meaning that can and do inhabit one and the same psychic space at once. To recall Freud's example in *Civilization and Its Discontents*, while the various historical and archaeological sediments of the city of Rome allow for only one structure, even a ruin, to occupy the space at the top of the earth, thereby relegating into archaeological obscurity all the previous buildings that over the centuries have occupied that same spot, the psyche alone is capable of providing the space for several localizations of the meaning of an experience *at the same time*.[2] The psyche is an active simultaneity of various historical and structural determinations, a living palimpsest more than an orderly archive of succession. Freud's insistence on this active simultaneity conforms, in the realm of psychoanalysis, to Hume's epistemological view that decouples the silkworm—butterfly model from a more human-specific movement of succession and tacit replacement.

Yet, as Arendt's reference to Hume's image suggests, at certain moments in one's experience, such as historical catastrophes or traumatic events of a more personal nature, there is a scission or rupture in what is no longer simply an after or a before. She gives this scission the name "empty space," a no-man's-land in which time is out of joint and in which there no longer can be a question of returning (as in the recuperative movement of nostalgia) or of leaping forward into futurity (as in the hopeful movement of various utopianisms). Because under certain extreme conditions there can be no credible continuity, not even the kind of continuity that assures us that it works to break with continuity in order to continue differently (but still to continue). A new space of experience opens up, an empty space in which the relationship between the "no longer" and the "not yet" has not yet ossified into legibility—and therefore predictability. This empty space is devoid of determined meanings; in fact, not even its emptiness can be fully "filled" or comprehended after the fact. Empty space, the one that unfolds after the after and before the before, incessantly calls attention to itself, wishes to be read *as* something while at the same time resisting any such efforts at conceptual and experiential translation.

Locating one iteration of empty space in the margins between the literary creation of Proust and that of Kafka, Arendt works to articulate the aesthetic contours of this space. According to her reading, Proust and his incessant melancholic farewells to the nineteenth century are "written in the key of the 'no longer,'" while Kafka's creation speaks to us "as though he wrote from the vantage point of a distant future, as though he were or could have been at home only in a world which is 'not yet.'"[3] It is here, between Proust and Kafka, that Arendt locates the achievement of Broch, who emerges as "something like a missing link between Proust and Kafka, between a past which we have irretrievably lost and a future which is not yet at hand."[4] By extension, *The Death of Virgil* "is, by itself, the kind of bridge with which Virgil tries to span the abyss of empty space between the no longer and the not yet."[5] Broch's novel, which chronicles with a singular philosophical rigor and lyrical beauty the last twenty-four hours of Virgil's life, is concerned with the last things, with giving an account of oneself, at the end of one's life, primarily to oneself. For Arendt, this "judgment is not self-accusation, for it is too late for that, nor self-justification, for it is, in a way, too early for that."[6] This state of affairs in Broch's novel "makes of the last judgment a human affair, to be settled by man himself, though at the limits of his forces and possibilities—as if he wanted to spare God this whole trouble." She continues: "The 'no longer and not yet' on this level means the no longer alive and the not yet dead; and the task is the conscious achievement of judgment and truth."[7] According to the logic of this perspective, Broch creates an aesthetic form in which the empty space between the no longer and the not yet is staged as a struggle with questions of judgment, justice, and the truth of a life. Unlike a prayer, which cannot simply be true or false, the possibility of a life's truth or falsity is to be negotiated, in an exasperated yet ethically inflected register, in the empty space of language itself.

Yet, Arendt is no literary historian, nor does she wish her argument to be understood in literary-historical terms. Rather, Broch's lyrical prose serves her as the rhetorical condition of possibility that propels into thinkability certain aspects of the empty space or no-man's-land of the no longer and the not yet. To have experienced a coming after always also is to have experienced oneself as a survivor, as the one who was alive at the time, witnessed something there and then, yet, unlike so many others, is still alive here and now, after the fact. It is no accident that Arendt's friend Benjamin emphasizes the concepts of *Überleben*, or "surviving the death or loss of something," and *Fortleben*, or "simply living on, continuing to live." In his final interview, *Learning to Live Finally*, Derrida returns to this Benjaminian distinction, calling attention to the idea of "this theme of survival, the meaning of which is *not to be added on* to living and dying" but rather is "originary: life *is* living on, life *is* survival [*la vie* est *survie*]. To survive in the usual sense of the term means to continue to live, but also to live after death."[8] Evoking the ancient Greek view on philosophy, that it is a learning how to die, he states: "Learning to live should mean learning to die, learning to take into account absolute mortality (that is, without salvation, resurrection, or redemption—neither for oneself nor for the other). That's been the old philosophical injunction since Plato: to philosophize is to learn to die. I believe in this truth without being able to resign myself to it."[9] If, for Derrida, speaking from his deathbed, "survival is not simply what remains but the most intense life possible," he can admit that he is "never more haunted by the necessity of dying than in moments of happiness and joy. To feel joy and to weep over the death that awaits me are for me the same thing."[10] To live fully and intensely, then, is *always already* to experience life in terms of a survival. The experience of survival not simply is derived from this or that actual death or loss, but is originary to the extent that mourning and finitude are inscribed in every moment of existence, will inflect every stance that could be assumed in relation to what is. Even, and especially, in moments of happiness and joy, their future absence is intuited as a constitutive element of what first makes them possible.

Is the self that inhabits Arendt's empty space between the no longer and the not yet not also the subject of survival? Is the experience of a coming after—in which one cannot have emancipated oneself fully from what one has left behind without belonging to it any longer, and in which futurity nevertheless remains out of reach—not also a way of articulating an important dimension of survival, both before and after loss? Is afterness itself, in all the ways in which it has been articulated in the course of this book, not always also a name for the impossible possibility of survival? To survive, to live on, to come "after" in an afterness that cannot be fully after—are the lessons of these peculiar forms of afterness not also the lessons of survival? In the end, is the empty space of afterness a form of survival?

To survive loss, departure, and mourning can be a crisis beyond and after crisis. As Cathy Caruth puts it in relation to Freud's explication of the shifting psychoanalytical relations between trauma and survival, "for those who undergo trauma, it is not only the moment of the event, but of the passing out of it that is traumatic; that *survival itself*, in other words, *can be a crisis.*"[11] If survival, whether understood in the more usual sense of surviving a particular traumatic event or in the extended sense as an originary and abiding experience of the thrownness of *Dasein*, can be a crisis, we might ask to what extent afterness is always also a crisis, a crisis of and in survival. To experience afterness—whether in the aesthetic terms of Adorno's philosophy of art; the language of the image in Benjamin, Derrida, Deleuze, Blanchot, and others; or the problems of translation in Heidegger, to recall just a few of the instances of afterness that we have encountered—is always also to be a survivor and to have encountered a certain crisis. But this survival and this crisis, too, always will have been a matter of yet another afterness, not the one that gave rise to them but the one that they will in turn engender. This latter afterness, the afterness to come, the afterness that is therefore both after and before, regardless of whether it is experienced first in the empty space of the no longer and the not yet, is eminently future-directed, as though it conformed to the sentiment that Derrida expresses in his final conversation, when he states that "it's utopic, but I'm already setting a date!"[12] The afterness that engages survival, the incomprehensible form of living on, even within the fundamental incomprehensibility of our finitude, continues to question, lives on in a kind of *vigilance* that will not rest and that will continue to refuse to take things for granted or assume them to be self-evident. The empty space of the afterness of survival allows for an experience of freedom in which the last word has not been spoken. Not content to affirm the "logic" by which a disfigured world perpetuates the injustices of unfreedom, unnecessary human suffering, superstitions of various stripes, and habitual environmental catastrophes, an opening up to the unsettling experience of afterness as survival and crisis, and, by extension, an opening up to critical survival and the survival of critique, still remains to be thought.

This remaining to be thought, especially when read through the lens of Arendt's reflections, extends both forward to the unthought of the not yet and backward to the no longer (for the no longer never will have been able to be "understood" once and for all, finished and closed, safely archived in personal or cultural memory). The not yet of which she speaks also resonates, in spite of all her differences from this contemporary, with Bloch's philosophy of the not yet, *des Noch-Nicht-Seins*, as he puts it, in which one's move into the open, what Bloch calls *das Offene*, cannot be thought in isolation from the promise of the not yet. "The not as a not yet moves across that which has become and beyond [*Das Nicht als Noch-Nicht zieht quer durchs Gewordensein und darüber hinaus*]," we read in his Tübingen lecture on the ontology of the not yet.[13] The not yet, for both Bloch and Arendt, is charged with future possibility precisely because it remains out of reach for now. By resisting our hermeneutic efforts, the not yet refuses to betray that in whose name it deserves to live on, to survive as its own afterness and therefore as the name of a radically unknown futurity to come. Unwilling to betray by affirming too quickly, this afterness of survival and the survival of afterness cannot do without the Hegelian labor of the concept, just as it cannot do without the articulation of that which, within the conceptual, is irrevocably at odds with it.

To return, one final time, to the orbit of Arendt's empty space, this time to her exposition of the extended dialogue in Broch's novel between Virgil and Octavian around the question of sacrifice, we, the survivors of afterness, understood in the double sense of the preposition "of," become witnesses of an end without end, an appropriate breaking off without closure, that makes afterness what it is:

> Then comes death, the boat ride down to the depths of the elements when gently, one after another, the friends disappear, and man returns in peace from a long voyage of freedom into the quiet waiting of an inarticulate universe. His death seemed to him a happy death: for he had found the bridge with which to span the abyss that yawns between the "no longer and not yet" of history, between the "no longer" of the old laws and the "not yet" of the new saving word, between life and death: "Not quite here but yet at hand; that is how it has sounded and how it would sound."[14]

Afterwards
After-Words

    This study has pivoted on the obsessive engagement with a concept that has been expressed by the texts of modernity in many guises—for instance, by Georg Büchner in his play *Leonce and Lena* (1836), in which he writes, "*a posteriori*—that is how everything begins."[1] Unwilling to content itself with a model that imagines a linear succession between an alleged origin and that which is believed to issue forth from that primal instance, the study has worked to concretize, in a variety of conceptual registers, the question as to what kind of a "beginning" the concept and experience of afterness always will have been—and always will be on the verge of becoming.

    Our readings have attempted to make vivid the implications of this and related questions for a reconsideration of the aesthetic and intellectual stakes of modernity itself. Yet, *concluding* a book on following and afterness presents a special challenge when the book has argued that, in the realms of reading, writing, creating, experiencing, and thinking, there can be no closure, no finished business, no stable sense—only an afterness that both follows and inaugurates one more time. And in the German context in particular, it is advisable to mind the uses and abuses of the word *After* in intellectual history. For, in German, the noun *der After* refers not to a temporal dimension—as in the preposition *nach*—but to the human posterior, the anus. After the upstart philologist Ulrich von Wilamowitz-Moellendorff had viciously attacked Nietzsche's first book, *The Birth of Tragedy*, one of Nietzsche's friends, Erwin Rhode, responded by characterizing Wilamowitz-Moellendorff's treatise as the work of *Afterphilologie*—that is, as an especially perverse, pretentious, and misguided form of hackneyed philology. The rhetorical gesture that Rhode employs in his defense of Nietzsche against the attacks of *Afterphilologie* belongs to a German tradition that dates back at least as far as Luther, who mobilized *After* as a prefix in various word combinations as he worked to formalize what would become the modern German language; Kant self-consciously employed the term in his explications of religion; and Schopenhauer sarcastically derided academic philosophy as *Afterphilosophie* because of the way it was being practiced at German universities.[2] To have traveled a long distance along the path of the after, beginning in the Greek *krinein* and ending squarely in the condition of modernity itself, also means to ask, always one more time and from ever-shifting vantage points, what it would mean to orient one's thinking in such a way that a necessary philosophy of afterness would not of necessity result in the dead end of *Afterphilosophie*. "*A posteriori*—that is how everything begins"—but not with a posterior.

The implications of the concept of afterness that we have developed over the course of this study remain a matter of ever-renewed openings and forms of critical vigilance. These openings and forms of vigilance can lead to engagements with the act of following and the experience of coming after in a variety of unexpected modulations. For instance, in his reflections on the question of the animal from a posthumanist point of view, *The Animal That Therefore I Am*—which was published after his death and as such constitutes its own form of afterness—Derrida weaves in a kind of subtext that shows itself sensitive to issues of following. Exploiting the multiple valences of the French phrase *je suis*—which, when read as a conjugation of the verb *être*, means "I am" and, when read as the first-person-singular form of the verb *suivre*, means "I follow"—he emphasizes the intimate relation between the experience of being and that of following. Indeed, being-in-the-world is always already the condition of a kind of following. Derrida confesses that "I am (following) this suite [*je suis cette suite*], and everything in what I am about to say will lead back to the question of what 'to follow' or 'to pursue' means, as well as 'to be after,' back to the question of what I do when 'I am' or 'I follow,' when I say *Je suis*."³ If, from this perspective, being and following are always imbricated, always make us who we are, in terms that we never fully control or comprehend, we might say that such issues "involve thinking about what is meant by living, speaking, dying, being, and world as in being-in-the-world or being-within the world, or being-with, being-before, being-behind, being-after, being and following, being followed or being following."⁴ Derrida's remarks are intended as reflections on his central concern in that text—the problematic category of "the animal" as it has been mobilized in Western thought since Descartes—but they also exceed the orbit or terrain of the animal precisely by providing a testimony to the ways in which Being cannot be thought in isolation from following, that is, from all the forms and experiences of the afterness implied by the one who, like all of us, says "*je suis*"—even when we are not speaking French.

The outcome of any reflection on the concept of afterness cannot be reduced to the stability of achieved hermeneutic knowledge or even to a propaedeutic for reading, thinking, and living. Rather, following and the after are the names of perpetual question marks that call on us to employ them again and again in different ways. As Derrida reminds us, the "only question today would be, if one wanted to reduce it to a word, the question, of which more to follow [*à suivre*], of the 'to be followed': what is meant by 'to follow,' 'more to follow,' 'to pursue [*poursuivre*],' even 'to persecute.'" He continues: "What does one do when one follows? What is it I am doing when I am (following)? When I am (following) *after* someone or something . . . ? What does 'to be after' mean?"⁵ One might now say, having traversed the terrain of our readings in this book, that what we are after is precisely the after as such. We are after it, in the sense of pursuing it, thinking about it, even writing books about it, and also in the sense that we ourselves, as the perpetual aftercomers, live after the after—that is, can be said to be products of the after and continue to be altered by the after and its multiple languages in unforeseen ways.

If being and following invite us to think them as one thing—that is, if they suggest an inextricable interpenetration of living and coming after—then the question arises what kind of knowledge might be owned concerning life's variegated and always-interrupted modes of afterness. Is ownership over an experience of the after possible? In his Zürau aphorisms from 1917/1918, Kafka records the following observation: "The word '*sein*' in German means both: being-in-the-world or existence and belonging-to-him [*Das Wort 'sein' bedeutet im Deutschen beides: Da-Sein und Ihm-gehören*]."⁶ The fact that German uses the same word for "being" and "his" or "its" suggests, among many other things, that a being is primarily imagined as an entity in its relation to property, to something that is owned. This ownership of something—be it a sense of self, a language, an idea, or even a minimal differential relation to all other beings—is what allows being to be spoken of. As a noun, *Sein* names Being as such, figuring, so to speak, as the noun of all nouns, since it designates the very concept of Being and therefore the very idea, and necessity, for a language to "have" nouns in the first place. The convergence of possession and being in the quadruple function of *sein* as a verb (to be), as a noun (Being), and as two distinct possessive pronouns (his and its) invites the question what one might in fact "possess" in a life that is inflected by the experience and condition of afterness, a life in which Being is prevented from knowing what it possesses, perpetually bound up with its own to-come structure, an irreducibly *future* intelligibility that will have been grounded in a certain late-coming, an after-the-fact-ness, an after-thought. The mode of being-in-the-world that the experience and analysis of afterness gives us to interpret is one in which Being can at no point be in full possession of an experience, a relationship, even a meaning—for the meaning of all that a being can know and experience is at some future point subject to revision and reinterpretation. The "owning" being does not actually own, not even its knowledge of afterness itself, because any interpretation of afterness is itself to be reread and rethought at an unforeseen future point; that is, it will not remain self-identical but rather will change in time and space to assume a different significance. This open-endedness of the relation between Being and the knowledge and experience of itself that it both possesses and fails to possess is the condition of modernity itself. It is perhaps no accident that in his *Trauerspiel* book, Benjamin provides a critical allegory of a postlapsarian modernity in which "any person, any thing, any relation can mean absolutely anything else [*kann ein beliebiges anderes bedeuten*]."[7] To experience afterness in modernity is always also an act of radical expropriation, in which the self's ownership of itself—the relation between *Sein* as Being and *Sein* as the possession of self-possession—is continually suspended.

To the extent that the thinking of afterness gives rise to a retroactive and always belated cognition of what will have been after the fact, it also disturbs the very time and location in which it can be thought. That is to say, there can be no work of thinking, reading, writing, and creating that will not have been touched by the ways in which it is already inscribed in an unforeseeable context of future appropriations, reinterpretations, and reworkings. Even prior to any execution and any actuality of experience, the work of afterness is visited by the potentiality of the specters that one day will have come to haunt it, will have made it something else, will have been faithful to it and broken with it at the same time. In a letter from October 1803, Kleist records his engagement with this intimation of afterness: "I step back before someone who does not yet exist, and I bow, a millennium in advance, before his spirit [*Ich trete vor einem zurück, der noch nicht da ist, und beuge mich, ein Jahrtausend im voraus, vor seinem Geiste*]."[8] To understand one's life and one's work as subject to an uncontrollable afterness, an aleatory futurity *avant la lettre*, is to respond to a call exhorting one to learn to relate responsibly and freely to a difficulty whose terms one does not dictate or even fully understand. In reading and writing critically, and in creating a conceptual work or a work of art, we are called on to bow before an unpredictable afterness, even one that is still a thousand years in the future—but silently already at work. The intellectual experience of such an afterness calls forth a thinking that cannot be reduced to conventional metaphysical categories but is compelled to reinvent, always one more time, what it means to think rigorously and responsibly. It is no accident that Heidegger refers to this passage by Kleist when he differentiates between traditional philosophy, which has come to an end, and the path of a future, unknown thinking that is yet to come—as both the result of and the impetus for careful reinterpretation and perpetual, caring, and incorruptible reinvention.[9]

There can, ultimately, be no other to the after, nothing to sublate or overcome, nothing to rescue, nothing to redeem. After all, after the after comes the after. Yet, having encountered the manifold workings of the after throughout this study, we are now in a position to understand the productive necessity of reformulating the phrase by Lyotard that figured at the opening of our reflections: "After philosophy comes philosophy. But it is altered by the after."[10] That is, we are now at last, and at least, capable of understanding more fully the implications of saying that, in the experience of modernity, rather than *Afterphilosophie*, after the after comes the after, but it has been altered by the after.

Afterness begins *now* because, like being-in-the-world itself, it has always already begun.

More to follow on the mo(u)rning after . . .

Acknowledgments

I am pleased to record my gratitude for the material support I received from the Alexander von Humboldt Foundation, the Deutscher Akademischer Austauschdienst (DAAD), and the Faculty Research Grant Program at the University of California, Davis, during the writing of this book. Early versions of some portions of the introduction and of chapter 2 appeared in German as "Zu spät? Nachheit und Kritik," *Weimarer Beiträge* 55, no. 1 (2009): 99–118. Robert Savage prepared an excellent draft translation of this text. A version of chapter 3 originally appeared under the title "Aesthetic Theory and Nonpropositional Truth Content in Adorno," *New German Critique* 97 (2006): 119–135. Copyright 2006, New German Critique, Inc. All rights reserved. Reprinted by permission of the publisher, Duke University Press. A version of chapter 4 appeared as "Can Anything Be Rescued by Defending It? Benjamin with Adorno," *differences* 31, no. 3 (2010): 34–52. Copyright 2010, Duke University Press. All rights reserved. Reprinted by permission of the publisher. A version of chapter 6 was published under the title "Unsettling Photography: Kafka, Derrida, Moses," *CR: The New Centennial*

Review 7, no. 2 (2007): 155–173. A few pages of this chapter also integrate material that appeared in a prior incarnation as a part of "A Portrait of Non-Identity," *Monatshefte* 94, no. 1 (2002): 1–9. © 2002 by the Board of Regents of the University of Wisconsin System. Reproduced courtesy of the University of Wisconsin Press. Earlier partial versions of chapters 8 and 9 were published, respectively, as "Can Hope Be Disappointed? Contextualizing a Blochian Question," *Symploke* 14, nos. 1–2 (2006): 42–54, reprinted by permission of the publisher, University of Nebraska Press, and as "Crude Thinking Rethought: Reflections on a Brechtian Concept," *Angelaki* 10, no. 3 (2005): 3–13, reprinted by permission of the publisher, Taylor & Francis. Finally, a version of chapter 10 was included under the title "Acts of Memory and Mourning: Derrida and the Fictions of Anteriority," in *Memory: Histories, Theories, Debates*, ed. Susannah Radstone and Bill Schwarz (New York: Fordham University Press, 2010), 150–160, 483–485.

The index was prepared by Karen Embry.

Notes

Introduction

Unless indicated otherwise, translations throughout the book are my own. In cases where published English translations are cited, I have occasionally modified them to enhance their fidelity to the original.

1. Georges Didi-Huberman, "Artistic Survival: Panofsky vs. Warburg and the Exorcism of Impure Time," trans. Vivian Rehberg and Boris Belay, *Common Knowledge* 9, no. 2 (2003): 273–285, here 273, 275.

For the earliest systematic account of the general relationship between the Warburg School and Walter Benjamin, see Wolfgang Kemp, "Fernbilder: Benjamin und die Kunstwissenschat," in *Walter Benjamin im Kontext*, 2nd ed., ed. Burkhardt Lindner (Königstein/Ts: Athenäum, 1985), 224–257, esp. 240–254. More recently, compare further Sigrid Weigel, "Bildwissenschaft aus dem 'Geiste wahrer Philologie': Benjamins Wahlverwandtschaft mit der neuen Kunstwissenschaft und der Warburg-Schule," in *Schrift Bilder Denken: Walter Benjamin und die Künste*, ed. Detlev Schöttker (Frankfurt am Main: Suhrkamp, 2004), 112–127.

2. Walter Benjamin, *Das Passagen-Werk*, in *Gesammelte Schriften*, ed. Rolf Tiedemann and Hermann Schweppenhäuser (Frankfurt am Main: Suhrkamp, 1991), 5:574–575; *The Arcades Project*, trans. Howard Eiland and Kevin McLaughlin (Cambridge, Mass.: Harvard University Press, 1999), 460.

3. Benjamin, *Das Passagen-Werk*, 588; *Arcades Project*, 471.

4. Benjamin, *Das Passagen-Werk*, 596; *Arcades Project*, 476.

5. Benjamin, *Das Passagen-Werk*, 593; *Arcades Project*, 474.

6. Walter Benjamin, "Die Aufgabe des Übersetzers," in *Gesammelte Schriften*, ed. Rolf Tiedemann and Hermann Schweppenhäuser (Frankfurt am Main: Suhrkamp, 1991), 4:9–21; "The Task of the Translator," trans. Harry Zohn, in *Selected Writings*, ed. Marcus Bullock and Michael W. Jennings (Cambridge, Mass.: Harvard University Press, 1996), 1:253–263.

7. Walter Benjamin, *Berliner Kindheit um neunzehnhundert* (Fassung letzter Hand), in *Gesammelte Schriften*, ed. Rolf Tiedemann and Hermann Schweppenhäuser (Frankfurt am Main: Suhrkamp, 1991), 7:385–430, here 395–396; *Berlin Childhood around 1900*, trans. Howard Eiland (Cambridge, Mass.: Harvard University Press, 2006), 57.

8. Hans Blumenberg, *Theorie der Unbegrifflichkeit*, ed. Anselm Haverkamp (Frankfurt am Main: Suhrkamp, 2007), 32.

9. On this performative tension in the Declaration of Independence, see Jacques Derrida, "Declarations of Independence," trans. Thomas Keenan and Thomas Pepper, *New Political Science* 15 (1986): 3–19.

10. These etymological remarks are based on the entries for the word *nach* in Jacob and Wilhelm Grimm, *Deutsches Wörterbuch* (Munich: Deutscher Taschenbuch Verlag, 1999), 13:9–16; Wolfgang Pfeifer et al., eds., *Etymologisches Wörterbuch des Deutschen* (Munich: Deutscher Taschenbuch Verlag, 1997), 905–906; and Günther Drosdowski, Paul Grebe, et al., eds., *Duden Etymologie: Herkunftswörterbuch der deutschen Sprache* (Mannheim: Duden Verlag, 1963), 459–460.

11. Cathy Caruth, "Introduction: Trauma and Experience," in *Trauma: Explorations in Memory*, ed. Cathy Caruth (Baltimore: Johns Hopkins University Press, 1995), 3–12, here 7–8.

12. Ibid., 9.

13. I am grateful to Bernhard Greiner for having reminded me of the significance of this myth in relation to the figure of afterness. For a sustained examination of myth's gesture of circular self-foundation of speech and speaker, see Bernhard Greiner, "Mythische Rede als Echo-Rede: die Lorelei (Ovid—Brentano—Heine)," in *Mythenkorrekturen: Zu einer paradoxalen Form der Mythenrezeption*, ed. Martin Vöhler and Bernd Seidensticker (Berlin: de Gruyter, 2005), 243–261.

14. In the wake of what some have called "the turn to religion" in the humanities in recent years, the literature on the topics of secularization, theological motifs in philosophy, the dialectic of religion, and the complex afterlife of faith has grown to enormous proportions. Excellent overviews of the various positions generally held

within these debates are offered in Martin Treml and Daniel Weidner, eds., *Nachleben der Religionen: Kulturwissenschaftliche Untersuchungen zur Dialektik der Säkularisierung* (Munich: Fink, 2007); Hent de Vries, *Philosophy and the Turn to Religion* (Baltimore: Johns Hopkins University Press, 1999); Hent de Vries and Lawrence E. Sullivan, eds., *Political Theologies: Public Religions in a Post-Secular World* (New York: Fordham University Press, 2006); and John D. Caputo, *On Religion* (London: Routledge, 2001), and *What Would Jesus Deconstruct? The Good News of Postmodernism for the Church* (Ada, Mich.: Baker Academic, 2007).

15. Karlheinz Stierle and Rainer Warning, "Vorwort," in *Das Ende: Figuren einer Denkform*, ed. Karlheinz Stierle and Rainer Warning (Munich: Fink, 1996), ix–x, here ix.

16. Ibid.

17. Georg Wilhelm Friedrich Hegel, *The Difference Between Fichte's and Schelling's System of Philosophy*, trans. H. S. Harris and Walter Cerf (Albany: State University of New York Press, 1977), 179. In this context of an aesthetically conceived end, see also Alexander García Düttmann, *Kunstende: Drei ästhetische Studien* (Frankfurt am Main: Suhrkamp, 2000).

18. Martin Heidegger, *Über den Anfang*, vol. 70 of *Gesamtausgabe*, ed. Paola-Ludovika Coriando (Frankfurt am Main: Klostermann, 2005); Edward Said, *Beginnings: Intention and Method* (New York: Basic Books, 1975).

19. Robert Musil, *Nachlaß zu Lebzeiten* (Reinbek bei Hamburg: Rowohlt, 1962); Maurice Blanchot, *Après Coup, precede par Le ressassement éternal* (Paris: Minuit, 1983). After I had already completed my study, Michael Wetzel drew my attention to his comprehensive and intellectually kindred study *Die Wahrheit nach der Malerei* (Munich: Fink, 1997).

20. Samuel Weber, *Theatricality as Medium* (New York: Fordham University Press, 2004), 19.

21. Ibid.

22. The idea of an afterness that convenes with the logic of a parting-with as both departure from and perpetuation of is illuminated further by a remarkable example from an unexpected source: modern Tibetan. This issue in modern Tibetan, a language I do not speak, was first brought to my attention years ago by a former undergraduate student of mine at the University of Wisconsin–Madison. I am also grateful to Karma Ngodup, who leads the Tibetan program at the University of California, Berkeley, for allowing me to confer with him on the linguistic marvels of Tibetan. In modern Tibetan, the so-called associative case expressed in conjunction with the particle *thang/-tang* performs an action of simultaneous commonality and separation: "This particle is used mainly as a coordinating conjunction (or connective), meaning 'and'; however, it also corresponds to a case, the associative, which is generally translated as 'with' or 'against,' or else not translated at all" (Nicolas Tournadre and Sangda Dorje, *Manual of Standard Tibetan* [Ithaca, N.Y.: Snow Lion, 2003], 154). Or else not

translated at all—in this disturbance of the binary "with" and "against" is lodged a logic that works subtly to defy translation, which is to say, comprehension and legibility. This associative case, we learn, in which the particle *thang/-tang*, depending on its context, performs a certain undecidability between "with" and "against," is not common in spoken modern Tibetan but occurs more frequently in literary contexts. "In the spoken language," we read, "the associative case applies to a very limited number of verbs. Furthermore, it may sometimes be replaced by other cases such as the absolutive or the oblique." Among the examples given by the *Manual of Standard Tibetan* for verbs that continue to employ this case in spoken discourse are *thünpo*, meaning "to get along with," and *kha'ka' che'*, "to separate from" (155). The associative case in classical Tibetan grammar is used in five main contexts. Of these contexts, one relates to the idea of "gathering," another to "distributing" (according to a private communication from Karma Ngodup). A gathering that sometimes is a distributing, a togetherness that is also a break-up, a with that is also an against: the logic inherent in the parting-with and in afterness as that which does but is finally unable to depart is beautifully inscribed in the spirit (and specter) of this linguistic system. What is afterness, after all, but a perpetual "with" and "against," a gathering and a dissemination, which unfold in and as the experience of the vicissitudes of temporality itself?

23. Jean-François Lyotard, "Foreword: After the Words," in Joseph Kosuth, *Art After Philosophy and After: Collected Writings, 1966–1990*, ed. Gabriele Guercio (Cambridge Mass.: MIT Press, 1991), xv–xviii, here xv.

24. Jacques Derrida, *Specters of Marx: The State of the Debt, the Work of Mourning, and the New International*, trans. Peggy Kamuf (New York: Routledge, 1994), 16.

25. Ibid.

26. Some of the ways in which a Derridean thinking of legacy and inheritance opens up new perspectives on the problems posed by the concept of a "tradition" have been analyzed in Michael Naas, *Taking on the Tradition: Jacques Derrida and the Legacies of Deconstruction* (Stanford, Calif.: Stanford University Press, 2003).

27. Martin Heidegger, *Aus der Erfahrung des Denkens* (Stuttgart: Klett-Cotta, 2005), 19.

28. Martin Heidegger, "Die Sprache im Gedicht," in *Unterwegs zur Sprache* (Stuttgart: Klett-Cotta, 2003), 35–82, here 57.

29. Martin Heidegger, "Language in the Poem," in *On the Way to Language*, trans. Peter D. Hertz (San Francisco: Harper & Row, 1982), 157–198, here 176–178.

30. For an discussion of this passage in terms of Heidegger's investments in the perfection and perfectibility of futurity and mortality, see David Farrell Krell, "The Perfect Future: A Note on Heidegger and Derrida," in *Deconstruction and Philosophy: The Texts of Jacques Derrida*, ed. John Sallis (Chicago: University of Chicago Press, 1987), 114–121, here 118. Compare further David Farrell Krell, *Intimations of Mortality: Time, Truth, and Finitude in Heidegger's Thinking of Being* (University Park: Pennsylvania State University Press, 1991), 27–46, 47–63.

31. Martin Heidegger, *Der Begriff der Zeit: Votrag vor der Marburger Theologenschaft* (Tübingen: Niemeyer, 1995), 24–25.

32. Georg Wilhelm Friedrich Hegel, *Phänomenologie des Geistes*, in *Werke* (Frankfurt am Main: Suhrkamp, 1986), 3:35; *Phenomenology of Spirit*, trans. A. V. Miller (Oxford: Oxford University Press, 1979), 18.

33. Ibid.

34. Theodor W. Adorno, *Negative Dialektik*, in *Gesammelte Schriften*, ed. Rolf Tiedemann (Frankfurt am Main: Suhrkamp, 1997), 6:391; *Negative Dialectics*, trans. E. B. Ashton (New York: Continuum, 1973), 398.

1. *Afterness and Modernity*

1. Marshall Berman, *All That Is Solid Melts into Air: The Experience of Modernity* (New York: Penguin, 1988), 15. In his reading of Berman's text, the historian Perry Anderson comes to the radical conclusion that the "vocation of a socialist revolution . . . would be neither to prolong nor to fulfill modernity, but to abolish it" ("Modernity and Revolution," *New Left Review* 144 [1984]: 96–113, here 113).

2. See, for instance, the political critique of the term offered in Jost Hermand, "Moderne, Zeitgeist, Generation: Verschleierungstaktiken pseudodemokratischer Ideologiebildungen," in *Die Utopie des Fortschritts: 12 Versuche* (Cologne: Böhlau, 2007), 66–78, and "Zur Problematik des Begriffs 'Moderne,'" in *Nach der Postmoderne: Ästhetik heute* (Cologne: Böhlau, 2004), 43–69.

Among the most influential sociological and institutional accounts of modernity are Anthony Giddens, *The Consequences of Modernity* (Stanford, Calif.: Stanford University Press, 1991); and Ulrich Beck, *Risikogesellschaft: Auf dem Weg in eine andere Moderne* (Frankfurt am Main: Suhrkamp, 2007).

3. Bruno Latour, *We Have Never Been Modern*, trans. Catherine Porter (Cambridge, Mass.: Harvard University Press, 1993).

4. Jacques Derrida, *Positions*, trans. Alan Bass (Chicago: University of Chicago Press, 1982), 71.

5. Immanuel Kant, *Kritik der reinen Vernunft*, in *Werkausgabe*, ed. Wilhelm Weischedel (Frankfurt am Main: Suhrkamp, 1974), 3:13–14; *Critique of Pure Reason*, trans. Paul Guyer and Allen W. Wood (Cambridge: Cambridge University Press, 1998), 101.

6. Heinrich von Kleist, "Brief an Wilhelmine von Zenge, 22. März 1801," in *Sämtliche Werke und Briefe*, ed. Helmut Sembdner (Munich: Hanser, 1985), 2:630–636, here 634.

7. Friedrich Hölderlin, "Brief vom 1. Januar 1799," in *Sämtliche Werke und Briefe*, ed. Michael Knaupp (Munich: Hanser, 1992), 2:725–730, here 726.

8. Georg Wilhelm Friedrich Hegel, *Phänomenologie des Geistes*, in *Werke* (Frankfurt am Main: Suhrkamp, 1986), 3:18–19; *Phenomenology of Spirit*, trans. A. V. Miller (Oxford: Oxford University Press, 1979), 6–7.

9. Ibid.

10. Hegel, *Phänomenologie*, 36; *Phenomenology*, 19.

11. Hegel, *Phänomenologie*, 72; *Phenomenology*, 49.

12. Hegel, *Phänomenologie*, 74; *Phenomenology*, 51.

13. Hegel, *Phänomenologie*, 81; *Phenomenology*, 57.

14. Friedrich Nietzsche, *Menschliches, Allzumenschliches*, in *Kritische Studienausgabe*, ed. Giorgio Colli and Mazzino Montinari (Munich: Deutscher Taschenbuch Verlag; Berlin: de Gruyter, 1999), 2:25.

15. Friedrich Nietzsche, *Der Antichrist*, in *Kritische Studienausgabe*, ed. Giorgio Colli and Mazzino Montinari (Munich: Deutscher Taschenbuch Verlag; Berlin: de Gruyter, 1999), 6:167.

16. Walter Benjamin, *Ursprung des deutschen Trauerspiels*, in *Gesammelte Schriften*, ed. Rolf Tiedemann and Hermann Schweppenhäuser (Frankfurt am Main: Suhrkamp, 1991), 1:350.

17. I take up and situate many of these terms in Benjamin's overall theoretical and political concerns in *Walter Benjamin and the Corpus of Autobiography* (Detroit: Wayne State University Press, 2000). See also Gerhard Richter, ed., *Benjamin's Ghosts: Interventions in Contemporary Literary and Cultural Theory* (Stanford, Calif.: Stanford University Press, 2002).

18. Jürgen Habermas, *The Philosophical Discourse of Modernity: Twelve Lectures*, trans. Frederick Lawrence (Cambridge, Mass.: MIT Press, 1987), 7.

19. Robert B. Pippin, "Nietzsche's Alleged Farewell: The Premodern, Modern, and Postmodern Nietzsche," in *The Cambridge Companion to Nietzsche*, ed. Bernd Magnus and Kathleen M. Higgins (Cambridge: Cambridge University Press, 1996), 252–278, here 253.

2. Afterness and Critique

1. Many of the primary documents of this remarkable "other" strain of the German tradition of criticism since Johann Christoph Gottsched and the Enlightenment were collected by the literary historian Hans Mayer in the roughly four thousand pages of his four-volume *Deutsche Literaturkritik* (Frankfurt am Main: Fischer, 1978). For a contextualization of the historical trajectory of this tradition of criticism, compare further Peter Uwe Hohendahl, *The Institution of Criticism* (Ithaca, N.Y.: Cornell University Press, 1982), and his edited volume, *A History of German Literary Criticism, 1730–1980* (Lincoln: University of Nebraska Press, 1988).

2. Maurice Blanchot, "Preface: What Is the Purpose of Criticism?," in *Lautréamont and Sade*, trans. Stuart Kendall and Michelle Kendall (Stanford, Calif.: Stanford University Press, 2004), 1–6, here 2.

3. Michel Foucault, "What Is Critique?," in *The Essential Foucault*, ed. Paul Rabinow and Nikolas Rose (New York: New Press, 2003), 263–278, here 263.

4. Ibid.

5. Ibid., 265.

6. Ibid., 263.

7. In this matter see, alongside Foucault's analysis, Kurt Röttgers's still valuable study, *Kritik und Praxis: Zur Geschichte des Kritikbegriffs von Kant bis Marx* (Berlin: de Gruyter, 1975), on whose historical periodization I draw here. See also Reinhart Koselleck, *Kritik und Krise: Eine Studie zur Pathogenese der bürgerlichen Welt* (Frankfurt am Main: Suhrkamp, 1973); and Werner Schneider, "Vernünftiger Zweifel und wahre Eklektik: Zur Entstehung des modernen Kritikbegriffs," *Studia Leibnitiana* 17, no. 2 (1985): 146–150. For a more recent approach, see the circumspect historical and comparative reconstruction of the concept of critique undertaken by Martin Fontius, "Kritisch/Kritik," in *Ästhetische Grundbegriffe: Historisches Wörterbuch in sieben Bänden*, ed. Karlheinz Bark, Martin Fontius, Dieter Schlenstedt, Burkhart Steinwachs, and Friedrich Wolfzettel (Stuttgart: Metzler, 2001), 3:450–489. For a reading of the concept of critique in German Romanticism—particularly Schelling and Schlegel—see Philippe Lacoue-Labarthe and Jean-Luc Nancy, "Criticism: The Formation of Character," in *The Literary Absolute: The Theory of Literature in German Romanticism*, trans. Philip Barnard and Cheryl Lester (Albany: State University of New York Press, 1988), 101–119.

8. On the distinction between critique, deconstruction, and genealogy with particular reference to questions of political equality, see Christoph Menke, *Spiegelungen der Gleichheit: Politische Philosophie nach Adorno und Derrida* (Frankfurt am Main: Suhrkamp, 2004), 75–97. See also Rodolphe Gasché, "Critique, Hypercriticism, Deconstruction: The Case of Benjamin," *Cardozo Law Review* 13 (1991): 1115–1132.

9. The precise sense in which critique works fatefully to perpetuate that which it negates should also be considered in relation to a very different system of thought, sociologist Niklas Luhmann's general theory of autopoietic, or self-referential and self-producing, systems. While Luhmann's theory of self-producing systems has often been accused of departing from the concept of critique entirely and of recasting critique as a system-immanent category of observation rather than acknowledging its *operative* specificity, what systems theory would seem to share with an expanded concept of afterness is a general awareness of the ways in which critique threatens to remain indelibly inscribed in the relays of that from which it had set to out to depart. Consider, for instance, this passage from Luhmann's magnum opus, *Soziale Systeme*:

> One cannot expect counter-cultural forms in a functionally oriented system to be as well-defined as those in a hierarchical one. Obviously, no established framework

for fulfilling functions can be completely satisfactory. A functionally oriented system encourages critique because its unity resides in the principle that all its figures can be replaced under certain conditions. As a formula for critique, the search for an "alternative" becomes a formula for legitimation as such. . . . Alternative and rejective lifestyles are conspicuously present. Their language, wherever there is talk of "criticism" and "alternatives," is precisely that of the dominant order. One cannot formulate in the domain of latency an alternative order oriented to function because precisely this has long been the principle of the system one would reject. . . . The reason for this might be that a systemic order oriented to function cannot functionalize what must remain latent without including it in the order itself. The only possible remaining form for latency is then a sort of blind, speechless, functionless terrorism: a counter-contingency reduced to existence itself. (*Soziale Systeme: Grundriß einer allgemeinen Theorie* [Frankfurt am Main: Suhrkamp, 1987], 464–465; *Social Systems*, trans. John Bednarz Jr., with Dirk Baecker [Stanford, Calif.: Stanford University Press, 1995], 339–340)

10. Immanuel Kant, *Kritik der reinen Vernunft*, in *Werkausgabe*, ed. Wilhelm Weischedel (Frankfurt am Main: Suhrkamp, 1974), 3:13; *Critique of Pure Reason*, trans. Paul Guyer and Allen W. Wood (Cambridge: Cambridge University Press, 1998), 100–101.

11. Fontius, "Kritisch/Kritik," 457.

12. Paul de Man, "Criticism and Crisis," in *Blindness and Insight: Essays in the Rhetoric of Contemporary Criticism*, 2nd rev. ed. (Minneapolis: University of Minnesota Press, 1983), 3–19, here 8.

13. William K. Wimsatt and Monroe Beardsley, "The Intentional Fallacy," in *The Verbal Icon: Studies in the Meaning of Poetry* (Lexington: University of Kentucky Press, 1954), 3–18.

14. Walter Benjamin, "Goethes Wahlverwandtschaften," in *Gesammelte Schriften*, ed. Rolf Tiedemann and Hermann Schweppenhäuser (Frankfurt am Main: Suhrkamp, 1991), 1:123–201, here 125; "Goethe's Elective Affinities," trans. Stanley Corngold, in *Selected Writings*, vol. 1, *1913–1926*, ed. Marcus Bullock and Michael W. Jennings (Cambridge, Mass.: Harvard University Press, 2004), 297–360, here 297.

15. Benjamin, "Goethes Wahlverwandtschaften," 126; "Goethe's Elective Affinities," 298.

16. Immanuel Kant, *Kritik der Urteilskraft*, in *Werkausgabe*, ed. Wilhelm Weischeidel (Frankfurt am Main: Suhrkamp, 1974), 10:213. I am grateful to my friend Sam Weber for reminding me of this passage.

17. Ibid.

18. Ibid.

19. Rodolphe Gasché, *The Honor of Thinking: Critique, Theory, Philosophy* (Stanford, Calif.: Stanford University Press, 2007), 13. See also Klaus Düsing, "Immanuel

Kant: Aufklärung und Kritik," in *Philosophen des 18. Jahrhunderts. Eine Einführung*, ed. Lothar Kreimendahl (Darmstadt: WBG, 2000), 198–208.

20. Martin Heidegger, *Die Frage nach dem Ding: Zu Kants Lehre von den transzendentalen Grundsätzen*, vol. 41 of *Gesamtausgabe* (Frankfurt am Main: Klostermann, 1984), 122. My understanding here is indebted to Gasché's insightful interpretation of this Heideggerean passage in *Honor of Thinking*, 14.

21. Heidegger, *Die Frage nach dem Ding*, 122.

22. Ibid.

23. Ibid.

24. Ibid., 123.

25. Martin Heidegger, "Das Ende der Philosophie und die Aufgabe des Denkens," in *Zur Sache des Denkens* (Tübingen: Niemeyer, 1969), 61–90, here 61; "The End of Philosophy and the Task of Thinking," trans. Joan Stambaugh, in *Basic Writings*, ed. David Farrell Krell (New York: Harper & Row, 1993), 431–449, here 431.

26. Ibid.

27. Heidegger, "Das Ende der Philosophie," 90; "End of Philosophy," 449.

28. Heidegger refers to several possible such paths of thinking in texts such as "Was heißt Denken?" (1952), "Überwindung der Metaphysik" (1951), and "Die Frage nach der Technik" (1954), each of which attempts in its own singular way to bring to language the after of a future thinking. These three texts are gathered in Martin Heidegger, *Vorträge und Aufsätze*, ed. Friedrich-Wilhelm von Herrmann (Stuttgart: Klett-Cotta, 2000).

29. Theodor W. Adorno, "Kritik," in *Gesammelte Schriften*, ed. Rolf Tiedemann (Frankfurt am Main: Suhrkamp, 1997), 10:785–793, here 785–786; "Critique," in *Critical Models: Interventions and Catchwords*, trans. Henry W. Pickford, introduction by Lydia Goehr (New York: Columbia University Press, 2005), 281–288, here 282.

30. Adorno, "Kritik," 793; "Critique," 288. A more contemporary version of this suspicion may be said to reside in Slavoj Žižek's assessment of the resistance to the American war on Iraq under the presidency of George W. Bush:

> The big demonstrations in London and Washington against the U.S. attack on Iraq a few years ago offer an exemplary case of this strange symbiotic relationship between power and resistance. Their paradoxical outcome was that both sides were satisfied. The protesters saved their beautiful souls: they made it clear that they don't agree with the government's policy on Iraq. Those in power calmly accepted it, even profited from it: not only did the protests in no way prevent the already-made decision to attack Iraq; they also served to legitimize it. Thus George Bush's reaction to mass demonstrations protesting his visit to London, in effect: "You see, this is what we are fighting for, so that what people are doing here—protesting against their government policy—will be possible also in Iraq!"

("Resistance Is Surrender," *London Review of Books*, November 15, 2007, www.lrb.co.uk/v29/n22/zize01_.html)

31. Theodor W. Adorno, *Negative Dialektik*, in *Gesammelte Schriften*, ed. Rolf Tiedemann (Frankfurt am Main: Suhrkamp, 1997), 6:15; *Negative Dialectics*, trans. E. B. Ashton (New York: Continuum, 1973), 3.

32. Theodor W. Adorno, *Ästhetische Theorie*, in *Gesammelte Schriften*, ed. Rolf Tiedemann (Frankfurt am Main: Suhrkamp, 1997), 7:387; *Aesthetic Theory*, trans. Robert Hullot-Kentor (Minneapolis: University of Minnesota Press, 1999), 261.

33. Max Horkheimer, "Traditionelle und kritische Theorie," *Zeitschrift für Sozialforschung* 6, no. 2 (1937): 245–294; "Traditional and Critical Theory," in *Critical Theory: Selected Essays*, trans. Matthew J. O'Connell et al. (New York: Continuum, 1999), 188–243.

34. Adorno, *Negative Dialektik*, 30; *Negative Dialectics*, 19.

35. Ibid.

36. Ibid.

37. Sven Kramer, for example, offers a concise overview of this consciousness in "'Wahr sind die Sätze als Impuls . . .': Begriffsarbeit und spachliche Darstellung in Adornos Reflexion auf Auschwitz," *Deutsche Vierteljahrsschrift* 70 (1996): 501–523.

38. Menke, *Spiegelungen der Gleichheit*, 199. On the theoretical connection between Adorno's meditations on consciousness after Auschwitz and ethico-political questions, see also J. M. Bernstein, *Adorno: Disenchantment and Ethics* (Cambridge: Cambridge University Press, 2001), esp. 371–414; and Gerhard Richter, "Nazism and Negative Dialectics: Adorno's Hitler in *Minima Moralia*," in *Thought-Images: Frankfurt School Writers' Reflections from Damaged Life* (Stanford, Calif.: Stanford University Press, 2007), 147–190, 217–227.

39. Martin Seel, "'Jede wirklich gesättigte Anschauung': Das positive Zentrum der negativen Philosophie Adornos," in *Adornos Philosophie der Kontemplation* (Frankfurt am Main: Suhrkamp, 2004), 20–28.

40. Adorno, *Negative Dialektik*, 355; *Negative Dialectics*, 363.

41. Adorno, *Negative Dialektik*, 357; *Negative Dialectics*, 364.

42. Ibid.

43. Adorno, *Negative Dialektik*, 358; *Negative Dialectics*, 365.

3. *Afterness and Aesthetics*

1. Theodor W. Adorno, *Vorlesung über "Negative Dialektik,"* in *Nachgelassene Schriften*, vol. 16, sec. 4, *Vorlesungen* (Frankfurt am Main: Suhrkamp, 2003).

2. Theodor W. Adorno, "Kulturkritik und Gesellschaft," in *Gesammelte Schriften*, ed. Rolf Tiedemann (Frankfurt am Main: Suhrkamp, 1997), 10:11–30, here 30.

3. Theodor W. Adorno, "Auf die Frage: Was ist deutsch," in *Gesammelte Schriften*, ed. Rolf Tiedemann (Frankfurt am Main: Suhrkamp, 1997), 10:691–701, here 701, and *Berg: Der Meister des kleinsten Übergangs*, in *Gesammelte Schriften*, ed. Rolf Tiedemann (Frankfurt am Main: Suhrkamp, 1997), 13:321–494.

4. Theodor W. Adorno, *Ästhetische Theorie*, in *Gesammelte Schriften*, ed. Rolf Tiedemann (Frankfurt am Main: Suhrkamp, 1997), 7:140.

5. Martin Heidegger, *Hölderlins Hymne "Andenken,"* vol. 52 of *Gesamtausgabe* (Frankfurt am Main: Klostermann, 1992).

6. I borrow this delightful image from Stanley Corngold.

7. Theodor W. Adorno, *Beethoven: Philosophie der Musik*, in *Nachgelassene Schriften*, (Frankfurt am Main: Suhrkamp, 1993), 1, sec. 1:39.

8. Christine Eichel, *Vom Ermatten der Avantgarde zur Vernetzung der Künste: Perspektiven einer interdisziplinären Asthetik im Spätwerk Theodor W. Adornos* (Frankfurt am Main: Suhrkamp, 1993); Hauke Brunkhorst, "Kritik statt Theorie: Adornos experimentelles Freiheitsverständnis," in *Impuls und Negativität: Ethik und Ästhetik bei Adorno*, ed. Gerhard Schweppenhäuser and Mirko Wischke (Berlin: Argument-Verlag, 1995), 117–135. Adorno mentions his notion of *Verfransung*, for instance, in his late essay "Die Kunst und die Künste," in *Ohne Leitbild: Parva Aesthetica*, in *Gesammelte Schriften*, 10:432–453.

9. Rüdiger Bubner, "Kann Theorie ästhetisch werden? Zum Hauptmotiv der Philosophie Adornos," in *Materialien zur Ästhetischen Theorie Theodor W. Adornos: Konstruktionen der Moderne*, ed. Burkhardt Lindner and W. Martin Lüdke (Frankfurt am Main: Suhrkamp, 1980), 108–137, here 133.

10. Adorno, *Ästhetische Theorie*, 113.

11. Adorno, *Vorlesung über "Negative Dialektik,"* 115.

12. J. Hillis Miller, "'Reading' Part of a Paragraph in *Allegories of Reading*," in *Theory Now and Then* (Durham, N.C.: Duke University Press, 1991), 341–358, here 348.

13. It would also be necessary in this context to examine in some detail Adorno's relationship to Walter Benjamin's philosophical transformation of allegory as ruin and otherness in *Ursprung des deutschen Trauerspiels*. That the early Adorno already was deeply familiar with Benjamin's 1928 study, originally designed as a *Habilitation* thesis, is well known. He even offered a seminar on Benjamin's text at the University of Frankfurt in 1931/1932, the first university course on Benjamin ever. Compare further the surviving class minutes prepared by various participants in Adorno's seminar: "Adornos Seminar vom Sommersemester 1932 über Benjamins Ursprung des deutschen Trauerspiels. Protokolle," *Frankfurter Adorno Blätter* 4 (1995): 52–77. For a general discussion of Adorno's seminar on Benjamin, see Stefan Müller-Doohm, *Adorno: Eine Biographie* (Frankfurt am Main: Suhrkamp, 2003), 220–228.

14. These problems deserve to be inflected by Adorno's warning against "the illusion that what is said is immediately what is meant [*die Illusion, es wäre, was geredet wird, unmittelbar das Gemeinte*]." Instead, the character of language as an elusive token

(*Spielmarke*) reveals "the way that all words behave: that language imprisons its speakers one more time; that language, as the proper medium of its speakers, is a failure" (Theodor W. Adorno, "Wörter aus der Fremde," in *Noten zur Literatur* [Frankfurt am Main: Suhrkamp, 1997], 11:216–232, here 221).

15. Theodor W. Adorno, "Parataxis: Zur späten Lyrik Hölderlins," in ibid., 447–491, here 452.

16. In the original, the rich passage reads: "Ich verspräche gerne diesem Buche die Liebe der Deutschen. Aber ich fürchte, die einen werden es lesen, wie ein Compendium, und um das *fabula docet* sich zu sehr bekümmern, indem die andern gar zu leicht es nehmen, und beede Theile verstehen es nicht. Wer blos an meiner Pflanze riecht, der kennt sie nicht, und wer sie pflückt, blos, um daran zu lernen, kennt sie auch nicht. Die Auflösung der Dissonanzen in einem gewissen Charakter ist weder für das bloße Nachdenken, noch für die leere Lust" (Friedrich Hölderlin, *Hyperion oder der Eremit in Griechenland*, in *Sämtliche Werke und Briefe*, ed. Michael Knaupp [Munich: Hanser, 1992], 1:609–760, here 611).

17. Adorno, *Ästhetische Theorie*, 27.

18. Ibid., 199.

19. Christoph Menke, *Die Souveränität der Kunst: Ästhetische Erfahrung nach Adorno und Derrida* (Frankfurt am Main: Suhrkamp, 1991).

20. Simon Jarvis, "Art, Truth, and Ideology," in *Adorno: A Critical Introduction* (New York: Routledge, 1998), 90–123, here 90. As Jarvis suggests, the idea of a nonpropositional truth content is tied to the intuition that the cognitive significance of an artwork or a philosophical text "is not exhausted by the sum of the correct propositions contained in it, because it depends also on the relations between these propositions and the way in which they are organized." Adorno terms this differential or relational structure the work's *Sprachähnlichkeit* (similarity to language or language-likeness), its *Sprachcharakter* (lingusitic character), in short, its status as *Schrift* (writing or script) (103).

21. Andreas Bernard and Ulrich Raulff, *Theodor W. Adorno: "Minima Moralia" neu gelesen* (Frankfurt am Main: Suhrkamp, 2003).

22. Theodor W. Adorno, "Zum Ende," in *Minima Moralia: Reflexionen aus dem beschädigten Leben*, in *Gesammelte Schriften*, ed. Rolf Tiedemann (Frankfurt am Main: Suhrkamp, 1997), 4:283.

23. I am grateful to Elke Siegel for reminding me of the third meaning of the preposition. I also thank Liliane Weissberg for suggesting to me that the translator may have attempted to "out-Adorno" Adorno by choosing a technical term drawn from music. And, indeed, the Italian term *finale* can signify the concluding movement or part of a musical piece or performance, such as an opera, a symphony, a sonata, or a concert more generally. Given the high esteem in which Adorno holds composers such as Mozart and Beethoven, for whom the "finale" is especially significant, this is an intriguing possibility. If this musical inflection had been the marching

plan of Adorno's text, however, he doubtless would have employed the word "finale" in his original text, as he does throughout his musicological writings.

24. Theodor W. Adorno, *Negative Dialektik*, in *Gesammelte Schriften*, ed. Rolf Tiedemann (Frankfurt am Main: Suhrkamp, 1997), 6:148.

25. Adorno, "Kulturkritik und Gesellschaft," 27.

26. Theodor W. Adorno, "Aus einem Schulheft ohne Deckel: Bar Harbor, Sommer 1939," *Frankfurter Adorno Blätter* 4 (1995): 7.

27. Theodor W. Adorno, "Thesen über die Sprache des Philosophen," in *Philosophische Frühschriften*, in *Gesammelte Schriften* (Frankfurt am Main: Suhrkamp, 1997), 1:366–371, here 368.

28. Ibid.

29. J. M. Bernstein, "Fragment, Fascination, Damaged Life: 'The Truth About Hedda Gabler,'" in *The Actuality of Adorno: Critical Essays on Adorno and the Postmodern*, ed. Max Pensky (Albany: State University of New York Press, 1997), 154–182, here 155.

30. For a reading of this Adornian extension of a Marxian transformation of Kantian aesthetics in the context of his essay "On Lyric Poetry and Society," see Robert Kaufman, "Adorno's Social Lyric, and Literary Criticism Today: Poetics, Aesthetics, Modernity," in *The Cambridge Companion to Adorno*, ed. Thomas Huhn (Cambridge: Cambridge University Press, 2004), 354–375.

31. Adorno, *Negative Dialektik*, 21.

32. Ibid., 27.

33. Martin Heidegger, *Über den Humanismus* (Frankfurt am Main: Klostermann, 2000), 49.

4. *Afterness and* Rettung

1. Friedrich Hölderlin, "Patmos," in *Sämtliche Werke und Briefe*, ed. Michael Knaupp (Munich: Hanser, 1992), 1:447–453, here 447.

2. Theodor W. Adorno and Walter Benjamin, *Briefwechsel, 1928–1940*, ed. Henri Lonitz (Frankfurt am Main: Suhrkamp, 1994), 243.

3. These etymological remarks are based on the entries for the words *Rettung* and *retten* in Jacob and Wilhelm Grimm, *Deutsches Wörterbuch* (Leipzig: Hirzel, 1893), 14:825–828; Günther Drosdowski, Paul Grebe, et al., eds., *Duden Etymologie: Herkunftswörterbuch der deutschen Sprache* (Mannheim: Duden Verlag, 1963), 566–567; and Wolfgang Pfeifer et al., eds., *Etymologisches Wörterbuch des Deutschen* (Munich: Deutscher Taschenbuch Verlag, 1997), 1121.

4. Walter Benjamin, *Das Passagen-Werk*, in *Gesammelte Schriften*, ed. Rolf Tiedemann and Hermann Schweppenhäuser (Frankfurt am Main: Suhrkamp, 1991), 5:587.

5. An excellent start has been made by Heinrich Kaulen, "Rettung," in *Benjamins Begriffe*, ed. Michael Opitz and Erdmut Wizisla (Frankfurt am Main: Suhrkamp,

2000), 619–664. This essay provides a brief but circumspect historical overview of the term as it recurs in Benjamin's work. Among earlier studies, see especially Ullrich Schwarz, *Rettende Kritik und antizipierte Utopie: Zum geschichtlichen Gehalt ästhetischer Erfahrung in den Theorien von Jan Mukarovsky, Walter Benjamin und Theodor W. Adorno* (Munich: Fink, 1981); and Norbert Bolz and Richard Faber, eds., *Walter Benjamin: Profane Erleuchtung und rettende Kritik* (Würzburg: Königshausen & Neumann, 1985). For a consideration of *Rettung* in a broader historical framework, compare further R. Glei, S. Natzel, and R. Tiedemann, "Rettung," and Th. Rehbock, "Die Rettung der Phänomene," both in *Historisches Wörterbuch der Philosophie*, ed. Joachim Ritter and Karlfried Gründer (Basel: Schwabe, 1992), 8:932–941, 941–944.

6. Kaulen, "Rettung," 620–629.

7. Adorno and Benjamin, *Briefwechsel*, 336.

8. Ibid., 336–337.

9. Ibid., 337.

10. Ibid.

11. In fact, the first sentence of his *Trauerspiel* book, published in 1928, unambiguously announces this concern with textual self-reflexivity: "It is the property of philosophical writing to confront with each turn the question of presentation anew" (Walter Benjamin, *Ursprung des deutschen Trauerspiels*, in *Gesammelte Schriften*, ed. Rolf Tiedemann and Hermann Schweppenhäuser [Frankfurt am Main: Suhrkamp, 1991], 1:1). For meditations on some of the ways in which Benjamin approaches this demand of what he calls a new *schriftstellerische Form* in his own textual practice, see Gerhard Richter, "Acts of Self-Portraiture: Benjamin's Confessional and Literary Writings," in *The Cambridge Companion to Walter Benjamin*, ed. David Ferris (Cambridge: Cambridge University Press, 2002), 221–237; Hans-Jost Frey, "On Presentation in Benjamin," trans. Michael Shae, in *Walter Benjamin: Theoretical Questions*, ed. David Ferris (Stanford, Calif.: Stanford University Press, 1996), 139–164; and Hans Heinz Holz, "Prismatisches Denken" (1965), in *Über Walter Benjamin* (Frankfurt am Main: Suhrkamp, 1968), 62–110, especially 62–70.

12. Benjamin, *Das Passagen-Werk*, 591.

13. Adorno and Benjamin, *Briefwechsel*, 337.

14. Kaulen, "Rettung," 652.

15. Adorno and Benjamin, *Briefwechsel*, 345.

16. Jürgen Habermas, "Bewußtmachende oder rettende Kritik—die Aktualität Walter Benjamins," in *Zur Aktualität Walter Benjamins*, ed. Siegfried Unseld (Frankfurt am Main: Suhrkamp, 1972), 173–223. In what follows, quotations of Habermas will be taken from "Walter Benjamin: Consciousness-Raising or Rescuing Critique," trans. Frederick G. Lawrence, in *Walter Benjamin: Critical Evaluations in Cultural Theory*, ed. Peter Osborne (London: Routledge, 2005), 1:107–136.

17. Among the variegated critical responses to Habermas's critique of Benjamin are, for instance, Peter Bürger, "Benjamins 'rettende Kritik': Vorüberlegungen zum

Entwurf einer kritischen Hermeneutik," in *Vermittlung—Rezeption—Funktion: Ästhetische Theorie und Methodologie der Literaturwissenschaft* (Frankfurt am Main: Suhrkamp, 1979), 160–172; and Rolf Tiedemann, "Historischer Materialismus oder politischer Messianismus? Zur Interpretation der Thesen 'Über den Begriff der Geschichte,'" in *Dialektik im Stillstand: Versuche zum Spätwerk Walter Benjamins* (Frankfurt am Main: Suhrkamp, 1983), 99–142, most explicitly 141n.74.

18. Habermas, "Consciousness-Raising," 124.

19. Ibid., 113.

20. Ibid., 127.

21. Walter Benjamin, *Nachträge*, in *Gesammelte Schriften*, ed. Rolf Tiedemann and Hermann Schweppenhäuser (Frankfurt: Suhrkamp, 1991), 7:766.

22. Theodor W. Adorno, *Negative Dialetik*, in *Gesammelte Schriften*, ed. Rolf Tiedemann (Frankfurt am Main: Suhrkamp, 1997), 6:384.

23. Compare also the thoughtful commentary on this passage by Alexander García Düttmann, who relates it to Adorno's general concept of critique and compares it with recent arguments in the field of moral philosophy such as those advanced by Raimond Gaita and Joseph Margolis, in "Without Soil: A Figure in Adorno's Thought," trans. Robert Savage, in *Language Without Soil: Adorno and Late Philosophical Modernity*, ed. Gerhard Richter (New York: Fordham University Press, 2010), 10–16.

24. It is in this sense, too, that Benjamin's relation to so-called tradition and to the idea of rescuing something in and of the past can be understood. Tradition and the past, for Benjamin, can become objects of a rescuing critique only to the extent that they are read as problems, as open questions, rather than as a self-identical property to be ruled over. Krista R. Greffrath therefore has it right when she suggests that "Benjamin was no traditionalist, but he loved what the traditionalists administer as though it were their property. It is for the sake of traditional culture that Benjamin becomes an opponent of tradition. The idea of a *Rettung* of what has come to pass is an expression of this contradiction" ("Der historische Materialist als dialektischer Historiker," in *Materialien zu Benjamins Thesen "Über den Begriff der Geschichte": Beiträge und Interpretationen*, ed. Peter Bulthaup [Frankfurt am Main: Suhrkamp, 1975], 193–230, here 217).

25. Michel Foucault, *Society Must Be Defended: Lectures at the Collège de France, 1975–76*, trans. David Macey (New York: Picador, 2003).

26. Andrea Köhler, ed., *Kleines Glossar des Verschwindens: Von Autokino bis Zwischengas* (Munich: Beck, 2003).

27. Walter Benjamin, "Pariser Passagen I," in *Das Passagen-Werk*, 993–1038, here 1001.

28. Benjamin, *Ursprung des deutschen Trauerspiels*, 350.

29. Benjamin, *Das Passagen-Werk*, 591.

30. Theodor W. Adorno, "Charakteristik Walter Benjamins," in *Gesammelte Schriften*, ed. Rolf Tiedemann (Frankfurt am Main: Suhrkamp, 1997), 10:238–253, here 240.

31. Benjamin, *Passagen-Werk*, 588.

32. The most sustained and insightful analysis of Benjamin's engagement with photography and its relation to history, mourning, and philosophy remains Eduardo Cadava, *Words of Light: Theses on the Photography of History* (Princeton, N.J.: Princeton University Press, 1997).

33. Benjamin, *Das Passagen-Werk*, 595–596.

34. Walter Benjamin, "Goethes Wahlverwandtschaften," in *Gesammelte Schriften*, 1:123–201, here 126.

5. *Afterness and Translation*

1. Günter Figal, "Chronik," in *Heidegger Lesebuch*, ed. Günter Figal (Stuttgart: Klostermann, 2007), 374–382, here 379.

2. Rüdiger Safranski, *Ein Meister aus Deutschland: Heidegger und seine Zeit* (Frankfurt am Main: Fischer, 1997), 303.

3. This unpublished entry from Heidegger's so-called *Schwarze Hefte* (Black notebooks) is partially cited in Günter Figal, "Einleitung," in *Heidegger Lesebuch*, ed. Figal, 9–43, here 25. It was made available to Figal for perusal by Heidegger's son, Dr. Hermann Heidegger.

4. Otto Pöggeler, *Philosophie und Politik bei Heidegger* (Freiburg: Alber, 1972); Dominique Janicaud, *The Shadow of That Thought*, trans. Michael Gendre (Evanston, Ill.: Northwestern University Press, 1996); David Farrell Krell, "'You in front of me, I in front of you': Heidegger in the University of Life," in *Daimon Life: Heidegger and Life-Philosophy* (Bloomington: Indiana University Press, 1992), 137–170; Berel Lang, *Heidegger's Silence* (Ithaca, N.Y.: Cornell University Press, 1996); Jean-François Lyotard, *Heidegger and "the Jews*," trans. Andreas Michel and Mark S. Roberts (Minneapolis: University of Minnesota Press, 1990).

5. Odo Marquard, "Der Schritt in die Kunst: Über Schiller und Heidegger," in Martin Heidegger, *Übungen für Anfänger: Schillers Briefe über die ästhetische Erziehung des Menschen, Wintersemester 1936/37*, transcribed by Wilhelm Hallwachs, ed. Ulrich von Bülow, with an essay by Odo Marquard (Marbach am Neckar: Deutsche Schillergesellschaft, 2005), 191–206, here 191.

6. Ibid., 202.

7. Philippe Lacoue-Labarthe, *Heidegger, Art, and Politics*, trans. Chris Turner (Oxford: Blackwell, 1990).

8. Jacques Derrida, *Of Spirit: Heidegger and the Question*, trans. Geoffrey Bennington and Rachel Bowlby (Chicago: University of Chicago Press, 1989).

9. Regarding the first of these issues—the one that speaks most directly to the political perspective that Marquard emphasizes—the literature is now extensive. For a representative and selective sample, see the thoughtful accounts by Otto Pöggeler,

Der Denkweg Martin Heideggers, 2nd ed. (Pfullingen: Neske, 1983); Hugo Ott, *Martin Heidegger: Unterwegs zu seiner Biographie* (Frankfurt am Main: Campus, 1988); Silvio Vietta, *Heideggers Kritik am Nationalsozialismus und an der Technik* (Tübingen: Niemeyer, 1989); Peter Kemper, ed., *Martin Heidegger—Faszination und Erschrecken: Die politische Dimension einer Philosophie* (Frankfurt am Main: Campus, 1990); Tom Rockmore, *On Heidegger's Nazism and Philosophy* (Berkeley: University of California Press, 1992); Christopher Fynsk, "Postface: The Legibility of the Political," in *Heidegger: Thought and Historicity*, 2nd ed. (Ithaca, N.Y.: Cornell University Press, 1993), 230–249; Thomas Sheenan, "Reading a Life: Heidegger and Hard Times," in *The Cambridge Companion to Martin Heidegger*, ed. Charles Guigon (Cambridge: Cambridge University Press, 1993), 70–96; Julian Young, *Heidegger, Philosophy, Nazism* (Cambridge: Cambridge University Press, 1997); and Miguel de Beistegui, *Heidegger and the Political: Dystopias* (London: Routledge, 1998). Most recently, the basic facts as well as the major positions in the scholarship concerning Heidegger's involvement with National Socialism are circumspectly summarized in Dieter Thomä, "Heidegger und der Nationalsozialismus: In der Dunkelkammer der Seinsgeschichte," in *Heidegger-Handbuch: Leben, Werk, Wirkung*, ed. Dieter Thomä (Stuttgart: Metzler, 2003), 141–162. Thomä also offers his own original and even-handed perspective on the relation between Heidegger and National Socialism.

10. The factual information in this paragraph follows the editor's philological remarks: Ulrich von Bülow, "Zu dieser Ausgabe," in Heidegger, *Schillers Briefe*, 169–177.

11. Quoted in Samuel Weber, "Translating the Untranslatable," translator's introduction to Theodor W. Adorno, *Prisms*, trans. Samuel Weber and Shierry Weber (Cambridge, Mass.: MIT Press, 1983), 9–15, here 12.

12. "Translating Heidegger's Sein und Zeit," special issue, *Studia Phenomenologica* 5 (2005).

13. Martin Heidegger, *Was heißt Denken?* (Tübingen: Niemeyer, 1954), 107–108.

14. Martin Heidegger, *Parmenides*, vol. 54 of *Gesamtausgabe* (Frankfurt am Main: Klostermann, 1982), 17.

15. Hans-Georg Gadamer, "Lesen ist wie Übersetzen," in *Ästhetik und Politik 1: Kunst als Aussage*, vol. 8 of *Gesammelte Werke* (Tübingen: Mohr, 1993), 279–285.

16. Jacques Derrida, reply to Christie McDonald, "The Passage into Philosophy," in "Roundtable on Translation," in *The Ear of the Other: Otobiography, Transference, Translation—Texts and Discussions with Jacques Derrida*, ed. Christie McDonald, trans. Peggy Kamuf (Lincoln: University of Nebraska Press, 1985), 116–126, here 120.

17. Martin Heidegger, *Hölderlins Hymne "Der Ister*,*"* vol. 53 of *Gesamtausgabe* (Frankfurt am Main: Klostermann, 1984), 100.

18. Heidegger, *Schillers Briefe*, 9.

19. Ibid., 10.

20. Paul de Man, "Kant and Schiller," in *Aesthetic Ideology*, ed. Andrzej Warminski (Minneapolis: University of Minnesota Press, 1996), 129–162.

21. Martin Heidegger, "Die Frage nach der Technik," in *Vorträge und Aufsätze* (Pfullingen: Neske, 2000), 9–40, here 9.

22. Günter Figal, "Seinserfahrung und Übersetzung: Hermeneutische Überlegungen zu Heidegger," in *Interpretation und Wahrheit—Interprétation et vérité*, Studia Philosophica 57, ed. Emil Angehrn and Bernard Baertschi (Berne: Verlag Paul Haupt, 1998), 177–188, here 186.

23. Martin Heidegger, "Überwindung der Metaphysik," in *Vorträge und Aufsätze*, 67–95.

24. Figal, "Seinserfahrung und Übersetzung," 187.

25. Martin Heidegger, "Der Ursprung des Kunstwerkes," in *Holzwege* (Frankfurt am Main: Klostermann, 1980), 1–72, here 7.

26. Ibid., 8.

27. Rodolphe Gasché, "The Operator of Difference," in "Roundtable on Translation," in *Ear of the Other*, ed. McDonald, 110–115, here 113.

28. Martin Heidegger, *Über den Anfang*, vol. 70 of *Gesamtausgabe* (Frankfurt am Main: Klostermann, 2005), 122.

29. Martin Heidegger, "The Nature of Language," in *On the Way to Language*, trans. Peter D. Hertz (San Francisco: Harper & Row, 1971), 57–108, here 59; "Vom Wesen der Sprache," in *Unterwegs zur Sprache* (Stuttgart: Klett-Cotta, 2003), 157–216, here 161.

30. Martin Heidegger, "Language," in *Poetry, Language, Thought*, trans. Albert Hofstadter (New York: HarperCollins, 2001), 185–208, here 207; "Die Sprache," in *Unterwegs zur Sprache*, 9–33.

31. David Wood, *Thinking After Heidegger* (Cambridge: Polity, 2002), 21. For a complementary account, compare further Robert Bernasconi, *The Question of Language in Heidegger's History of Being* (Atlantic Highlands, N.J.: Humanities Press, 1985).

32. Martin Heidegger, *Der Satz vom Grund*, vol. 10 of *Gesamtausgabe* (Frankfurt am Main: Klostermann, 1997), 145.

33. John Sallis, *On Translation* (Bloomington: Indiana University Press, 2002), 17.

34. Heidegger, *Der Satz vom Grund*, 153.

35. Ibid., 154.

36. Heidegger, *Schillers Briefe*, 38.

37. Ibid., 41.

38. Ibid., 47.

39. Ibid., 24.

40. Ibid., 26

41. Immanuel Kant, *Kritik der reinen Vernunft*, in *Werkausgabe*, ed. Wilhelm Weischedel (Frankfurt am Main: Suhrkamp, 1974), 3:63.

42. Heidegger, *Schillers Briefe*, 55.

43. Ibid., 57.

44. The rhetoric of the deliberate step is echoed in other Heideggerean texts in which a series of related figures are mobilized to similar effect. For instance, in the

1957 Freiburg lecture "Der Satz der Identität," Heidegger speaks of the *Sprung*, or "jump," by means of which the principle of identity is carried over into the abyss in which Being is no longer simply the ground or reason (*Grund*) of beings of that which is (*des Seienden*). As is the case in Heidegger's interpretation of Schiller's *Schritt* (step) back, this is not a matter of *falling* into an abyss, but a deliberate and thinking jump into it. The step back is a figure of thinking, an unknown thinking to come, in which metaphysics itself is confronted with its having forgotten Being. See "Der Satz der Identität," in *Identität und Differenz* (Pfullingen: Neske, 1990), 9–30, here 28.

45. Walter Benjamin, "Die Aufgabe des Übersetzers," in *Kleine Prosa und Baudelaire-Übertragungen*, in *Gesammelte Schriften*, ed. Rolf Tiedemann and Hermann Schweppenhäuser (Frankfurt am Main: Suhrkamp, 1991), 4:9–21, here 12–13.

46. Jacques Derrida, "Living On/Borderlines," in *Deconstruction and Criticism* (New York: Seabury, 1979), 75–176, here 102–103.

47. Heidegger, "Die Frage nach der Technik," 15.

48. Martin Heidegger, *Einführung in die Metaphysik*, vol. 40 of *Gesamtausgabe* (Frankfurt am Main: Klostermann, 1983), 159–162; *Introduction to Metaphysics*, trans. Gregory Fried and Richard Polt (New Haven, Conn.: Yale University Press, 2000), 159–162.

49. Martin Heidegger, *Hölderlin's Hymn "The Ister,"* trans. William McNeill and Julia Davis (Bloomington: Indiana University Press, 1996), 61–63; *Hölderlins Hymne "Der Ister,"* 74–76.

50. Thomas Bernhard, *Eine Begegnung: Gespräche mit Krista Fleischmann* (Vienna: Verlag der Österreichischen Staatsdruckerei, 1991), 210; Derrida, "Living On/Borderlines," 101.

51. Walter Benjamin, "Diary Entries, 1938," trans. Gerhard Richter and Michael W. Jennings, in *Selected Writings*, vol. 3, *1935–1938*, ed. Howard Eiland and Michael W. Jennings (Cambridge, Mass.: Harvard University Press, 2002), 335–343, here 335.

52. The general difference between error and mistake, particularly as it relates to the rhetorical criticism of Paul de Man, is pursued in Stanley Corngold, "Error in Paul de Man," in *The Yale Critics: Deconstruction in America*, ed. Jonathan Arac, Wlad Godzich, and Wallace Martin (Minneapolis: University of Minnesota Press, 1983), 90–108.

53. Ernst Bloch, "Something's Missing: A Discussion Between Ernst Bloch and Theodor W. Adorno on the Contradictions in Utopian Longing," in *The Utopian Function of Art and Literature: Selected Essays*, trans. Jack Zipes and Frank Mecklenburg (Cambridge, Mass.: MIT Press, 1988), 1–17, here 15. One must no doubt feel honest sympathy for the cautionary note that appears in the volume's "Notes on Translation and Acknowledgments": "Due to the fact that it is sometimes impossible to understand Bloch, even when one has a firm command of German, there are no doubt mistranslations. One is never on firm ground when reading Bloch" (vii–x, here ix). This, one might add, is the experience of all language and all translation.

54. Theodor W. Adorno, *Minima Moralia: Reflections from Damaged Life*, trans. E. F. N. Jephcott (London: Verso, 1974), 46. Thomas Pepper first pointed out this mistranslation in "Guilt By (Un)free Association," in *Singularities: Extremes of Theory in the Twentieth Century* (Cambridge: Cambridge University Press, 1997), 20–48, here 21.

55. Theodor W. Adorno, *Minima Moralia: Refexionen aus dem beschädigten Leben*, in *Gesammelte Schriften*, ed. Rolf Tiedemann (Frankfurt am Main: Suhrkamp, 1997), 4:51.

56. Zukofsky and Jandl are mentioned in Klaus Reichert, *Die unendliche Aufgabe: Zum Übersetzen* (Munich: Hanser, 2003), 20–21.

57. For instance, the first line of Hölderlin's poem traverses the following stages of linguistic transformation: Denn, wie wenn hoch von der herrlichgestimmeten, der Orgel // Then we went, high hooked from the hardly edged dimness, dark orgulous // Dann gingen wir, hoch gehakt von der kaum gerandeten Trübheit, dunkel stölzern // Darn kinky, we. O harken wonder cow gay run debt, tree bite. Doom-kelt stole the urn // Ziemlich schräg, wir. O hör Wunderkuh schwul verschulde dich beiß Baum. Untergangskelte hat Urne gestohlen" (Schuldt and Robert Kelly, *Friedrich Hölderlin: "Am Quell der Donau,"* 2 vols. [Göttingen: Steidl Verlag, 1998], 2:7). For a theoretical reflection on this project, see Schuldt's afterword (2:75–78), in which he writes, among other things:

> Languages once come out of the unfolding of sense and sound, out of their twisting and twirling and tweaking each other. They still do. Two siamese worlds where correspondence and caricature, separation and reflection, mockery and resonance are playing hide-and-seek while we listeners, adrift in the din, go on dreaming of reassuring tautologies. Sound is the soul of language while the meanings of words form the body. The five voices or incarnations that constitute the present work are switching back and forth between speaking and listening, mouth and ear. . . . Am Quell der Donau arises from a simple situation: What one person is saying in one language, in German, is overheard by another in a second language, in English. Whatever he hears is entirely different from what is being said. We cannot even determine whether he has heard the wrong copy. But he certainly heard the wrong language. It is, however, the only language he knows or notices. It is in this language that he fashions for himself a speech from what came to his hearing. What else can he do? He has to make up this speech from scratch, in his language, with his sense. He is speaking." (75)

58. Martin Heidegger, "Building Dwelling Thinking," in *Poetry, Language, Thought*, 141–159, here 150; "Bauen Wohnen Denken," in *Vorträge und Aufsätze*, 139–156, here 146.

59. Martin Heidegger, *Heraklit*, vol. 55 of *Gesamtausgabe* (Frankfurt am Main: Klostermann, 1979), 44.

60. In a suggestive meditation, Ludger Heidbrink devotes himself to the question concerning the extent to which Heidegger's thoughts on translation can be read

as a form of carrying oneself over toward an other in the scene of recognition. The question opens one of the ethico-political dimension of Heidegger's engagement with translation. See "Das Eigene im Fremden: Martin Heideggers Begriff der Übersetzung," in *Übersetzung und Dekonstruktion*, ed. Alfred Hirsch (Frankfurt am Main: Suhrkamp, 1997), 349–372.

61. Figal, "Seinserfahrung und Ubersetzung," 184.

62. Martin Heidegger, "Der Spruch des Anaximander," in *Holzwege*, 317–368, here 342–343.

63. Heidegger, *Parmenides*, 16.

64. I am indebted on this point to the excellent discussion, in the context of a reading of Lacan as a translator of Heidegger, by Hans-Dieter Gondek, "Logos und Übersetzung: Heidegger als Übersetzer Heraklits—Lacan als Übersetzer Heideggers," in *Übersetzung und Dekonstruktion*, ed. Hirsch, 263–348, here 272.

65. On the topological dimensions that relate Heidegger's thinking of language to his thinking of place and space, see Otto Pöggeler, "Heidegger's Topology of Being," in *On Heidegger and Language*, ed. Joseph Kockelmans (Evanston, Ill.: Northwestern University Press, 1972), 107–146; Adam Sharr, *Heidegger's Hut* (Cambridge, Mass.: MIT Press, 2006); and Jeff Malpas, *Heidegger's Topology: Being, Place, and World* (Cambridge, Mass.: MIT Press, 2007). In a different tonality, two other recent publications provide a less theoretical but empirically saturated account of Heidegger's more quotidian inscriptions in his native topologies, including a remarkable range of previously unknown facts and documents: Hans Dieter Zimmermann, *Martin und Fritz Heidegger: Philosophie und Fastnacht* (Munich: Beck, 2005); and Alfred Denker and Elsbeth Büchin, *Martin Heidegger und seine Heimat* (Stuttgart: Klett-Cotta, 2005).

66. Barbara Johnson was the first critic to suggest a link between Heidegger's image of the bridge and the general problem of translation, in "Taking Fidelity Philosophically," in *Difference in Translation*, ed. Joseph Graham (Ithaca, N.Y.: Cornell University Press, 1985), 142–148, here 148.

6. *Afterness and the Image (I)*

1. Graham Clarke, *The Photograph* (Oxford: Oxford University Press, 1997), 24. Clark's account should be supplemented by Bernd Stiegler's recent history of the theory of photography, *Theoriegeschichte der Photographie* (Munich: Fink, 2006), and by Martin Schulz's investigation of whether there can be a "science" of the image or only of images in *Ordnungen der Bilder: Eine Einführung in die Bildwissenschaft* (Munich: Fink, 2005).

2. André Bazin, "The Ontology of the Photographic Image," trans. Hugh Gray, *Film Quarterly* 13, no. 4 (1960): 4–9.

3. Franz Kafka, *Letters to Felice*, ed. Erich Heller and Jürgen Born, trans. James Stern and Elisabeth Duckworth (London: Penguin, 1978), 202.

4. Jean-Luc Nancy reminds us of this etymology of photography in "*Nous Autres*," in *The Ground of the Image*, trans. Jeff Fort (New York: Fordham University Press, 2005), 100–107, here 104.

5. Susan Sontag, *Regarding the Pain of Others* (New York: Farrar, Straus and Giroux, 2003); Vilém Flusser, *Für eine Philosophie der Fotografie* (Berlin: European Photography Verlag, 2000); Geoffrey Batchen, *Each Wild Idea: Writing, Photography, History* (Cambridge, Mass.: MIT Press, 2001); Hubertus von Amelunxen, "Fotografie *nach der Fotografie*," in *Fotografie nach der Fotografie*, ed. Hubertus von Amelunxen, Stefan Iglhaut, and Florian Rötzer, with Alexis Cassel (Dresden: Verlag der Kunst, 1995), 116–123.

6. Jacques Derrida, *Right of Inspection*, with photographs by Marie-François Plissart, trans. David Wills (New York: Monacelli Press, 1998). The pages of this edition, both those containing Plissart's photographic plates and those containing Derrida's commentary, are unnumbered. Quotations from this work therefore appear without page numbers in the text.

7. Jacques Derrida. "The Deaths of Roland Barthes," trans. Pascale-Anne Brault and Michael Naas, in *The Work of Mourning*, ed. Pascale-Anne Brault and Michael Naas (Chicago: University of Chicago Press, 2001), 31–67; *Athens, Still Remains*, trans. Pascale-Anne Brault and Michael Naas (New York: Fordham University Press, 2010); *Copy, Archive, Signature: A Conversation on Photography*, trans. Jeff Fort, ed., with an introduction, Gerhard Richter (Stanford, Calif.: Stanford University Press, 2010); *The Truth in Painting*, trans. Geoff Bennington (Chicago: University of Chicago Press, 1987); and *Memoirs of the Blind: The Self-Portrait and Other Ruins*, trans. Pascale-Anne Brault and Michael Naas (Chicago: University of Chicago Press, 1993). For a more extensive discussion of the entire range of Derrida's work on photography, see my "Between Translation and Invention: The Photograph in Deconstruction," introduction to *Copy, Archive, Signature*, ed. Richter, ix–xxxviii, 55–64.

8. Derrida, "Deaths of Roland Barthes," 48.

9. Ibid., 57.

10. Ibid., 49.

11. Kafka, *Letters to Felice*, 255.

12. A representative selection of this series is now available in Stefan Moses, *Die Monographie*, ed. Ulrich Pohlmann and Matthias Harder (Munich: Schirmer/Mosel, 2002). This magnificent volume of Moses's photographs includes numerous essays and other texts by such critics as Ilse Eichinger, Hans Magnus Enzensberger, and Alexander Kluge, among many others.

13. Paul de Man, *Allegories of Reading: Figural Language in Rousseau, Nietzsche, Rilke, and Proust* (New Haven, Conn.: Yale University Press, 1979), epigraph without pagination.

14. Nancy, "*Nous autres*," 104.

15. Ibid., 104–105.

16. Matthias Harder, "Bilder einer deutschen Gesellschaft: Das fotografisch-epische Theater des Stefan Moses," in Moses, *Die Monographie*, 13–26, here 23.

17. Roland Barthes, *Camera Lucida: Reflections on Photography*, trans. Richard Howard (New York: Noonday, 1993), 12.

18. An early version of part of the following paragraphs devoted to a close reading of Moses's portrait of Adorno appeared in Gerhard Richter, "A Portrait of Non-Identity," *Monatshefte* 94, no. 1 (2002): 1–9. Long after composing these lines, I found out that my friend Hubertus von Amelunxen, in the context of his meditation on the relays between photography and the figure of the echo, had devoted a paragraph to the discussion of these Adorno portraits, in "Das Echo: Zu einem Zustand der Fotografie," *Fotogeschichte* 40 (1991): 31–39. I thank Hubertus von Amelunxen for making a reprint of his illuminating essay available to me and am glad (and amazed) to see that there appears to be such a strong, quasi-objective pull in the logic of the matter itself, a pull capable of being shared, invisibly, by a community of kindred spirits.

19. Barthes, *Camera Lucida*, 10–13.

20. Derrida, *Copy, Archive, Signature*, 31–32

21. Theodor W. Adorno, *Negative Dialektik* (Frankfurt am Main: Suhrkamp, 1970), 148.

22. Theodor W. Adorno, *Zur Metakritik der Erkenntnistheorie*, in *Gesammelte Schriften* (Frankfurt am Main: Suhrkamp, 1997), 5:32.

23. Jacques Derrida, *Archive Fever: A Freudian Impression*, trans. Eric Prenowitz (Chicago: University of Chicago Press, 1996).

24. Dirk Reinartz, *Totenstill: Bilder aus den ehemaligen deutschen Konzentrationslagern* (Göttingen: Steidl, 1994).

25. Kafka, *Letters to Felice*, 161.

26. Barthes, *Camera Lucida*, 97. Derrida expands on Barthes's conjunction of photography and death when he writes that

> it is the modern possibility of photography (whether art or technique matters little here) that combines death and the referent in the same system. It was not for the first time, and this conjugation of death and the referent did not have to wait for the Photograph to have an essential relationship to reproductive technique, or to technique in general, but the immediate proof given by the photographic apparatus or by the structure of the *remains* it leaves behind are irreducible events, ineffaceably original. . . . By the time—at the instant—that the *punctum* rends space, the reference and death are in it together in the photograph. ("Deaths of Roland Barthes," 53)

27. Kafka, *Letters to Felice*, 191.

28. Martin Heidegger, "Der Ursprung des Kunstwerkes," in *Holzwege* (Frankfurt am Main: Klostermann, 1980), 1–72, here 65.

29. Ibid.

30. Derrida's last words were first recorded for us by David Farrell Krell, "Shudder Speed: The Photograph as Ecstasy and Tragedy," *Mosaic: A Journal for the Interdisciplinary Study of Literature* 37, no. 4 (2004): 21–37, here 21n.1. Krell's essay also represents a fine meditation in its own right on various experiential and conceptual aspects of photography.

7. Afterness and the Image (II)

1. Jacques Rancière, "Are Some Things Unrepresentable?" in *The Future of the Image*, trans. Gregory Elliot (London: Verso, 2007), 109–138; Thierry de Duve, *Kant After Duchamp* (Cambridge, Mass.: MIT Press, 1996).

2. It remains to be investigated how this specifically imagistic or iconographic self-resistance relates to the self-resistance of language itself. For a recent discussion of the relation between the figurative logic of the image and that of language more generally, see Gottfried Boehm, "Jenseits der Sprache? Anmerkungen zur Logik der Bilder," in *Wie Bilder Sinn erzeugen: Die Macht des Zeigens* (Berlin: Berlin University Press, 2007), 34–53. Concerning the ways in which the aesthetic specificity of the language of the photographic image inflects the philosophy of history as a question of the medium itself, see, most recently, the essays in Robin Kelsey and Blake Stimson, eds., *The Meaning of Photography* (New Haven, Conn.: Yale University Press, 2008).

3. Theodor W. Adorno, *Minima Moralia: Reflexionen aus dem beschädigten Leben*, in *Gesammelte Schriften*, ed. Rolf Tiedemann (Frankfurt am Main: Suhrkamp, 1997), 4:27.

4. Walter Benjamin, *Charles Baudelaire: Ein Lyriker im Zeitalter des Hochkapitalismus*, in *Gesammelte Schriften*, ed. Rolf Tiedemann and Hermann Schweppenhäuser (Frankfurt am Main: Suhrkamp, 1991), 1:511–604, here 590.

5. Walter Benjamin, "Pariser Passagen I," in *Das Passagen-Werk*, in *Gesammelte Schriften*, ed. Rolf Tiedemann and Hermann Schweppenhäuser (Frankfurt am Main: Suhrkamp, 1991), 5:993–1038, here 1001.

6. Walter Benjamin, *Ursprung des deutschen Trauerspiels*, in *Gesammelte Schriften*, 1:203–430, here 345.

7. Theodor W. Adorno, "Nachwort," in Walter Benjamin, *Berliner Kindheit um neunzehnhundert* (Frankfurt am Main: Suhrkamp, 1950), 176–180, here 177.

8. Walter Benjamin, "Das Kunstwerk im Zeitalter seiner technischen Reproduzierbarkeit (Dritte Fassung)," in *Gesammelte Schriften*, 1:471–508, here 473. For an extended analysis of the logic and possibilities of the "useless" in Benjamin's work, see Gerhard Richter, *Walter Benjamin and the Corpus of Autobiography* (Detroit: Wayne State University Press, 2000).

9. Wolfgang Ullrich, "Bruchwerk," in *Verwindungen: Arbeit an Heidegger*, ed. Wolfgang Ullrich (Frankfurt am Main: Fischer, 2003), 111–121, here 111. Albert Speer's

reflections on the ruin are recorded in his memoirs, *Erinnerungen* (Berlin: Ullstein, 1969), 69. For a recent analysis that places Speer's obsession with the ruin in the context of the philosophies of art and theories of history developed by Hegel, Adorno, and Arthur Danto, see Lydia Goehr, "The Pastness of the Work: Albert Speer and the Monumentalism of Intentional Ruins," in *Elective Affinities: Musical Essays on the History of Aesthetic Theory* (New York: Columbia University Press, 2008), 136–170.

10. Walter Benjamin, "Über den Begriff der Geschichte," in *Gesammelte Schriften*, 1:691–704, here 695.

11. Martin Heidegger, *Heraklit*, vol. 55 of *Gesamtausgabe* (Frankfurt am Main: Klostermann, 1979), 137. Wolfgang Ullrich proceeds from this passage to analyze the various ways in which Heidegger *himself* was turned into an image, especially with regard to the many photographs taken over the years by such photographers as Digne Meller Marcovicz, François Fédier, and Felix H. Man that show him in his preferred "thinker poses" and in the context of his famous hut, in "Heidegger im Bild," in *Verwindungen: Arbeit an Heidegger*, ed. Wolfgang Ullrich (Frankfurt: Fischer, 2003), 9–43. Many of these remarkable images have been collected in Digne Meller Marcovicz, *Martin Heidegger: Photos 23. September 1966/17. + 18. Juni 1968* (Frankfurt am Main: Klostermann, 1985); and François Fédier, *Soixante-deux photographies des Martin Heidegger* (Paris: Gallimard, 1999).

12. Martin Heidegger, *Platon: Sophistes*, vol. 19 of *Gesamtausgabe* (Frankfurt am Main: Klostermann, 1992), especially 388–405.

13. Martin Heidegger, "Die Zeit des Weltbildes," in *Holzwege* (Frankfurt am Main: Klostermann, 1980), 73–110.

14. For instance in his 1957 Freiburg lecture on identity and difference: Martin Heidegger, *Identität und Differenz* (Pfullingen: Neske, 1990), 24–25.

15. This paragraph summarizes the historical remarks made by Wlad Godzich, "The Tiger on the Paper Mat," foreword to Paul de Man, *The Resistance to Theory* (Minneapolis: University of Minnesota Press, 1989), ix–xviii, here xiii–xv.

16. Heidegger takes up the trope of the "imageless" at various other points in his writing as well—for instance, in his late poem-like meditation (a lyrical form to which he himself referred as *Gedachtes*, or "that which has been thought") "Denken—als Weg," in which he evokes a thinking (*Denken*) that "poeticizes imagelessly [*bildlos dichtet*]" ("Denken—als Weg," in *Gedachtes* [Frankfurt am Main: Klostermann, 2007], 43).

17. Martin Heidegger, ". . . dichterisch wohnet der Mensch . . . ," in *Vorträge und Aufsätze* (Stuttgart: Neske, 2000), 181–198, here 194–195.

18. Maurice Blanchot, "Two Versions of the Imaginary," in *The Space of Literature*, trans. Ann Smock (Lincoln: University of Nebraska Press, 1982), 254–263, here 254.

19. Ibid., 255.

20. Ibid.

21. Ibid., 255–256.

22. Ibid., 260.

23. Ibid., 254.

24. Gilles Deleuze, *Difference and Repetition*, trans. Paul Patton (New York: Columbia University Press, 1994), xv–xvii, here xvi.

25. Ibid.

26. Ibid.

27. Ibid., xvii.

28. Ibid., 167.

29. Sigmund Freud, *Der Mann Moses und die monotheistische Religion: Drei Abhandlungen*, in *Studienausgabe*, ed. Alexander Mitscherlich, Angela Richards, and James Strachey (Frankfurt am Main: Fischer, 2000), 9:455–581; Max Weber, *Wirtschaft und Gesellschaft: Grundriß der verstehenden Soziologie* (Tübingen: Mohr Siebeck, 1980).

30. Walter Benjamin, *Einbahnstraße*, in *Gesammelte Schriften*, ed. Rolf Tiedemann and Hermann Schweppenhäuser (Frankfurt am Main: Suhrkamp, 1991), 4:83–148, here 94.

8. *Afterness and Experience (I)*

1. Alphonso Lingis and Mary Zournazi, "Murmurs of Life: A Conversation with Alphonso Lingis," in *Hope: New Philosophies for Change*, ed. Mary Zournazi (New York: Routledge, 2002), 22–41, here 23.

2. Ibid.

3. Ibid., 23–24.

4. Ibid., 41.

5. Peter Szondi, "Hoffnung im Vergangenen: Über Walter Benjamin," in *Schriften* (Frankfurt am Main: Suhrkamp, 1978), 2:278–294.

6. Andrew Benjamin, *Present Hope: Philosophy, Architecture, Judaism* (London: Routledge, 1997), 153.

7. Reinhard Lettau, "Zu Herbert Marcuses Tod," in *Zerstreutes Hinausschaun: Vom Schreiben über Vorgänge in direkter Nähe oder in der Entfernung von Schreibtischen* (Frankfurt am Main: Fischer, 1982), 203–205, here 204–205.

8. Jochen Hörisch, *Die ungeliebte Universität: Rettet die Alma Mater!* (Munich: Hanser, 2006); Marc Bousquet, *How the University Works: Higher Education and the Low-Wage Nation* (New York: New York University Press, 2008).

9. Many of these documents are conveniently collected in Ehrhard Bahr, ed., *Was ist Aufklärung?* (Stuttgart: Reclam, 1974); and James Schmidt, ed., *What Is Enlightenment? Eighteenth-Century Answers and Twentieth-Century Questions* (Berkeley: University of California Press, 1996).

10. This is the term proposed by the historian Peter Gay in *The Enlightenment: The Science of Freedom* (New York: Norton, 1996).

11. Immanuel Kant, "An Answer to the Question: What Is Enlightenment?," trans. James Schmidt, in *What Is Enlightenment?*, ed. Schmidt, 58–64, here 58.

12. Ibid., 60.

13. See Max Horkeimer's foundational essay, "Traditional and Critical Theory," in *Critical Theory: Selected Essays*, trans. Matthew J. O'Connell et al. (New York: Continuum, 1999), 188–243.

14. For recent assessments of some of the dilemmas encountered by serious writing that aims to be public and transformative, see the nuanced accounts by John McCumber, "The Metaphysics of Clarity and the Freedom of Meaning," and Michael Warner, "Styles of Intellectual Publics," both in *Just Being Difficult? Academic Writing in the Public Arena*, ed. Jonathan Culler and Kevin Lamb (Stanford, Calif.: Stanford University Press, 2003), 58–71, 106–125.

15. Judith Butler, *Precarious Life: The Powers of Mourning and Violence* (London: Verso, 2004); Samuel Weber, *Targets of Opportunity: On the Militarization of Thinking* (New York: Fordham University Press, 2005).

16. Kant, "What Is Enlightenment?," 58.

17. Friedrich Schlegel, "Concerning the Essence of Critique," in *Theory as Practice: A Critical Anthology of Early German Romantic Writings*, ed. and trans. Jochen Schulte-Sasse, Haynes Horne, Elizabeth Mittman, and Lisa C. Roetzel (Minneapolis: University of Minnesota Press, 1997), 268–277, here 276–277.

18. Theodor W. Adorno, "Critique," in *Critical Models: Interventions and Catchwords*, trans. Henry W. Pickford (New York: Columbia University Press, 1998), 281–288, here 288.

19. Michel Foucault, "What Is Critique?," trans. Kevin Paul Geiman, in *What Is Enlightenment?*, ed. Schmidt, 382–398, here 391.

20. Martin Heidegger, "Hölderlin's Earth and Heaven," in *Elucidations of Hölderlin's Poetry*, trans. Keith Hoeller (Amherst, N.Y.: Humanity Books, 2000), 175–207, here 176.

21. Brod's recollection, from his 1921 article on Kafka in *Die neue Rundschau*, is cited in Walter Benjamin, "Franz Kafka: On the Tenth Anniversary of His Death" (1934), trans. Harry Zohn, in *Selected Writings*, vol. 2, *1927–1934*, ed. Michael Jennings, Howard Eiland, and Gary Smith (Cambridge, Mass.: Harvard University Press, 1999), 794–818, here 789.

22. Ernst Bloch, "Can Hope Be Disappointed?," in *Literary Essays*, trans. Andrew Joron et al. (Stanford, Calif.: Stanford University Press, 1998), 339–45 (hereafter cited by page number in the text).

9. *Afterness and Experience (II)*

1. For a sustained reflection on the elusive concept of situatedness, see David Simpson, *Situatedness, or, Why We Keep Saying Where We're Coming From* (Durham, N.C.: Duke University Press, 2002).

2. This is the title Martin Heidegger gives to his imbrication of poetry and thinking, his 1947 lyric poems collected in *Aus der Erfahrung des Denkens* (Stuttgart: Klett-Cotta, 2005).

3. Plato, "Theaetetus," in *Collected Dialogues*, ed. Edith Hamilton and Huntington Cairns (Princeton, N.J.: Princeton University Press, 1989), 845–919, here 860 (155d).

4. Edward Said, "Millennial Reflections: Heroism and Humanism," *Al-Ahram Weekly On-Line* 463 (January 6–12, 2000): 1–4, http://weekly.ahram.org.eg/2000/463/op10.htm, quoted in Jacques Lezra, "Unrelated Passions," *Differences* 14, no. 1 (2003): 74–87, here 86.

5. One also thinks of the Foucauldian notion of those "founders of discursivity," such as Marx and Freud, who author not merely their own texts but enable new and potentially endless discursive possibilities.

6. Barbara Johnson, "An Interview with Barbara Johnson, conducted by Michael Payne and Harold Schweizer," in *The Wake of Deconstruction* (Oxford: Blackwell, 1994), 76–103, here 100–101.

7. See, for instance, Gilles Deleuze and Félix Guattari, *What Is Philosophy?*, trans. Hugh Tomlison and Graham Burchell (New York: Columbia University Press, 1994), 88.

8. Christopher Norris, "What Are the Questions that Fascinate You? What Do You Want to Know? (A Roundabout Answer to Some Straightforward Questions)," *SubStance* 32, no. 1 (2003): 44–49, here 49.

9. Martin Heidegger, "Was heißt Denken?," in *Vorträge und Aufsätze* (Stuttgart: Neske, 2000), 123–137, here 124.

10. Theodor W. Adorno, "Resignation," in *Gesammelte Schriften*, ed. Rolf Tiedemann (Frankfurt am Main: Suhrkamp, 1997), 10, bk. 2:794–799, here 789–790.

11. Friedrich Hölderlin, "In lieblicher Bläue . . . ," in *Sämtliche Werke und Briefe*, ed. Michael Knaupp (Munich: Hanser, 1992), 1:908–909, here 908.

12. Bertolt Brecht, *Dreigroschenroman*, in *Große kommentierte Berliner und Frankfurter Ausgabe*, vol. 16, *Prosa I*, ed. Werner Hecht, Jan Knopf, Werner Mittenzwei, and Klaus-Detlev Müller (Frankfurt: Suhrkamp, 1990), 173.

13. Fredric Jameson, "Criticism and History," in *The Ideologies of Theory: Essays, 1971–1986*, vol. 1, *Situations of Theory* (Minneapolis: University of Minnesota Press, 1988), 119–136, here 119–120.

14. It is necessary as well to consider additional repressed modes of knowledge encrypted in crude thinking, such as the terms of psychoanalysis. As Kalliopi Nikolopoulou reminds me,

> [P]sychoanalysis as a body of knowledge has been the stage of much of this tension between practical (crude) and theoretical thinking (speculative, most notably in the Lacanian branch of it). At the same time, Freud, and even more Lacan, seem to locate the knowledge that comes out of analytic practice as a dialectical knowl-

edge between the *plumpes Denken* (itself often somatic) of the analysand (though it itself can also be dialectizable) and the more refined knowledge of the analyst. Freud himself has often outlined the very nature, questions, and principles of psychoanalysis in a "crude" style. Phrases that come to mind are the definition of psychoanalysis as the project that tries to answer the question "what do women want," or even particular empirical descriptions of his concepts such as "his majesty the baby" for primary narcissism. (Personal correspondence with the author)

15. In these etymological remarks, I follow once again Jacob and Wilhelm Grimm, *Deutsches Wörterbuch* (Munich: Deutscher Taschenbuch Verlag, 1999), 13:1939–1941; and Wolfgang Pfeifer et al., eds., *Etymologisches Wörterbuch des Deutschen* (Munich: Deutscher Taschenbuch Verlag, 1995), 1021.

16. Martin Heidegger, *Hölderlins Hymne "Der Ister"* (Frankfurt am Main: Klostermann, 1984).

17. This emphasis on the perpetual *learning* of *plumpes Denken* rather than its mere execution from a standpoint of mastery is also encoded in Brecht's preference for calling his dramatic works *Lehrstücke*, or "teaching pieces."

18. Walter Benjamin, "Brechts Dreigroschenroman," in *Versuche über Brecht*, ed. Rolf Tiedemann (Frankfurt am Main: Suhrkamp, 1971), 54–63, here 60.

19. Giorgio Agamben, *Idea of Prose*, trans. Michael Sullivan and Sam Whitsitt (Albany: State University of New York Press, 1995), 138.

20. Jean-François Lyotard, *The Inhuman: Reflections on Time*, trans. Geoffrey Bennington and Rachel Bowlby (Stanford, Calif.: Stanford University Press, 1991), 73.

21. According to recollections by his son Hermann Heidegger, who notes that Heidegger repeatedly made this confession to him. Cited in Rüdiger Safranski, *Ein Meister aus Deutschland: Heidegger und seine Zeit* (Frankfurt am Main: Fischer, 1997), 352.

22. Theodor W. Adorno, *Quasi una fantasia*, in *Gesammelte Schriften*, vol. 16, *Musikalische Schriften I–III*, ed. Rolf Tiedemann (Frankfurt am Main: Suhrkamp, 1997), 249–642, here 540.

10. *Afterness and Experience (III)*

1. Johann Wolfgang von Goethe, *Briefe*, vol. 1, *Briefe der Jahre 1764–1786*, ed. Karl Robert Mandelkow (Munich: Deutscher Taschenbuch Verlag, 1988), 99.

2. Jacques Derrida, "'Dialanguages,'" in *Points . . . Interviews, 1974–1994*, ed. Elisabeth Weber, trans. Peggy Kamuf et al. (Stanford, Calif.: Stanford University Press, 1995), 132–155, here 143–144.

3. David Farrell Krell, *The Purest of Bastards: Works of Mourning, Art, and Affirmation in the Thought of Jacques Derrida* (University Park: Pennsylvania State University Press, 2000), 146.

4. Friedrich Nietzsche, *Menschliches, Allzumenschliches*, in *Kritische Studienausgabe*, ed. Giorgio Colli and Mazzino Montinari (Munich: Deutscher Taschenbuch Verlag; Berlin: de Gruyter, 1999), 2:430.

5. Georg Wilhelm Friedrich Hegel, *Enzyklopädie der philosophischen Wissenschaften*, part 3, vol. 10 of *Werke*, ed. Eva Moldenhauer and Karl Markus Michel (Frankfurt am Main: Suhrkamp, 1986), 282.

6. Jacques Derrida, *Specters of Marx: The State of the Debt, the Work of Mourning, and the New International*, trans. Peggy Kamuf (New York: Routledge, 1994), for instance, 91–92. Compare further Derrida's remarks on the question of learning how to inherit responsibly—that is, aporetically—in his reply to various critics of *Specters of Marx*: "Marx & Sons," trans. G. M. Goshgarian, in *Ghostly Demarkations: A Symposium on Jacques Derrida's Specters of Marx*, ed. Michael Sprinker (London: Verso, 1999), 213–269.

7. Rodolphe Gasché, *Inventions of Difference: On Jacques Derrida* (Cambridge, Mass.: Harvard University Press, 1994), 20–21.

8. Jacques Derrida, *Memoires for Paul de Man*, rev. ed., trans. Cecile Lindsay, Jonathan Culler, Eduardo Cadava, and Peggy Kamuf (New York: Columbia University Press, 1989), 11.

9. Ibid., 14.

10. Ibid., 20.

11. Ibid.

12. Ibid., 123.

13. Ibid., 29.

14. Friedrich Hölderlin, "Die Titanen," in *Sämtliche Werke und Briefe*, ed. Michael Knaupp (Munich: Hanser, 1992), 1:390–394, here 391.

15. Jacques Derrida, "Rams: Uninterrupted Dialogue—Between Two Infinities, the Poem," in *Sovereignties in Question: The Poetics of Paul Celan*, ed. Thomas Dutoit and Outi Pasanen (New York: Fordham University Press, 2005), 135–163, here 163.

16. Jacques Derrida, "Rams: Uninterrupted Dialogue—Between Two Infinities, the Poem," and "Aus den Fugen," trans. Sigrid Vagt, *Heiner Müller Archiv*, Stiftung Archiv der Akademie der Künste (1998): 17–18.

17. Geoffrey Bennington and Jacques Derrida, *Jacques Derrida* (Chicago: University of Chicago Press, 1993).

18. Jacques Derrida, "The Taste of Tears," in *The Work of Mourning*, ed. Pascale-Anne Brault and Michael Naas (Chicago: University of Chicago Press, 2001), 105–110, here 107.

19. Hegel, *Enzyklopädie*, 282.

20. A general account of Hegel's engagement with memory can be found in Martin Donougho, "Hegel's Art of Memory," in *Endings: Questions of Memory in Hegel and Heidegger*, ed. Rebecca Comay and John McCumber (Evanston, Ill.: Northwestern University Pres, 1999), 139–159. For a nuanced reading of the distinction between the two modes of memory, *die Erinnerung* and *das Gedächtnis*, within the framework of Hegel's system, see David Farrell Krell, "Of Pits and Pyramids: Hegel on Memory, Remembrance, and Writing," in *Of Memory, Reminiscence, and Writing: On the Verge* (Bloomington: Indiana University Press, 1990), 205–239. Together with Edward Casey's far-reaching *Remembering: A Phenomenological Study*, 2nd ed. (Bloomington: Indiana University Press, 2000), Krell's book also is one of the most consistently illuminating guides in the vast sea of recent studies concerning the theoretical debates over the history of Western thinking about memory, from Plato via Descartes, Hobbes, and Locke to Nietzsche, Freud, Heidegger, and Derrida. An important supplement is Maurice Halbwachs's classic account, *On Collective Memory*, trans. Lewis A. Coser (Chicago: University of Chicago Press, 1992), originally published in French in 1950, five years after the author's death in Buchenwald.

21. Derrida, *Memoires for Paul de Man*, 56.

22. Ibid., 58.

23. Ibid., 65.

24. Ibid., 58.

25. Ibid., 58–59. Derrida's notions of the past that has never been present—that is, the past that "is" only in the passing of the trace—should also be thought in terms of his understanding of an "absolute past," a past without a real past conceived as presence, in other texts, such as *Of Grammatology*. For a discussion of this aspect of *Of Grammatology*, see, especially, Krell, "Mourning Ultratranscendence," in *Purest of Bastards*, 103–116.

26. Derrida, *Memoires for Paul de Man*, 59.

27. Martin Heidegger, *Übungen für Anfänger: Schillers Briefe über die ästhetische Erziehung des Menschen, Wintersemester 1936/37*, transcribed by Wilhelm Hallwachs, ed. Ulrich von Bülow, with an essay by Odo Marquard (Marbach am Neckar: Deutsche Schillergesellschaft, 2005), 9.

11. *Afterness and Empty Space*

1. Hannah Arendt, "No Longer and Not Yet," in *Essays in Understanding, 1930–1954*, ed. Jerome Kohn (New York: Harcourt, Brace, 1993), 158–162, here 158–159.

2. Sigmund Freud, *Civilization and Its Discontents*, trans. James Strachey (New York: Norton, 1989), 17–18.

3. Arendt, "No Longer and Not Yet," 159.

4. Ibid.
5. Ibid.
6. Ibid., 161.
7. Ibid.
8. Jacques Derrida, *Learning to Live Finally: An Interview with Jean Birnbaum*, trans. Pascale-Anne Brault and Michael Naas (Hoboken, N.J.: Melville House, 2007), 26.
9. Ibid., 24.
10. Ibid., 52.
11. Cathy Caruth, "Trauma and Experience: Introduction," in *Trauma: Explorations in Memory*, ed. Cathy Caruth (Baltimore: Johns Hopkins University Press, 1995), 3–12, here 9.
12. Derrida, *Learning to Live Finally*, 44.
13. Ernst Bloch, "Logikum/Zur Ontologie des Noch-Nicht-Seins," in *Werkausgabe*, vol. 13, *Tübinger Einleitung in die Philosophie* (Frankfurt am Main: Surkamp, 1985), 210–300, here 219. See also Bloch, *Philosophische Grundfragen I: Zur Ontologie des Noch-Nicht-Seins: Ein Vortrag und zwei Abhandlungen* (Frankfurt am Main: Suhrkamp, 1961).
14. Arendt, "No Longer and Not Yet," 162.

Afterwards

1. Georg Büchner, *Leonce und Lena*, in *Werke und Briefe* (Munich: DTV, 1967), 85–111, here 95, cited in Michael Levine, "*Pendant*: Büchner, Celan, and the Terrible Voice of the Meridian," *MLN* 122 (2007): 573–601, here 573.
2. Walter Kaufmann, "Translator's Introduction," in *The Birth of Tragedy*, in *Basic Writings of Nietzsche*, ed. and trans. Walter Kaufmann (New York: Modern Library, 2000), 3–13, here 5.
3. Jacques Derrida, *The Animal That Therefore I Am*, ed. Marie-Louise Mallet, trans. David Wills (New York: Fordham University Press, 2008), 3.
4. Ibid., 11.
5. Ibid., 55.
6. Franz Kafka, *Die Zürauer Aphorismen*, ed. Roberto Calasso (Frankfurt am Main: Suhrkamp, 2006), 57.
7. Walter Benjamin, *Ursprung des deutschen Trauerspiels*, in *Gesammelte Schriften*, ed. Rolf Tiedemann and Hermann Schweppenhäuser (Frankfurt am Main: Suhrkamp, 1991), 1:203–430, here 350; *Origin of German Tragic Drama*, trans. John Osborne (London: Verso, 1977), 175.
8. Heinrich von Kleist, "Brief an Ulrike Kleist vom 5. Oktober 1803," in *Sämtliche Werke und Briefe*, ed. Helmut Sembdner (Munich: Hanser, 1985), 2:735–737, here 736.

9. Martin Heidegger, *Martin Heidegger im Gespräch*, ed. Richard Wisser (Freiburg: Alber, 1970), 77.

10. Jean-François Lyotard, "Foreword: After the Words," in Joseph Kosuth, *Art After Philosophy and After: Collected Writings, 1966–1990*, ed. Gabriele Guercio (Cambridge, Mass.: MIT Press, 1991), xv–xviii, here xv.

Index

Adorno, Theodor W.: aesthetic theory of, 55–60, 80, 203, 211, 225n.30; "after Auschwitz" of, 2, 50–52, 55, 222nn.37,38; on afterness and critique, 22, 42, 161–162, 227n.23; allegorical thinking of, 64, 65, 67; and Benjamin, 22, 74–79, 81, 85, 223n.13; and Bloch, 112; on communication, 141, 223n.14; on constellation, 135, 144; critique of enlightenment by, 51, 56, 158, 162; debt to, 6; on dialectic of culture and barbarism, 55; and *finale*, 224n.23; on Hölderlin, 59; (mis)translation of work of, 62, 64–68, 82, 113, 232n.54; on negative dialectics, 48, 52, 54, 69, 70, 75, 131–132, 176, 222n.38; and Nietzschean *Nachgesang* of modernity, 38; oppositional spirit of, 70; on philosophical structure, 78; photographic self-portrait of, with Stefan Moses, 124, 127–134, 235n.18; and *plumpes Denken*, 178, 185; and political action, 176; and redemption, 68–69; and *Rettung*, 82, 85, 91, 211; and Speer, 237n.9; on *Spiegelschrift*, 66; on splinter in one's eye, 136; on *Sprachähnlichkeit*, 224n.20; on utopian thinking, 70, 112, 176, 185, 231n.53; on *Verfransung*, 56, 223n.8

WORKS OF: *Aesthetic Theory* (*Ästhetische Theorie*), 22, 49, 56, 59, 64, 130, 162, 222n.32, 223nn.4,10, 224n.17; "Afterword" ("Nachwort" [in

248 Index

Adorno, Theodor (*continued*)
Benjamin, *Berliner Kindheit um neunzehnhundert*]), 236n.7; *Alban Berg: Master of the Smallest Transition* (*Berg: Der Meister des kleinsten Übergangs*), 223n.3; "Art and the Arts" (Die Kunst und die Künste), 223n.8; "Aus einem Schulheft ohne Deckel: Bar Harbor, Sommer 1939," 69, 79, 225n.26; *Beethoven: The Philosophy of Music* (*Beethoven: Philosophie der Musik*), 223n.7; *Correspondence* (*Briefwechsel* [with Benjamin]), 225n.2, 226nn.7,14,15; "Critique" (Kritik), 48, 162, 221nn.29,30, 239n.18; "Cultural Criticism and Society" (Kulturkritik und Gesellschaft), 55, 67, 222n.2, 225n.25; *Dialectic of Enlightenment*, 49, 60, 66, 67; *In Search of Wagner* (*Versuch über Wagner*), 76, 79; Lecture on "Negative Dialectics" (*Vorlesung über "Negative Dialektik"*), 222n.1, 223n.11; *Minima Moralia: Reflections from Damaged Life* (*Minima Moralia: Reflexionen aus dem beschädigten Leben*), 22, 50, 60–63, 69, 72, 113, 222n.38, 224nn.21,22, 232nn.54,55, 236n.3; *Negative Dialectics* (*Negative Dialektik*), 22, 25, 49, 50, 55, 63, 64, 70, 79, 81, 83, 130, 162, 217n.34, 222nn.31,34,40,41,43, 225nn.24,31, 227n.22, 235n.21; *Notes to Literature* (*Noten zur Literatur*), 56, 224n.14; *On the Metacritique of Epistemology* (*Zur Metakritik der Erkenntnistheorie*), 131, 235n.22; "On the Question: What Is German?" (Auf die Frage: Was ist deutsch?), 223n.3; "Parataxis," 59, 224n.15; "Portrait of Walter Benjamin" (Charakteristik Walter Benjamins), 227n.30; *Prisms*, 229n.11; *Quasi una fantasia*, 241n.22; "Resignation," 240n.10; "Theses on the Language of the Philosopher" (Thesen über die Sprache des Philosophen), 69, 225n.27; "Words from Abroad" (Wörter aus der Fremde), 223n.14
Agamben, Giorgio, 183, 241n.19
aletheia. *See* Heidegger, Martin: on aletheia
allegory, 15, 36, 58–59, 61, 63–66, 75, 144, 190–191, 209, 223n.13
Althusser, Louis, 192
Amelunxen, Hubertus von, 121, 122, 234n.5, 235n.18
Anderson, Perry, 217n.1
Arendt, Hannah, 24, 38, 199–205, 243nn.1,3, 244n.14
Aristotle, 19
Azin, André, 119

Barthes, Roland, 122–123, 127, 129–130, 136, 139, 192, 235nn.17,19, 26
Batchen, Geoffrey, 121, 234n.5
Baudelaire, Charles, 5, 30, 36, 75, 77, 81, 120, 143, 231n.45, 236n.4
Bauer, Felice. *See* Kafka, Franz: and Felice Bauer
Baumgarten, Alexander Gottlieb, 46
Bazin, André, 233n.2
Beardsley, Monroe, 43, 220n.13
Beck, Ulrich, 217n.2
Beckett, Samuel, 38, 58, 156–157
Beethoven, Ludwig van, 56, 223n.7, 224n.23
Beistegui, Miguel de, 229n.9
Benjamin, Andrew, 156, 238n.6
Benjamin, Walter: and Adorno, 22, 74–79, 81, 85, 223n.13; on allegory, 36, 75, 144, 209, 223n.13; on angel of history, 75, 78; on Baudelaire, 5, 77, 143; and blotting paper, 85–86; and

Brecht, 5, 24, 182; canonical concepts of, 75; and communicative rationality, 81; and critique, 22, 44; on dialectic of culture and barbarism, 75, 79; and discourse of modernity, 7; on *Fortleben*, 6, 107, 202; on Fuchs, 79; and German baroque mourning play, 5, 36, 75, 84–85, 144, 209, 223n.13, 226n.11; and Habermas, 79–80, 82, 226nn.16,17; and historical materialism, 5, 80, 86; on hope, 155; on the image, 23, 77–78, 85–87, 143–144, 150–153, 203; and intellectual history of modernity, 14; and *Jetztzeit*, 75, 80; and Jewish Messianism, 75; and Kracauer, 83; on music, 77–78; on *Nachleben*, 2–6, 215n.14; on *Nachreifen*, 6, 107; and Nietzschean *Nachgesang* of modernity, 38; on optical unconscious, 135; on photography, 5, 86, 134–135, 228n.32; on *plumpes Denken*, 24, 182–183; on *Rettung*, 77–87, 91, 211, 225n.5, 227n.24; on ruins of history, 37, 69, 75, 144, 218n.17, 223n.13; and theology, 5–6; on translation, 6, 101, 107, 112; on *Überleben*, 6, 107, 202; and Warburg School, 213n.1; on weak messianic power, 75, 80

WORKS OF: *The Arcades Project* (*Das Passagen-Werk*), 3, 36, 75, 78, 84, 85–86, 144, 214nn.2–5, 225n.4, 226n.12, 227nn.27,29, 228nn.31,33, 236n.5; *Berlin Childhood around 1900* (*Berliner Kindheit um neunzehnhundert*), 6, 75, 214n.7, 236n.7; "Brecht's Three-Penny Novel" (*Brechts Dreigroschenroman*), 241n.18; *Charles Baudelaire*, 236n.4; *Correspondence* (*Briefwechsel* [with Adorno]), 225n.2, 226nn.7,14,15; "Critique of Violence," 63; "Diary Entries, 1938," 231n.51; "Goethe's *Elective Affinities*" (Goethes Wahlverwandtschaften), 43, 75, 87, 220nn.14,15, 228n.34, 237n.9; "Little History of Photography," 86, 134; *One-Way Street* (*Einbahnstraße*), 238n.30; *Origin of German Tragic Drama* (*Ursprung des deutschen Trauerspiels*), 36, 75, 84–85, 144, 209, 218n.16, 223n.13, 226n.11, 227n.28, 236n.6, 244n.7; "The Paris of the Second Empire in Baudelaire" (Das Paris des Second Empire bei Baudelaire), 143; "Pariser Passagen I," 83, 143, 227n.27, 236n.5; "The Task of the Translator" (Die Aufgabe des Übersetzers), 6, 101, 107, 112, 214n.6, 231n.45; "Theses on the Philosophy of History" (Über den Begriff der Geschichte), 75, 79, 145, 237n.10; "The Work of Art in the Age of Its Technical Reproducibility (Third Version)" (Das Kunstwerk im Zeitalter seiner technischen Reproduzierbarkeit [Dritte Fassung]), 144, 236n.8

Bennington, Geoffrey, 193, 242n.17
Benoist, Jean-Marie, 193
Berg, Alban, 55, 58, 78, 223n.3
Berger, Anne, 187
Berlin Wall, 164
Berlin Wednesday Society, 157
Berman, Marshall, 28, 217n.1
Bernard, Andreas, 224n.21
Bernasconi, Robert, 230n.31
Bernhard, Thomas, 112, 231n.50
Bernstein, J. M., 222n.38, 225n.29
Blanchot, Maurice: "Après Coup," 13, 215n.19; on the image, 23, 149–152, 203; *Lautrémont and Sade*, 40, 218n.2;

Blanchot, Maurice (*continued*)
  "Preface: What Is the Purpose of Criticism?," 218n.2; *Le ressassement éternal*, 13; *The Space of Literature*, 143, 237n.18; "Two Versions of the Imaginary," 143, 149, 237n.18
Bloch, Ernst: aesthetic *Vorschein* of, 136; debt to, 6; on hope, 12, 23–24, 164–167, 212, 239n.22; and Nietzschean *Nachgesang* of modernity, 38; on the Open (*das Offene*), 204; philosophy of the not yet of, 204, 244n.13; photographic self-portrait of, with Stefan Moses, 124; on religion and faith, 12; on utopian thinking, 112, 164, 231n.53
Bloom, Harold, 8
Blumenberg, Hans, 7, 37, 214n.8
Boehm, Gottfried, 236n.2
Böschenstein, Bernhard, 61
Bousquet, Marc, 157, 238n.8
Braque, Georges, 126
Brecht, Bertolt, 5, 24, 120, 178–185, 212, 240n.12, 241n.17
Breton, André, 120
Broch, Hermann, 199, 202, 205
Brod, Max. *See* Kafka, Franz: and Max Brod
Brunkhorst, Hauke, 223n.8
Bubner, Rüdiger, 57, 223n.9
Büchin, Elsbeth, 233n.65
Büchner, George, 206, 244n.1
Bülow, Frieda von, 139
Bülow, Ulrich von, 229n.10
Bürger, Peter, 226n.17
Bush, George W., 221n.30
Butler, Judith, 159

Cadava, Eduardo, 228n.32
Caputo, John D., 12, 215n.14
Caruth, Cathy, 10, 203, 214n.11, 244n.11
Casey, Edward, 243n.20
Catullus, Gaius Valerius, 113
Celan, Paul, 38, 242n.15, 244n.1
Christianity, 12, 35, 58, 74, 89, 152, 167, 214n.14
Clarke, Graham, 118, 233n.1
Clausewitz, Carl von, 83
Cohen, Herman, 75
Corngold, Stanley, 223n.6, 231n.52
critique, 39–53, 218n.1, 219nn.8,9

Damisch, Hubert, 118
Danto, Arthur, 237n.9
Dasein. *See* Heidegger, Martin: on *Dasein*
deconstruction: and critique, 42, 219n.8; and Derrida 68, 187–188, 216n.26; and dialectical concepts, 173–174; and memory, 187–188, 191, 195, 198
Deleuze, Gilles: and Derrida, 192; *Difference and Repetition*, 11, 143, 238n.24; on image of thought, 23, 151–152, 203; and Nietzschean *Nachgesang* of modernity, 38; on thought as deterritorialization, 175; *What Is Philosophy?*, 240n.7
de Man, Paul: on allegory, 15, 125, 234n.13; "Criticism and Crisis," 43, 220n.12; and Derrida, 186, 190–194; on *Erinnerung* and *Gedächtnis*, 195–197; on error and mistake, 231n.52; on Hölderlin, 192; and intellectual history of modernity, 14; "Kant and Schiller," 97, 229n.20; *The Resistance to Theory*, 237n.15
Denker, Alfred, 233n.65
Derrida, Jacques: debt to, 6; on following, 207–208; on Heidegger, 90, 120; on Hölderlin, 192; and the image, 122–123, 203; on inheritance, 216n.26; and intellectual history of modernity, 14; last words of, 138,

236n.30; on memory and mourning, 24, 186–198, 199, 212, 243n.20; on Narcissus, 186; and Nietzschean *Nachgesang* of modernity, 38; on paleonomy, 29; on *passé absolu*, 14–15, 243n.25; on photography, 23, 120–124, 130, 134–138, 211, 234n.7, 235n.26, 236n.30; on religion and faith, 12; son of, 138; on spectrality, 16; on survival, 203, 204; on translation, 95, 107, 112 WORKS OF: *The Animal That Therefore I Am*, 207–208, 244n.3; *Archive Fever: A Freudian Impression*, 135, 235n.23; *Athens, Still Remains*, 122, 234n.7; "Aus den Fugen," 242; *Cinders*, 188; *Copy, Archive, Signature*, 123, 234n.7, 235n.20; "The Deaths of Roland Barthes," 122–123, 234nn.7,8, 235n.26; "Declarations of Independence," 214n.9; "Dialanguages," 241n.2; "Faith and Knowledge: The Two Sources of 'Religion' at the Limits of Reason Alone," 12; *Glas*, 57; *Jacques Derrida*, 242n.17; *Learning to Live Finally*, 202, 244nn.8,12; "Living On/Borderlines," 231nn.46,50; *Memoires for Paul de Man*, 186, 190–194, 242n.8, 243nn.21,26; *Memoirs of the Blind: The Self-Portrait and Other Ruins*, 123, 234n.7; *Of Grammatology*, 187, 189, 243n.25; *Of Spirit: Heidegger and the Question*, 228n.8; "The Passage into Philosophy," 229n.16; *Positions*, 217n.4; "Rams: Uninterrupted Dialogue—Between Two Infinities, the Poem," 242nn.15,16; *Right of Inspection*, 234n.6; *Sovereignties in Question: The Poetics of Paul Celan*, 242n.15; *Specters of Marx*, 15, 189, 216n.24, 242n.6; *The Truth in Painting*, 121, 123, 234n.7; *The Work of Mourning*, 190, 191, 234nn.7,8, 242n.18

Descartes, René, 15, 36, 38, 49, 42, 145, 208, 243n.20
Didi-Huberman, Georges, 3, 213n.1
Dilthey, Wilhelm, 159
Donougho, Martin, 243n.20
Dorje, Sangda, 215n.22
Duchamp, Marcel, 141, 236n.1
Düsing, Klaus, 220n.19
Düttman, Alexander García, 215n.17, 227n.23
Duve, Thierry de, 141, 236n.1

Eichel, Christine, 223n.8
Eichinger, Ilse, 234n.12
Eisenberg, Daniel, 149
Engels, Friedrich, 31
enlightenment: and German tradition of critique, 218n.1; Habermas on Benjamin's view of, 80; hope beyond renewed enlightenment, 168; Horkheimer and Adorno on, 49, 51, 56, 60, 66–67; Kant on, 157–162; and *plumpes Denken*, 178; post-Enlightenment, 23
Enzensberger, Hans Magnus, 40, 234n.12
Ereignis. See Heidegger, Martin: on *Ereignis*
Erfahrung, 16, 36, 99, 136, 170, 216n.27, 224n.19, 226n.5, 230nn.23,24, 233n.61, 240n.2
Erinnerung, 24, 194–196, 237n.9, 243n.20
Erlebnis, 36, 136
es gibt, 142
Expressionism, German, 40

Fascism, 66, 90, 144
Fédier, François, 237n.11
Fichte, Johann Gottlieb, 7, 30, 42, 32, 33

252 *Index*

Figal, Günter, 115, 228nn.1,3, 230nn.22,24, 233n.61
Flusser, Vilém, 121, 234n.5
Fontius, Martin, 219n.7, 220n.11
Fortleben. *See* Benjamin, Walter: on *Fortleben*
Foucault, Michel, 22, 41, 83, 161–162, 192, 219nn.3,7, 227n.25, 239n.19, 240n.5
Frankfurt School, 42, 49, 80, 162, 176, 222n.38
French Revolution, 8, 90, 155
Freud, Sigmund: and discursivity, 240n.5; on the image, 152; and intellectual history of modernity, 14; and latency, 10; on memory, 243n.20; on *Nachträglichkeit*, 14; and *plumpes Denken*, 240n.14; on psychic structure of the self, 161; on religion and faith, 12; on ruins, 201; on trauma and survival, 203
WORKS OF: *Civilization and Its Discontents*, 201, 243n.2; *The Future of an Illusion*, 12; *The Interpretation of Dreams*, 11; *Moses and Monotheism (Der Mann Moses und die monotheistische Religion: Drei Abhandlungen)*, 238n.29
Freund, Gisèle, 126
Frey, Hans-Jost, 226n.11
fundamental ontology. *See* Heidegger, Martin: and fundamental ontology
Fynsk, Christopher, 229n.9

Gadamer, Hans-Georg, 95, 192–193, 229n.15
Gaita, Raimond, 227n.23
Gardner, Alexander, 136
Gasché, Rodolphe, 46, 100, 189, 219n.8, 220n.19, 221n.20, 230n.27, 242n.7
Gedächtnis, 24, 194–196, 243n.20

Geist, 30, 33, 35, 36, 81, 82, 90, 131, 153, 158, 159, 210
George, Stefan, 162
German Democratic Republic (GDR; East Germany), 164
Ge-stell. *See* Heidegger, Martin: on *Ge-stell*
Geworfenheit. *See* Heidegger, Martin: on *Geworfenheit*
ghosts and the ghostly, 2, 6, 15–16, 36, 82, 91, 101, 118, 196
Gianikian, Yervant, 149
Giddens, Anthony, 217n.2
Glei, R., 226n.5
God, 12, 73, 82, 106, 152, 165, 202
Godzich, Wlad, 146, 231n.52, 237n.15
Goehr, Lydia, 237n.9
Goethe, Johann Wolfgang von, 7, 15, 39, 43, 75, 87, 92, 186–188, 241n.1
Gombrich, Ernst, 3
Gondek, Hans-Dieter, 233n.64
Gottsched, Johann Christoph, 218n.1
Grass, Günter, 120
Greeks: and aesthetics, 39; *aletheia*, 161 (*see also* Heidegger, Martin: and critique); Heidegger on thought of, 94, 99–100, 109; Hölderlin on, 8, 113–114; *kairos*, 125; *krinein*, 22, 25, 40–44, 73, 79, 199, 207; and morality, 35; *philosophia*, 188; philosophy of, as learning to die, 202–203; and Romans, 7, 159; *thaumazein*, 170–172, 184; *theorein*, 146; translation of concepts of, into Latin, 100, 102, 109
Greffrath, Krista R., 227n.24
Greiner, Bernhard, 214n.13
Gross, Walter, 89
Guattari, Félix, 175, 240n.7
Gumbrecht, Hans Ulrich, 61, 83

Habermas, Jürgen: on Benjamin, 80, 226nn.16,17; critique of quietism by,

82; on Nietzsche and modernity, 37–38; on religion and faith, 12; on self-identical critical consciousness, 22
WORKS OF: *The Dialectics of Secularization: On Reason and Religion* (*Dialektik der Säkularisierung: Über Vernunft und Religion* [with Joseph Ratzinger, now Pope Benedict XVI]), 12; *The Philosophical Discourse of Modernity*, 37, 218n.18; "Walter Benjamin: Consciousness-Raising or Rescuing Critique" (Bewußtmachende oder rettende Kritik—die Aktualität Walter Benjamins), 79, 226n.16, 227n.18
Hahn, Otto, 125
Halbwachs, Maurice, 243n.20
Hallwachs, Wilhelm, 91–92, 228n.5, 243n.27
Harder, Matthias, 235n.16
haunting: as debt, 6; Derrida on, 203 (*see also* Derrida, Jacques: works of: *Specters of Marx*); and the future, 209–210; and Hegel, 34; and Heidegger, 20, 90, 184; and the image, 139, 150; and modernity, 21, 30; and Nietzschean *Nachgesang* of modernity, 36; photographic, 136; and *Rettung*, 87; of what has been "overcome," 15, 27; as a "yes, yes," 191
Heartfield, John, 120
Hegel, Georg Wilhelm Friedrich: and Adorno, 70, 81, 131; on aesthetics, 14; on art and culture, 40; on *Aufhebung*, 33–35; on critique, 42, 48; and determinate negation, 34; and dialectic, 33, 70; *The Difference Between Fichte's and Schelling's System of Philosophy* (*Differenzschrift*), 13, 215n.17; "Earliest Program for a System of German Idealism," 161; *Encyclopedia of the Philosophical Sciences* (*Enzyklopädie der philosophischen Wissenschaften*), 242nn.5,19; and Habermas, 38; on Hölderlin, 192; and Idealism, 30; and intellectual history of modernity, 14; after Kant, 32; and knowledge, 21; and labor of the concept, 205; on memory (*Gedächtnis* and *Erinnerung*), 24, 188–189, 194–196, 243n.20; and modernity, 33; *Phenomenology of Spirit* (*Phänomenologie des Geistes*), 21, 32, 33–34, 110, 217nn.8,32, 218nn.10–13; and the photograph, 121; and *plumpes Denken*, 178–179; and Speer, 237n.9
Heidbrink, Ludger, 232n.60
Heidegger, Hermann, 228n.3, 241n.21
Heidegger, Martin: on *aletheia*, 94, 109, 116; on *Andenken*, 17; on the beginning, 13; on concept of time, 18–19; and critique, 22, 42, 46–48; on *Dasein*, 14, 19–20, 93, 116, 203; debt to, 6; Derrida on, 90, 120; on *Ereignis*, 100, 116, 146, 163; and fundamental ontology, 47, 70, 91, 95, 146–147, 162, 176; and futurity, 216n.30; on *Gedachtes*, 237n.16; on *Ge-stell*, 100, 163; on *Geworfenheit*, 127, 203; on Heraclitus, 114–115, 143, 145–148; on Hölderlin, 23, 56, 88, 90, 95, 109–110, 113, 114, 147, 162–163, 181; on the image, 23, 145–148, 150, 152, 237n.11; and intellectual history of modernity, 14; and the *Kehre*, 90, 91; on Kleist, 210; on *Lichtung*, 138; on memory, 192, 243n.20; and National Socialism, 88–91, 228n.9; and Nietzsche, 34, 90, 189; on Parmenides, 23, 94, 116, 229n.14, 223n.63; philosophy of language of,

Heidegger, Martin (*continued*)
23, 233n.65; on Schiller's aesthetics, 23, 88–98, 103–109, 114, 116, 197–198; on the *Schritt zurük*, 97; on *Seinsvergessenheit*, 98, 162; on step/*Sprung*, 101, 230n.44; on thinking, 70, 94, 135, 175, 178, 184, 221n.28; on Trakl, 18; on translation, 22–23, 88–117, 199, 203, 232n.60, 233nn.64,66; on *Ur-sprung*, 85, 101; use of *Seyn* by, 17; on *das Vorbei*, 19–20; on *Zustand*, 104–106

WORKS OF: *Being and Time*, 18, 47, 89; *Black Notebooks* (*Schwarze Hefte*), 228n.3; "Building, Dwelling, Thinking" (Bauen Wohnen Denken), 23, 114, 232n.58; "The Concept of Time: Lecture Before the Marburg Theologians" (Der Begriff der Zeit: Vortrag vor der Marburger Theologenschaft), 19, 217n.31; "Denken—als Weg," 237n.16; "The End of Philosophy and the Task of Thinking" (Das Ende der Philosophie und die Aufgabe des Denkens), 47, 221nn.25,27; "The Essence of Language," 101; *Exercises for Beginners: Schiller's "Letters on the Aesthetic Education of Man"* (*Übungen für Anfänger: Schillers "Briefe über die ästhetische Erziehung des Menschen"*), 91, 215n.18, 228n.5; 229nn.10,18, 230nn.36,42 243n.27; *From the Experience of Thinking* (*Aus der Erfahrung des Denkens*), 16–17, 170, 216n.27; *Heraclitus* (*Heraklit*), 232n.59, 237n.11; "Hölderlin and the Essence of Poetry," 90; *Hölderlin's Hymn "Andenken,"* 223n.5; *Hölderlin's Hymn "The Ister"* (*Hölderlins Hymne "Der Ister"*), 23, 88, 95, 109, 231n.49, 241n.16; *Identity and Difference* (*Identität und Differenz*), 237n.14; *Introduction to Metaphysics* (*Einführung in die Metaphysik*), 109, 231n.48; "Language," 230n.30; "Language in the Poem" (Die Sprache im Gedicht), 18, 216nn.28,29; "The Law of Identity" (Der Satz der Identität), 230n.44; *Martin Heidegger in Conversation* (*Martin Heidegger im Gespräch*), 245n.9; "The Nature of Language," 230n.29; "Nietzsche: The Will to Power as Art," 90; *On Humanism* (*Über den Humanismus*), 225n.33; *On the Beginning* (*Über den Anfang*), 13, 100, 215n.18, 230n.28; *On the Way to Language* (*Unterwegs zur Sprache*), 216n.28; "The Origin of the Work of Art" (Der Ursprung des Kunstwerkes), 90, 98, 137, 230n.25, 235n.28; "Overcoming Metaphysics" (Überwindung der Metaphysik), 98, 221n.28, 230n.23; *Parmenides*, 23, 229n.14, 233n.63; *Plato's Sophist* (*Platon: Sophistes*), 237n.12; ". . . poetically man dwells . . ." (. . . dichterisch wohnet der Mensch . . .), 237n.17; "The Principle of Reason" (Der Satz vom Grund), 103, 230nn.32,34; "The Question Concerning Technology" (Die Frage nach der Technik), 23, 97, 109, 221n.28, 230n.21, 231n.47; *The Question Concerning the Thing* (*Die Frage nach dem Ding*), 221nn.20,21; "The Saying of Anaximander," 115, 233n.62; "The Time of the World Picture" (Die Zeit des Weltbildes), 145, 237n.13; "What Is Called Thinking?" (Was heißt Denken?), 94, 175, 221n.28, 229n.13, 240n.9

Heine, Heinrich, 40

Heraclitus, 35, 114–115, 143, 145–146, 148, 167
Hermand, Jost, 217n.2
Hitler, Adolf, 89, 144, 222n.38
Hobbes, Thomas, 243n.20
Hohendahl, Peter Uwe, 218n.1
Hölderlin, Friedrich: Adorno on, 59; and *Andenken*, 17; and complications for afterness, 8; "Earliest Program for a System of German Idealism," 161; Heidegger on, 23, 56, 88, 90, 95, 109–110, 113, 114, 147, 162–163, 181; *Hyperion*, 224n.16; "In Lovely Blue . . ." (In lieblicher Bläue . . .), 240n.11; on Kant, 32; "Letter of January 1, 1799" (Brief vom 1. Januar 1799), 217n.7; on memory and mourning, 192, 196; "Patmos," 73, 225n.1; and the thinking of thinking, 177; "The Titans" (Die Titanen), 242n.14; translation of poetry by, 113–114, 232n.57; use of *Seyn* by, 17
Holz, Hans Heinz, 226n.11
Hörisch, Jochen, 83, 157, 238n.8
Horkheimer, Max, 49, 51, 56, 60, 66–67, 158, 222n.33
Humboldt, Wilhelm von, 39, 92, 157, 159
Hume, David, 30, 200–201
Husserl, Edmund, 14, 78, 131, 145

Idealism, German, 32, 92, 161
ideology, critique of, 21, 80
image: and Adorno, 118–138; afterimage, 23, 138, 139–140, 142, 148; Benjamin on, 23, 77–78, 85–87, 143, 144, 150–153, 203; Blanchot on, 149–151; of critique, 44; Deleuze on, 23, 151–152, 203; Derrida on, 122–123, 203; dialectical, 75; *es gibt*, 142; Heidegger on, 23, 145–148, 150, 152, 237nn.11,16; imagelessness (*Bildlosigkeit*), 145, 147, 237n.16; Kafka on, 143, 187; and language, 236n.2; of modernity, 33, 36, 37; and *Nachleben*, 3; photographic, 23, 118–138, 233n.1; Rancière on, 141; of *Rettung*, 83; *Spiegelschrift* vs. *Spiegelbild* (mirror-writing vs. mirror-image), 66; thought, 13, 22, 60–61, 68, 143; and translation, 113; uncanniness of, 140; withdrawal of, 23, 139–153
inheritance, 15–16, 30, 32, 45, 103–104, 108–109, 170, 171, 189, 216n.26

Jameson, Fredric, 29, 178–179, 240n.13
Jandl, Ernst, 113, 232n.56
Janicaud, Dominique, 89, 228n.4
Jarvis, Simon, 60, 224n.20
Jaspers, Karl, 89, 125
Jens, Walter, 125
Johnson, Barbara, 172, 233n.66, 240n.6
Joyce, James, 93, 126
Jünger, Ernst, 125

Kafka, Franz: Arendt on, 201–202; debt to, 6; and Felice Bauer, 120, 124, 135–136, 233n.3, 234n.11, 235nn.25,27; and the image, 143, 187; "The Judgment," 163, 193; and Max Brod, 163, 239n.21; "The Metamorphosis," 163; and Nietzschean *Nachgesang* of modernity, 38; and other-directed hope, 161; and photography, 23, 120, 135–137, 138; and *plumpes Denken*, 183; on *sein* and ownership, 208; and the self, 163–164; *The Zürau Aphorisms* (*Die Zürauer Aphorismen*), 244n.6
Kant, Immanuel: on aesthetics, 104, 114, 225n.30; and afterness and critique, 22, 42, 44–48; "An Answer to the Question: What Is Enlightenment?," 157–164, 239nn.11,16; as-if mode of,

Kant, Immanuel (*continued*)
147; and *auto-nomia*, 34; binarisms of, 97; and central questions of philosophy, 121; Copernican turn in thinking of, 2, 29, 31–33, 36; *Critique of Pure Reason (Kritik der reinen Vernunft)*, 29–30, 42, 46, 106, 110, 217n.5, 220n.10, 230n.41; *Critique of the Power of Judgment (Kritik der Urteilskraft)*, 44, 70, 199, 220n.16; debt to, 6; de Man on, 97; Foucault on, 41; *Freiheit des Geistes*, 158; and German Idealism 32; and the image, 141; influence of, on Schiller's aesthetics, 106; Kleist's reaction to, 31–32; and *Nachahmung* and *Nachfolge*, 109; perpetual peace of, 185; post-Kantian modernity, 22, 37; on religion, 207; sublime of, 141; transcendental philosophy of, 30, 45, 106; turn against, 38
Kästner, Erich, 125
Kaufman, Robert, 225n.30
Kaufmann, Walter, 244n.2
Kaulen, Heinrich, 225n.5, 226nn.6,14
Keller, Gottfried, 7
Kelly, Robert, 113–114, 232n.57
Kemp, Wolfgang, 213n.1
Kierkegaard, Søren, 11
Kirchner, Ernst Ludwig, 126
Klee, Paul, 126
Kleist, Heinrich von, 31–32, 210, 217n.6, 244n.8
Klopstock, Friedrich Gottlieb, 39
Kluge, Alexander, 234n.12
Kofman, Sarah, 192
Köhler, Andrea, 227n.26
Körner, Gottfried, 92
Koselleck, Reinhart, 37, 219n.7
Kosuth, Joseph, 14, 216n.23, 245n.10
Kracauer, Siegfried, 74, 76, 83, 134
Kramer, Sven, 222n.37
Kraus, Karl, 78
Krell, David Farrell, 89, 188, 216n.30, 228n.4, 236n.30, 242n.3, 243nn.20,25
krinein. See Greeks: *krinein*

Lacan, Jacques, 126–127, 233n.64, 240n.14
Laclau, Ernesto, 171
Lacoue-Labarthe, Philippe, 90, 219n.7, 228n.7
La Mettrie, Julien Offray, 158
Lang, Berel, 89, 228n.4
Latour, Bruno, 29, 217n.3
Lebenswelt, 78, 140
Leibniz, Wilhelm, 46, 48
Lepenies, Wolf, 61
Lessing, Gotthold Ephraim, 39–40, 75
Lettau, Reinhard, 156, 172, 238n.7
Levinas, Emmanuel: and Derrida, 192; and intellectual history of modernity, 14; *Of God Who Comes to Mind*, 12; *Otherwise than Being or Beyond Essence*, 12; on religion and faith, 12; wholly other of, 164, 189
Levine, Michael, 244n.1
Lévi-Strauss, Claude, 57
Lingis, Alphonso, 154–155, 238n.1
Locke, John, 30, 243n.20
Lucchi, Angela Ricci, 149
Lucifer, 137
Luhmann, Niklas, 219n.9
Lukács, Georg, 40
Luther, Martin, 207
Lyotard, Jean-François: on "after philosophy," 14, 25, 210; and Derrida, 193; "Foreword: After the Words," 216n.23, 245n.10; on Heidegger, 89, 228n.4; *The Inhuman: Reflections on Time*, 241n.20; and intellectual history of modernity, 14; on master narratives, 169–170;

and Nietzschean *Nachgesang* of modernity, 38; on *passé absolu*, 14–15; and *plumpes Denken*, 184; on postmodern condition, 29

Malpas, Jeff, 233n.65
Man, Felix H., 237n.11
Mann, Thomas, 31, 40, 120
Mannheim, Karl, 200
Marcovicz, Digne Meller, 237n.11
Marcuse, Herbert, 60, 89, 156–157, 238n.7
Margolis, Joseph, 227n.23
Marquard, Odo, 88, 90–91, 228nn.5,9, 243n.27
Marx, Karl: and "all that is solid," 28, 73; Benjamin on, 80; Berman on, 28; on capital and human existence, 30; and critique, 42, 48, 173; Derrida on, 15, 189, 216n.24, 242n.6; and discursivity, 240n.5; eleventh thesis on Feuerbach by, 171; neo-Marxian aesthetics, 60; and *plumpes Denken*, 178–179; transformation of Kantian aesthetics by, 70, 225n.30
Mayer, Hans, 218n.1
McDonald, Christine, 229n.16
Mehring, Franz, 75
melancholia, 10, 36–37, 69, 75, 188
Mendelssohn, Moses, 157–158
Menke, Christoph, 51, 60, 219n.8, 222n.38, 224n.19
Mentré, François, 200
metaphysics: and Adorno, 50–51, 55; and Derrida, 197; and Heidegger, 47–48, 91, 98, 109, 162, 231n.44; Kantian, 29–30; and Nietzsche, 34–35; and photography, 119; translation of traditional, 94
Michelangelo, 187
Miller, J. Hillis, 58, 223n.12
Milton, John, 8

Mitscherlich, Alexander, 125, 238n.29
Moehsen, J. K. W., 157–158
Möllendorf, Wilhelm von, 88–89
Moloch, 167
Moses, 32, 238n.29
Moses, Stefan, 23, 120, 124–134, 138, 234n.12, 235nn.16,18
Mouffe, Chantel, 171
mourning: as alternative to violence, 159; always already, 203; Benjamin on, 5, 36, 75, 84–85, 144, 209, 228n.32; and memory, 24, 186–198; and modernity, 30–32; photographic, 130; radical afterness of, 168; space of, 199; and trauma of afterness, 10, 203
Mozart, Wolfgang Amadeus, 224n.23
Müller, Heiner, 193
Müller-Doohm, Stefan, 223n.13
Murry, Bill, 189
Musil, Robert, 13, 31, 215n.19

Naas, Michael, 216n.26
Nachahmung, 45, 109
Nachbild, 139, 147
Nachfolge, 9, 45, 109, 199
Nachkonstruktion, 61, 64–65
Nachleben. See Benjamin, Walter: on *Nachleben*
Nachreifen. See Benjamin, Walter: on *Nachreife*
Nancy, Jean-Luc, 126, 219n.7, 234nn.4,14
Narcissus and Echo, 11, 126, 186
National Socialism, German, 51, 88–90, 164, 222n.38, 228n.9
Natzel, S., 226n.5
Neo-Kantians, Marburg, 75
Nero, 167
Neumann, Gerhard, 61, 83
Ngodup, Karma, 215n.22
Niépce, Joseph Nicéphore, 118

Nietzsche, Friedrich: and Benjamin, 36–37; de Man on, 125; on figurative language, 140; genealogical project of, 42, 161; and Heidegger, 34, 90, 189; on human nature, 35; on memory, 189, 243n.20; on metaphysics, 34; on *Nachgesang*, 35–36, 38; and narrative voice, 63; on religion and faith, 12
WORKS OF: *The Anti-Christ (Der Antichrist)*, 35, 218n.15; *Beyond Good and Evil: Prelude to a Philosophy of the Future*, 35; *The Birth of Tragedy*, 207; *Ecce Homo*, 35; *Human, All Too Human (Menschliches, Allzumenschliches)*, 35, 57, 188, 218n.14, 242n.4; *Untimely Meditations*, 34; *The Will to Power*, 155
Nikolopoulou, Kalliopi, 240n.14
Nora, Pierre, 11
Norris, Christopher, 240n.8
Novalis (Georg Philipp Friedrich von Hardenberg), 57, 161

Octavian, 205
Offenbach, Jacques, 74, 76
Ott, Hugo, 229n.9
Ovid, 11

paleonomy, 29
Panofsky, Erwin, 3, 213n.1
Parmenides. *See* Heidegger, Martin: on Parmenides
Paul, Jean, 167
Pepper, Thomas, 232n.54
Pfeiffer, Michelle, 196
photography: and afterness, 118–138; Barthes on, 122–123, 127, 129–130, 136, 139, 235n.26; Benjamin on, 85–86, 228n.32; Derrida on, 23, 120–124, 130, 134–138, 234n.7, 235n.26, 236n.30; etymology of, 234n.4; history of, 118, 137, 233n.1; and the image, 139–140, 143; Kafka on, 23, 120, 135–137, 138; and *Nachleben*, 5; and philosophy of history, 236n.2; and psychoanalysis, 134–135; Stefan Moses and, 23, 120, 124–134, 138, 234n.12, 235n.18; as thinking, 119, 124, 135, 137–138; as translation, 118
Picasso, Pablo, 126
Pippin, Robert B., 37–38, 218n.19
Platen, August, 7
Plato, 57, 75, 145, 170, 203, 237n.12, 240n.3, 243n.20
Plissart, Marie-Françoise, 122, 132, 234n.6
plumpes Denken, 24, 178–185, 241nn.14,17
Poetics and Hermeneutics (German research group), 12
Pöggeler, Otto, 89, 228nn.4,9, 233n.65
"posthumanism," 135, 178, 207
"postmodernity," 15, 29, 215n.14, 217n.2, 218n.19, 225n.29
Proust, Marcel, 120, 125, 143, 201–202, 234n.13
psychoanalysis, 9, 10, 14, 134, 196, 201, 203, 240n.14

Raabe, Wilhelm, 7
Rancière, Jacques, 141, 236n.1
Ranke, Leopold von, 3
Ratzinger, Joseph (Pope Benedict XVI), 12
Raulff, Ulrich, 224n.21
redemption, 7, 34, 37, 62–69, 74, 203
Rehbock, Theda, 226n.5
Reichert, Klaus, 232n.56
Reinartz, Dirk, 135, 235n.24
reine Sprache, 6
religion, 11–12, 28, 36, 89, 152, 207, 214n.14, 238n.29
Rhode, Erwin, 207

Richter, Gerhard (the *other* one), 135
Rickert, Heinrich, 75
Rilke, Rainer Maria, 125, 139, 162, 234n.13
Rimbaud, Arthur, 29
Rockmore, Tom, 229n.9
Romans, 7, 99, 159
Romantics: British, 8; Jena, 57, 70, 161
Rorty, Richard, 12
Rosenberg, Alfred, 89
Röttger, Kurt, 219n.7
Rousseau, Jean-Jacques, 125, 234n.13
ruins, 7, 37, 69, 75, 98, 123, 136, 143–144, 201, 223n.13, 237n.9

Safranski, Rüdiger, 228n.2, 241n.21
Said, Edward, 13, 171, 215n.18, 240n.4
Sallis, John, 103, 230n.33
Sander, August, 126
Savage, Robert, 211
Saxl, Fritz, 3
Schapiro, Meyer, 120
Schelling, Friedrich Wilhelm Joseph: and critique, 219n.7; "Earliest Program for a System of German Idealism," 161; and Idealism, 30; after Kant, 32; on philosophy of nature, 33
Schiller, Friedrich: and bridge of translation, 116; debt to, 6; Heidegger on aesthetics of, 88, 90–98, 103–109, 198; Humboldt on, 39; and Kantian aesthetics, 114; *Letters on the Aesthetic Education of Mankind*, 23, 88, 108, 109, 197; on *Schritt*, 231n.44; *Wallenstein*, Hegel on, 40
Schlegel, Friedrich, 39, 42, 57, 75, 88, 161–162, 219n.7, 239n.17
Schleiermacher, Friedrich, 92
Schlemihl, Peter, 6
Schmeling, Max, 125
Schmitt, Carl, 170

Schneider, Werner, 219n.7
Scholem, Gershom, 75
Schönberg, Arnold, 38, 56, 58, 78
Schönkopf, Käthchen, 186–187
Schopenhauer, Arthur, 34, 207
Schuldt, 113–114, 232n.57
Schulz, Martin, 233n.1
Schwart, Ullrich, 226n.5
Schweppenhäuser, Hermann, 80
Sebald, W. G., 120
secret, 15–16, 104, 173
secularization, 7, 11–12, 36, 214n.14
Seel, Martin, 51, 222n.39
Shakespeare, William, 85
Sharr, Adam, 233n.65
Sheenan, Thomas, 229n.9
Shoah, 31, 55
Siegel, Elke, 224n.23
Sistine Chapel, 187
Socrates, 170
Sontag, Susan, 121, 234n.5
Sophocles, 181
Speer, Albert, 144, 236n.9
Spinoza, Baruch, 48
Stiegler, Bernd, 233n.1
Stierle, Karlheinz, 12, 215n.15
Stifter, Adalbert, 7
surrealism, 56
survival: as afterness, 2–6, 14; Blanchot on, 150; as crisis, 24, 203; future-directed, 204; of hope, 156; and memory, 187; and modernity, 31; as originary, 202–203; and *Rettung*, 84–85; and revolutionary politics, 90; of thinking, 176; translation as, 92, 107; and trauma, 10, 24; as a "yes, yes," 191
Szondi, Peter, 155, 238n.5

Talbot, William Henry Fox, 137
techné, 90, 121, 135, 195

Teutsche Merkur, Der (literary magazine), 157
thaumazein, 170–172, 184
Theaetetus, 170, 171
theologians, Marburg, 19, 217n.31
theology, 6, 75, 85–86
Thomä, Dieter, 229n.9
Tiedemann, Rolf, 80, 226n.5, 227n.17
Tournadre, Nicolas, 215n.22
Trakl, Georg, 18–19, 102, 162
translation: Benjamin on, 6, 101, 107, 112; of Bloch's work, 231n.53; Derrida on, 95, 107, 112; of empty space, 201; and *Fortleben*, 6; Heidegger on, 22–23, 88–117, 199, 203, 232n.60, 233nn.64,66; of Hölderlin's poetry, 113–114, 232n.57; and Kant, 45; and memory, 190; mistranslation, 93, 98, 99, 100, 109, 112–113, 231n.53, 232n.54; (mis)-translation of Adorno's work, 62, 64, 64–68, 82, 113, 232n.54; philosophy's, of art, 58; and photography, 118, 121, 135; and *plumpes Denken*, 180; of Tibetan "associative" case, 216n.22
trauma, 10–11, 14, 24, 31, 34, 66, 201, 203, 214n.11, 244n.11
Tucholsky, Kurt, 120

Überleben. See Benjamin, Walter: on *Überleben*
Ullrich, Wolfgang, 236n.9, 237n.11
Ur-sprung. See Heidegger, Martin: on *Ur-sprung*

Valéry, Paul, 163
Van Gogh, Vincent, 120
Vattimo, Gianno, 12
Vietta, Silvio, 229n.9

Virgil, 199, 202, 205
Vries, Hent de, 215n.14

Wagner, Richard, 34, 35, 76–78, 79
Warburg, Aby, 2–3, 231n.1
Warning, Rainer, 12, 215n.15
Weber, Max, 152, 238n.29
Weber, Samuel, 13, 159, 215n.20, 220n.16, 229n.11, 239n.15
Webern, Anton, 78
Wedekind, Frank, 40
Weigel, Sigrid, 213n.1
Weinrich, Harald, 83
Weiss, Peter, 156
Weissberg, Liliane, 224n.23
Wetzel, Michael, 122, 215n.19
Wieland, Christoph Martin, 157–158
Wilamowitz-Moellendorff, Ulrich von, 207
Wilkinson, Elizabeth M., 108
Willoughby, L. A., 108
Wimsatt, William, 43, 220n.13
Winkelmann, Johann Joachim, 39, 141
Witkacy (Stanisław Ignacy Witkiewicz), 127
Wolf, Erik, 89
Wolff, Christian, 48
Wölfflin, Heinrich, 141
Wood, David, 102, 230n.31
World War I, 30–31
World War II, 115, 144, 149

Young, Julian, 229n.9

Zeitraum, 24, 125, 199
Zenge, Wilhelmine von, 31, 217n.6
Zimmermann, Hans Dieter, 233n.65
Žižek, Slavoj, 61, 221n.30
Zöllner, Johann Friedrich, 157
Zukofsky, Louis, 113, 232n.56

COLUMBIA THEMES IN PHILOSOPHY, SOCIAL CRITICISM, AND THE ARTS
Lydia Goehr and Gregg M. Horowitz, Editors

Advisory Board
J. M. Bernstein
Noël Carroll
T. J. Clark
Arthur C. Danto
Martin Donougho
David Frisby
Boris Gasparov
Eileen Gillooly
Thomas S. Grey
Miriam Bratu Hansen
Robert Hullot-Kentor
Michael Kelly
Richard Leppert
Janet Wolff

Columbia Themes in Philosophy, Social Criticism, and the Arts presents monographs, essay collections, and short books on philosophy and aesthetic theory. It aims to publish books that show the ability of the arts to stimulate critical reflection on modern and contemporary social, political, and cultural life. Art is not now, if it ever was, a realm of human activity independent of the complex realities of social organization and change, political authority and antagonism, cultural domination and resistance. The possibilities of critical thought embedded in the arts are most fruitfully expressed when addressed to readers across the various fields of social and humanistic inquiry. The idea of philosophy in the series title ought to be understood, therefore, to embrace forms of discussion that begin where mere academic expertise exhausts itself, where the rules of social, political, and cultural practice are both affirmed and challenged, and where new thinking takes place. The series does not privilege any particular art, nor does it ask for the arts to be mutually isolated. The series encourages writing from the many fields of thoughtful and critical inquiry.

Lydia Goehr and Daniel Herwitz, eds., *The Don Giovanni Moment: Essays on the Legacy of an Opera*
Robert Hullot-Kentor, *Things Beyond Resemblance: Collected Essays on Theodor W. Adorno*
Gianni Vattimo, *Art's Claim to Truth*, edited by Santiago Zabala, translated by Luca D'Isanto
John T. Hamilton, *Music, Madness, and the Unworking of Language*

Stefan Jonsson, *A Brief History of the Masses: Three Revolutions*
Richard Eldridge, *Life, Literature, and Modernity*
Janet Wolff, *The Aesthetics of Uncertainty*
Lydia Goehr, *Elective Affinities: Musical Essays on the History of Aesthetic Theory*
Christoph Menke, *Tragic Play: Irony and Theater from Sophocles to Beckett*, translated by James Phillips
György Lukács, *Soul and Form*, translated by Anna Bostock and edited by John T. Sanders and Katie Terezakis with an introduction by Judith Butler
Joseph Margolis, *The Cultural Space of the Arts and the Infelicities of Reductionism*
Herbert Molderings, *Art as Experiment: Duchamp and the Aesthetics of Chance, Creativity, and Convention*
Whitney Davis, *Queer Beauty: Sexuality and Aesthetics from Winckelmann to Freud and Beyond*
Gail Day, *Dialectical Passions: Negation in Postwar Art Theory*